# MASTERING

KU-794-369

# BUSINESS COMMUNICATION

LEEDS BECKETT UNIVERSITY LIBRARY
DISCARDED

*Leeds Metropolitan University*

17 0094186 1

# MACMILLAN MASTER SERIES

Accounting
Arabic
Astronomy
Australian History
Background to Business
Banking
Basic Management
Biology
British Politics
Business Communication
Business Law
Business Microcomputing
C Programming
Catering Science
Catering Theory
Chemistry
COBOL Programming
Commerce
Computer Programming
Computers
Economic and Social History
Economics
Electrical Engineering
Electronics
English as a Foreign Language
English Grammar
English Language
English Literature
Financial Accounting
French 1
French 2
German 1
German 2

Hairdressing
Human Biology
Italian 1
Italian 2
Japanese
Keyboarding
Marketing
Mathematics
Modern British History
Modern European History
Modern World History
Nutrition
Office Practice
Pascal Programming
Philosophy
Physics
Practical Writing
Principles of Accounts
Psychology
Restaurant Service
Science
Secretarial Procedures
Social Welfare
Sociology
Spanish 1
Spanish 2
Spreadsheets
Statistics
Statistics with your Microcomputer
Study Skills
Typewriting Skills
Word Processing

# MASTERING
# BUSINESS COMMUNICATION

L.A. WOOLCOTT
AND
W.R. UNWIN

MACMILLAN

Text © Lysbeth A. Woolcott and Wendy R. Unwin 1983
© Illustrations: Barry Jackson 1983
© Text figures: The Macmillan Press Ltd

All rights reserved. No reproduction, copy or transmission
of this publication may be made without written permission.

No paragraph of this publication may be reproduced, copied or
transmitted save with written permission or in accordance with
the provisions of the Copyright, Designs and Patents Act 1988,
or under the terms of any licence permitting limited copying
issued by the Copyright Licensing Agency, 90 Tottenham Court
Road, London W1P 9HE.

Any person who does any unauthorised act in relation to
this publication may be liable to criminal prosecution and
civil claims for damages.

First published 1983 by
THE MACMILLAN PRESS LTD
Houndmills, Basingstoke, Hampshire RG21 2XS
and London
Companies and representatives
throughout the world

ISBN 0–333–33529–5

Printed in China

10    9
00   99   98   97   96   95   94   93   92

LEEDS METROPOLITAN
UNIVERSITY LIBRARY
1700941861
13123
88595  20·4·94
6567
12·5·94   £5·99

658·H5 WOO

# CONTENTS

# CONTENTS

# ILLUSTRATIONS

# ILLUSTRATIONS

# INTRODUCTION

**Communication** – an art, a science or a practical skill?

Communication is fundamental to all working relationships; inept or inadequate communication causes more controversy in business and industry than any other single factor.

Communication deteriorates as organisations get bigger. The public sector (government, public utilities, education) and the multinational groups (Ford, Shell, ICI, Sony) employ millions of people. Lines of communication are stretched; organisation structures become cumbersome; communication is remote, impersonal and anonymous. New technology, where computer speaks to computer, intensifies the trend.

Yet more than ever before people expect to be treated as individuals: to be consulted and informed; to express their views and have them respected.

This conflict between organisational complexity and individual needs can only be resolved by improving communication. Effective communication demands efficient management organisation, understanding of the effects of technological change, comprehensive interpersonal skills and mastery of communication techniques.

It is neither an art nor a science, but a basic practical skill which can be learnt and applied.

This book explains how to acquire and use such skill within the working context, at the same time taking into account examination requirements. The chapters are interrelated and cross-referenced so that the order in which you read can be varied to suit your own needs.

**One last word.** All successful communication depends on regarding what we are trying to say or write from the listener's or reader's point of view.

---

### FOCUS

Success means asking yourself
HOW WOULD I FEEL IF I WERE LISTENING TO WHAT I AM SAYING?
HOW WOULD I FEEL IF I WERE READING WHAT I AM WRITING?

---

**Another last word.** In this book the male form 'he' is used for convenience, and because the use of 'he/she', etc., is cumbersome. Any reference to 'he', therefore, means 'she' as well, unless it would be obviously inappropriate.

# CORRESPONDENCE

## 1.1 LETTERS

'Appollonius to Zeno, greeting. You did right to send the chick-peas to Memphis. Farewell.'

This letter, sent by an Egyptian civil servant thousands of years ago, contains all the essentials of a good modern business letter. Its very informality has a contemporary ring to it. It is simple, clear and concise — yet courtesy has not been sacrificed. Finally, it passes the essential test for any letter writer. How will the reader feel about it? Surely Zeno was well satisfied with this epistle?

Brevity is always a virtue in communication, but it has particular value in correspondence because letters are such costly items. It has been estimated that a letter will cost at least £10 and, if that seems an improbably large sum, think of the manager's time spent dictating, the secretary's time, plus overheads and other expenses, of which the stamp is probably the least. And the reader's time is also a cost.

In fact one American firm, Fluorocarbon Inc., has saved itself a great deal of money by almost abolishing letter-writing. If you write to them, their reply will be written on the margin of your original letter. A photocopier ensures that there is something for the Fluorocarbon files, and this firm, with a hundred million dollar turnover, keeps all its correspondence in one filing cabinet. All its filing is done on Friday morning by the receptionist. No doubt Fluorocarbon are delighted by the economies they have achieved, but if their practice became widespread there would soon be no letters in whose margins to reply!

None the less it might be wise as a first step in letter-writing to ask oneself: 'Is this letter really necessary?' Figure 1.1 should surely have been replaced by a compliments slip, for it says nothing but the obvious and unnecessary at expensive length.

Business organisations spend considerable sums of money on building,

Fig 1.1 *an unnecessary letter*

```
Dear Sir

I enclose a form for application for employment with
this organisation for you to complete and return to
me.

I understand that you are interested in working for
the Company in an engineering capacity and it will
be helpful if you can provide as much information as
possible.

I shall contact you again when I have received your
completed form with a probable view to arranging a
formal interview.

Yours faithfully
```

maintaining and projecting their image. Handsome buildings, decor and furniture, beautiful receptionists and glossy literature all help to impress clients with a picture of a flourishing, progressive concern. Very often, of course, our first contact with an organisation is via its letters, so it is important that they should also be designed to project an appropriate image.

Any letter carries two messages. The explicit message is what we say to the reader through the words we choose and use. The implicit message is conveyed by the *appearance* of the letter, i.e. by the way the words are arranged on the paper, by the quality of the typing, the quality of the paper, by the design of the letterhead. A letter which is badly typed, in one long paragraph, on rather poor-quality paper with an old-fashioned letterhead is not likely (however well chosen the words) to impress the reader or give him confidence in an organisation which pays so little attention to its image.

The three aspects of letter-writing considered in the following sections (format, planning, style and tone) are so arranged for convenience, but the divisions are somewhat artificial, for they are all interrelated. The presentation of the letter may include the use of headings, sub-headings, hanging paragraphs and possibly a numbering system. All these devices are closely related to the content of the letter, indeed their sole purpose is to help the reader understand what it is that the writer is saying. Similarly, the language, style and tone must match the message. A letter of complaint will be written in very different terms from those of a sales promotion letter.

**The conventions of format**
The layout of letters is largely determined by custom and convention. Because there are many acceptable variations possible, many firms produce

their own guidelines to a standard 'house style' which helps them to maintain a consistent image.

There are two main forms of layout currently in use: the older semi-blocked form and the fully blocked form, now very widely used. The fully blocked form of layout is often unpunctuated. Typed examples of the two styles are given in Figures 1.2 and 1.3 and these patterns can also be used for handwritten letters.

**Fig 1.2** *a semi-blocked letter*

```
                                        5 Green Lane,
                                           BURBERRY,
                                            Wilts.
                                          BB3 6XZ

                                     10th March, 19--


Contemporary Furnishings PLC,
11 James Square,
MANCHESTER
MC1 6BG

Dear Sirs,

     I should be grateful if you would send me further
information about the chairs you advertised in
'The Mercury' last week.

     I am particularly interested in your plywood
rocking chairs.

                    Yours faithfully,



                    W Penrose (Mrs)
```

Figure 1.2 shows a letter sent from a private address on unheaded notepaper. The sender's address is typed, indented, at the top right-hand corner. Note that the sender's name is not included. A telephone number could be inserted opposite this address on the left-hand margin, if required. So could the reader's reference, if applicable. The date appears beneath the address, and is neatly aligned with it. The recipient's name and address on the left-hand side is not indented but kept in line with the margin.

Although the letter is very short, it has been divided into two paragraphs, the first containing the topic of the letter, the second giving amplifying information. The start of each paragraph will normally be five spaces from the left-hand margin for a typed letter, or the equivalent for a handwritten one.

Fig 1.3 *a fully blocked letter*

# The Tin Can Preserving Co.

HUNSTON
LINCOLNSHIRE
HUF J7F                    Tel. Hunston 194

Our ref ABC/DE
Your ref GH/IJK

12 December 19--

A J Eyre Esq
Ideal Estates PLC
9 Timmins Lane
YARBOROUGH
Norfolk
YB1 6SZ

Dear Mr Eyre

Thank you for your letter of 1 December 19--, enclosing
detailed plans of Site No 12.

A preliminary sketch of our proposed new factory is
enclosed so that you may have time to consider it
before we meet.

I am pleased to confirm the tentative arrangements we
made on the telephone yesterday and shall look forward
to meeting you on Friday, 10 December, at 2.30 pm.

Yours sincerely

*J. Gott.*

J Gott
General Manager

Enclosure

The complimentary close, *Yours faithfully*, is centred on the page and the signature is aligned with it. Since so many people's signatures are illegible, it is courteous to print the name under the signature so that a reply can be correctly addressed.

The fully blocked letter shown in Figure 1.3 is typed on letterheaded paper. You will note that all the typing begins on the left-hand margin and that the layout has open punctuation (that is, no punctuation), though the content of the letter is, of course, conventionally punctuated.

This more streamlined layout is very much more economical of the typist's time than the more traditional form. No calculations are needed for neat presentation of dates, centred headings and complimentary close. The touch of a button on the typewriter aligns it on the margin ready to type the next line.

Nor is the lack of punctuation any disadvantage. The function of punctuation is to help make the meaning clear. In the format of letters the layout, each new item separated on a new line, makes the meaning perfectly clear and saves the time and thought necessary for the insertion of punctuation.

European law requires limited liability companies to include the following information in the letterhead: full name of the company, the names of the directors, the place of registration, the registered number and the address of the registered office. The telephone number and telex number are usually added. It is not many years since letterheads were so elaborately designed as to take up a significant proportion of the page but the current trend in letterheads is towards simplicity. Some firms prefer to print only the name of their organisation (or even simply a monogram) at the head of the page and to put all the other necessary information at the foot. This style gives an attractively uncluttered and modern impression. The style of letterhead should be related to the firm's activities: the same design would hardly suit the image of both a cosmetics firm and a heavy engineering firm, nor would ornate gothic lettering be very suitable for a computing firm.

If your correspondent uses a reference, it is important to quote it in your reply to save him time and inconvenience. A very large engineering firm complained of the difficulty they had in ensuring that their correspondents used their references, which were the only way of ensuring that letters went to the clerk dealing with that contract. Letters without a reference went into 'no-man's land', circulating from desk to desk until someone was able to identify them. The ensuing delays caused problems with customers, and on more than one occasion conciliatory visits were necessary, over long distances, to mollify customers whose own thoughtlessness had caused the delay.

Despite the modern taste for streamlining it is considered bad form to abbreviate the date. The most logical order is day, month and year, for example 1 *December 19--*. It is acceptable to write *1st* as merely *1*, but it is not acceptable to shorten *December* to *Dec.*, or even worse to write the date numerically as *1.12.19--*. (In Europe that would be interpreted as *12 January*.)

Conventions still link the recipient's name and address, the salutation and the complimentary close. Thus a letter addressed to a company, *Ideal Estates Plc*, should commence *Dear Sirs* (note the plural *Sirs*). A letter addressed to an individual by title will begin *Dear Sir*. The formal beginning *Dear Sir(s)* used invariably to be followed by the formal ending

*Yours faithfully* but now *Yours sincerely* is sometimes used, except for very formal letters. If you know the name of your correspondent, it is usual to address him by name rather than as *Dear Sir*. Letters to women, married or unmarried, begin *Dear Madam*, unless you are addressing them by name. If in doubt as to the sex of your correspondent use *Dear Sir* but never *Dear Sir or Madam*.

Letters to someone by name are usually addressed to *Mr J. Brown*; the form *J. Brown Esq.* is virtually obsolete — perhaps just as well since it was often used to emphasise class distinctions.

The signature block should include signature, the name (printed for legibility) and if a title, *Sales Manager, Sports Secretary*, is relevant it should be used to make clear the author's authority to write on behalf of the organisation. If a letter is signed on behalf of a superior, this should be indicated:

> *Yours faithfully*
>
> *Lesley Penworthy*
>
> *for James Golightly*
> *Sales Manager*

The expression *Dictated by Mr Golightly and signed in his absence* is sometimes used and it is a courtesy to the reader, since it indicates that his letter has had the manager's personal attention.

When a woman signs a letter she should indicate her status as follows:

(a) if she uses her forename in the signature, for example Jane Smith, and does not put *Mrs*, it will be assumed that she is *Miss*

(b) if she prefers to use an initial her name should be followed by her status, for example *J. Smith (Miss)*

(c) if she uses her forename and wishes to indicate her married status, then she signs herself *Jane Smith (Mrs)* — the expression *Ms* which is the equivalent of *Mr* and does not distinguish marital status is often preferred by women at work.

### Planning

All but the simplest of letters need to be planned carefully. The best way to do this is to make a list of the points to be covered, using a new line for each point. You can then arrange them in the best order by numbering them (see also Chapter 11, Example 1, p. 170). Some of the possibilities are given below.

(a) In a reply use the order of the original.

(b) Ascending order of importance. This implies that minor items will be presented first before one reaches the main topic of the letter.

(c) Descending order of importance. Here the main topic is presented first, followed by the minor details.

(d) Chronological order is often a logical choice. Thus a series of events will be presented in the order in which they happened.

Whatever sequence you think most suitable you need to consider: 'Suitable for whom?' The interests of your reader must be put first. Hence (a) above is particularly courteous to the reader since it uses his order of priorities. It incidentally saves the writer time and thought in planning!

As a very general guide, the following skeleton can be useful:

(a) state briefly what the letter is about
(b) amplify your brief opening statement
(c) purpose
(d) conclusion.

(a) *What the letter is about*

A heading can often be the ideal, concise way to announce the subject to the reader; otherwise the opening paragraph must immediately state the subject of the letter. It should be short, as indeed all the paragraphs of the letter should be. Frequently the letter will be a reply, when the simple opening sentence

> *Thank you for your letter of 15 June, 19--, about . . .*

is perhaps the most satisfactory form, though it *is* sterotyped.

(b) *Amplifying information*

Simply because you have kept your opening statement brief you will often find it necessary to add details in a succeeding paragraph or paragraphs to explain exactly what it is about.

(c) *The purpose*

This is the most important part of the letter. It may contain for example, a request for action, the statement of a decision, or the information requested.

(d) *Conclusion*

Don't use one unless you have something worth saying. Stereotyped expressions such as

> *I hope this information will be of interest to you*

are virtually meaningless. You should be sure by the choice of information and by the way it is expressed that the ending is of interest. A more constructive way of ending is to use the conclusion as a signpost to the reader, pointing him to the next step, the action required:

> *I shall be grateful if you will consider these choices and let me know which one you prefer.*

A positive expression of interest or concern can also be a useful way of signing off, for example

> *Please let me know if I can give you any further help.*

What do you think of these two endings?

> *I hope you will give this your careful consideration.*
>
> *Once again, we apologise . . .*

They are well meaning but ineffective. The first has an officious tone, the second is merely weak. If you are in doubt about the end of your letter, cover it up and see how the letter reads without it. If the letter loses no strength or energy, then omit your conclusion.

The letter in Figure 1.4 a real letter, is a splendid example of bad

**Fig 1.4** *a badly planned letter*

```
Dear Sirs

With reference to the telephone call of recent date
we wish to advise you that the information on your
outstanding items is as follows, 992945 has been
delivered on document number 267339 and we have asked
for Proof of Delivery from our Despatch Department
on this item.  U1300 is unfortunately back ordered
at the moment.  D104 is no longer in our range and
you were sent a letter advising you of the situation.
Item 994130 has been issued and should be with you
within the next 10 days.  A6005 and A6011 are both
back ordered at the moment.  A6007 has been issued
Thursday and Friday of this week and should be with
you within 10 days.  D315 has been issued to you
on document number 282390 and we have again asked
our Despatch Department for Proof of Delivery on this
item.  Items D996, D935 and D995 a letter was sent to
you advising you that these items must be ordered
in a minimum of 20.  Item 49493 HB pencils have been
have been issued and should be with you within the next
10 days.

We hope this clarifies the situation on these out-
standing items.

Yours faithfully,
```

planning. Clearly the writer compiled it from the notes jotted down during an unstructured telephone conversation. Such a mass of ill-assorted information in one long paragraph is very hard to understand.

On the other hand, the author of the letter shown in Figure 1.5 has taken pains not only to plan, but to display a long and complicated reply in a clear and readable way.

**Fig 1.5** *good planning and display*

```
Dear Mrs Unwin

COMMUNICATION FOR BUSINESS AND SECRETARIAL STUDENTS

Thank you for your letter of 3 June and for the parcel
of page proofs, typescript copy and galley proofs.

I have looked through your proofs, noting your
corrections and my answers to your queries 1-8 are
given below, in that order.

1. Spacing of Headings

The spacing of the section headings has now been
amended and the printer has been told what action
to take.


................et cetera
```

## Language, style and tone

Just as manners have become more informal in the past few decades, so generally has the language of business letters. However, there are still people to whom we shall need to use more formal language; when we write to those much higher or lower in status to ourselves perhaps. Similarly there are situations which call for formality: disciplinary letters, redundancy letters, requests for overdue payment, for example.

But there are never circumstances to justify the sort of language to be found in Figure 1.6. What sort of person do you imagine the writer to be? Pompous, for a start!

Our aim has to be to sound natural, friendly and fluent, and Figure 1.7 demonstrates that even the briefest letter can convey friendly concern. There are two key words in that very short letter which imply warm interest: *indeed* and *welcome*.

Opening the letter is often the most difficult part. Two beginnings to avoid are *With reference to . . .* and *I am writing . . . . With reference to* often leads the writer into either long and rambling sentences or incomplete ones such as *With reference to your letter of 1 March. I am writing* is simply stating the obvious.

**Fig 1.6** *a pompous letter*

```
Dear Sirs

We shall be pleased to receive at your earliest
convenience details of your organisation for dis-
tribution within our own organisation in order
to confirm these fact to members of our own staff.

If you could publish details of this organisation
in detail it will simplify our task to achieve
the objective of having the information available
at an early date.

We would suggest that a meeting be held at these
offices during January with your U K agents if
preferred on a date to be agreed to give you the
opportunity of outlining your proposals and ensuring
our interpretation is correct and in accordance
with our own interpretation of the main requirements.

Yours faithfully
```

**Fig 1.7** *a helpful letter*

```
Dear Mr X

CONFERENCE AT BLANK TECHNICAL COLLEGE

We are indeed interested in your Conference to
be held on 9th September and should be prepared
to man a display.

Further details of how you intend to run the
Exhibition would be welcome.

Yours sincerely
```

Consideration for the reader implies, among other things, that letters will be promptly replied to and that it should not be necessary to apologise for delay (if delay cannot be avoided then an acknowledgement should be sent). But if such an apology is necessary, then don't bore your reader by long explanations and excuses. In Figure 1.8 the writer's well-intentioned apology and explanation contrive to insult the reader by implying that he is rather low on the writer's list of priorities.

The style we choose will be a compromise between several different elements.

(a) *It will to some extent reflect our own personalities.* This is not to say that we should use too idiosyncratic a style, for we are seeking to project an image not only of ourselves but also of the organisation on whose behalf we may be writing. But an element of originality is desirable.

**Fig 1.8** *good intentions!*

```
Dear Mr X,

Thank you for your letter of 20th June,
and I apologise for the delay in answering
it.  I have recently returned from holiday
and have had a great many things to attend
to.  If you will be kind enough to give me
the address to which you would like the
material sent, I will despatch a quantity
of our latest catalogues and bulletins to
you.

                Yours sincerely,
```

Originality in this context implies that the letter will both avoid the use of stereotyped phrases or jargon and will also impress the reader as having been written with him in mind and to meet his particular needs.

The letter in Figure 1.9 is in fact a standard letter. It reflects the house style of the organisation from which it originated: friendly, efficient, informal – but not casual.

**Fig 1.9** *style and tone*

```
Dear Sirs,

            Our letter:

            Subject matter:

    We cannot trace having received a reply to our
letter.  It would help us if you could make enquiries
and let us have your comments.  If you have already
replied, we apologise for having troubled you - but
will you please let us have a copy of your answer?

    We shall be grateful for your co-operation.

                Yours faithfully,
```

(b) *Our style, in the choice of vocabulary, sentence structure, and so on, will aim primarily to be understood.* We shall need to adapt to different readers. A letter to ratepayers, explaining the need to increase rates, will use very different language from a report on the same subject circulated within the Treasurer's department.

(c) *Finally, the style must be suitable to the subject.* The comments made earlier on formality and informality are relevant here. A letter giving instructions will use a different approach from one that is asking a favour; a letter of adjustment will be conciliatory, a sales letter will need enthusiasm.

## Standard letters and paragraphs

To have a file of standard letters which can be used over and over again for routine recurring situations is a great time- and money-saver. A manager, instead of planning and dictating a letter, merely requests the typist to send, say, letter no. SR39. The typist who is familiar with the wording will also be speedier.

Some firms go to a great deal of trouble to compile such a file; one firm has six different letters for rejecting job applicants. Some are modified for the different types of job, other reject finally, some invite the applicant to apply again in the future. Although extra time needs to be spent on producing particularly good letters for regular re-use, this investment can ensure that the letters are truly effective.

There are some drawbacks to the use of standard letters: first, stock answers may not be quite appropriate to particular circumstances; and second, how does the customer who might receive several identical letters feel?

Standard paragraphs that can be fitted together as required are perhaps a little more flexible than standard letters but there is still the danger that the standard paragraph may not fit neatly into the newly composed 'special' parts of the letter.

The standard letter in Figure 1.10 shows time well spent on composing a difficult letter. Its tone is reasonable, persuasive, fair but firm, and the message is absolutely clear.

---

### FOCUS

Always read your letters through before you sign them
Ask yourself:
    Does it look attractive?
    Does it cover all essential points?
    Is the information correct?
    Is it clear, concise and courteous?
    Does it sound natural and sincere?
    Will the tone create the right impression?

IS IT THE KIND OF LETTER YOU WOULD LIKE TO RECEIVE IF YOU WERE IN YOUR CORRESPONDENT'S PLACE?

**Fig 1.10** *a standard letter*

Dear Sirs

**OVERDUE ACCOUNT**

As you know, we have already asked you to settle the overdue account detailed at the foot of this letter.

Your failure to do so has cost you the cash discount and is prejudicing future supplies.

**WITHDRAWAL OF CREDIT**

We regret that, from today, credit facilities on all your other outstanding accounts are withdrawn. These accounts, therefore, are also due for immediate payment.

**DEBT COLLECTION**

In view of our previous good business relationship, we are reluctant to pass your accounts to a debt collection agency, but such is the policy of our company. Thus, unless immediate payment is received you will unfortunately leave us no alternative.

Please, in your own interests, send us your payment in full, in the enclosed reply-paid envelope, **NOW**.

Yours faithfully


Accounts Manager

<u>Invoice Number</u>          <u>Date</u>                              <u>Amount</u>


Enclosure: SAE

## Types of letter

*Letters of complaint*

A dissatisfied customer who feels unfairly treated is likely to be angry. It is essential to overcome the temptation to show this by rudeness or sarcasm in a letter seeking redress. A moment's reflection shows that such a tone can hardly fail to antagonise the reader and is unlikely to persuade him to consider the complaint with sympathy.

The tone of a successful letter should therefore be reasonable but firm. All the relevant information should be presented clearly, and copies, not originals, of any documents involved should be included if possible. If the letter is about faulty goods, they should not be returned with the letter, but retained as evidence, or possibly returned personally.

Figure 1.11 shows a letter of complaint which carefully explains the

**Fig 1.11** *a letter of complaint*

```
                                        5 The Larches,
                                           BLANKTON,
                                             Exshire,
                                              BL5 4JS

                                        16th October, 19--

The Manager,
Blank Electricity Board,
BLANKTON,
Exshire.
BL1 6BD

Dear Sir,

              Electricity Account No.NB.456/H

     I was concerned to receive your final demand of
13th October, 19-- for payment of my quarterly elec-
tricity account of £35.78.

     I wrote to you on 25th September querying this
account and my letter was acknowledged by a card from you
stating that my letter was receiving attention.   I have
not yet received a full reply.

     In my earlier letter, of which I enclose a copy, I
questioned the amount of the account, which I believe is
far too high an estimate for a summer quarter during
which electricity was used only for cooking and lighting.

     The meter now reads 52405 units. Will you please
send me a revised account based on this actual reading
or, if this reading is unacceptable, send your meter
reader to check.

     In view of your threat to cut off my electricity, I
hope that you will reply promptly.

                    Yours faithfully,


                     B. Bloggs

Enclosure
```

problem but perhaps does not (justifiably?) succeed in avoiding an aggrieved tone. The letter shown in Figure 1.12 demanded much more skill from its writer. He might well have felt angry at the rejection of his claim but he sat down and carefully worked out how to appeal to the company's sense of fair play in order to succeed. His claim was met!

**Fig 1.12** *a letter seeking redress*

```
Dear Sirs

CLAIM ON HOUSEHOLD POLICY AX 468/43779

I have received your letter of 16 April  rejecting
my claim because you do not consider that the
terms of the Policy include accidental damage
to shower trays.

I sincerely believe that this is not fair.
It looks as if the wording of the Policy goes
back a number of years to a time when showers
were uncommon.  So it does not mention them.

You will agree that nowadays more and more
people have showers and that they are not at
all exceptional.  They are even officially
recommended as a way of saving fuel.

Because it seems to me that I am being penalised
by an unintentional omission from your Policy,
I feel justified in making a complaint of unfair
treatment to the British Insurance Association.

You are such an old and well-known insurance
company that, before doing this, it seems reason-
able to ask you first if you will reconsider
my claim.

Yours faithfully
```

## Letters of adjustment

Any complaint, justified or not, should receive a prompt reply. If you are wrong, then an apology is necessary and it should come early in the letter. One apology is enough. If the complaint is unjustified, then you can still, discreetly, express some sympathy with the inconvenience the customer has suffered. Tell the customer early in the letter if you are meeting his complaint with an adjustment satisfactory to him. This will conciliate him and ensure that he reads any following explanation with some sympathy.

If his request is unreasonable and you cannot meet it, explain carefully why this is so. You don't want to lose a customer.

It is helpful to avoid using negative expressions, for example by saying *We are pleased you have drawn our attention to* rather than *We have received your complaint about*. Figure 1.13 shows the reply which was sent to the complaint made in Figure 1.11.

**Fig 1.13** *a letter of adjustment*

```
19 October 19--

B Bloggs Esq
5 The Larches
BLANKTON
Exshire
BL5 4JS

Dear Mr Bloggs

Electricity account No NB 456/H

Thank you for your letter of 16 October 19-- about
the final demand for payment of this account.

We apologise both for the delay in replying to your
letter of 25 September 19--, which appears to have
been mis-filed, and for the final demand which you
were mistakenly sent.

Your meter reading of 52405 is indeed acceptable
and a revised account, which will replace the previous
estimated account, is being sent to you.

Yours sincerely


J Kincaid
Area Manager
```

## Letters of condolence

Perhaps these are the most difficult letters of all to write. They should be sent promptly and written with sincerity and restraint. Figure 1.14 is from the standard letter file of a large company. Do you approve of it?

**Fig 1.14** *a letter of condolence*

```
Dear Mrs X

We were all most shocked to hear of the sudden
death of your husband John last Wednesday and
I write on behalf of the Company to express our
deepest sympathy to you and your family.

In his nineteen years with the Company John had
proved a real asset and had made many friends;
his loss will be felt on all sides.

I realise only too well how much distress you
must have been caused and have asked Tom Smith
from our Personnel Department to keep in touch
with you to offer what assistance he can.

Yours most sincerely
```

## Letters of application

Many firms use job application forms or are so informal as to invite applicants to telephone to arrange an interview. But for many jobs, and especially more senior ones, we have to compose a letter. There are in fact two choices: a letter containing all the information; or a shorter covering letter together with a *curriculum vitae* containing information set out on a separate sheet.

The second choice is preferable. It looks more businesslike and the tabulation makes the information easier for the reader. The shorter covering letter is easier to compose effectively when it is not cluttered with miscellaneous detail about your qualifications, etc.

The *curriculum vitae* should be typed and can be planned as follows.

*Personal details*
Name
Address
Telephone number
Date of birth

*Details of education*
School/college/university
Examinations and qualifications

*Experience*

| Dates | Name of company | Job title |
|---|---|---|

*Any other relevant information*
Referees (1)
         (2)

Usually two referees are sufficient, though a third may be asked for. One will be a professional reference, possibly your current or a previous employer. The second may be called a character reference and you should choose someone of standing who has known you for a period of time.

Courtesy demands that your referees should have been asked to act for you *before* you give their names. If you are able to give them some information about the post for which you have applied, they will be able to make their reference more relevant and helpful.

The plan for the covering letter might be:

(i) reference to the advertisement and statement of application
(ii) reference to the enclosed *curriculum vitae*
(iii) amplification of details of *curriculum vitae*
(iv) complimentary close.

Your letter must sound like *you*, it must convey something of your own personality. However, if you are a very unassuming person, you will need to make the effort to sound a little more forceful than usual. After all you do have to speak for yourself on this occasion!

Remember that the aim of this letter is to ensure that your name goes on to the shortlist and takes you to the next stage, the interview. To do this you need to study the advertisement very carefully indeed, decide what sort of person with what qualifications, is being sought, and then show that you *are* that person. You need to show enthusiasm and interest in the company and the position (without being too overwhelming about it). Remember how many other applications your letter may have to compete against and try to ensure that it will stand out and compel attention.

The covering letter should be handwritten. Many employers like to see a specimen of your handwriting. Some large companies, especially in the USA, employ experts (graphologists) to examine applicants' handwriting.

Since every letter of application should be unique to the individual and specially written as a response to one particular advertisement, no model is given here.

## 1.2 MEMORANDA

Memoranda (*memos* for short) are the equivalent within a business of the letters sent to people outside it — internal correspondence, in fact.

They contribute largely to the impression we make on our fellow workers, subordinates and superiors, and therefore deserve a little more care than they are sometimes given. Because they are often notes to our colleagues they receive less attention than our missives to the outside world.

The paper on which they are written or typed is usually pre-printed and, so that staff may be encouraged to keep memos short, it is often of A5 size. Figure 1.15 shows some examples of printed memo forms, but there are many variations. One organisation uses a pre-printed set of three A4 size sheets, coloured white, blue and pink respectively, with no carbon required. The top half of the set is used for the original message, the white and blue sheets are sent to the recipient and the pink sheet is filed. The recipient writes his answer on the bottom half, returns the white sheet and files the blue one. This has the advantage that question and answer appear on the same sheet of paper.

If a memo is to be sent to several people, all their names should appear so that each knows who else has received it. Sometimes multiple copies are made, one for each recipient. Occasionally a circulation list is attached and each reader will tick his name on the list to indicate that the memo has been read.

Fig 1.15  *memo formats*

---

**MEMORANDUM**

---

                             DATE:
    TO:                   FROM:

---

**Name of Firm**

**Memorandum**

From: .................. To: ..................
Date: .................. Ref: ..................
Subject:......................................

---

FIRM          MEMORANDUM      FORM NO 632

---

TO        SUBJECT        FROM
                                 DATE

Sometimes memos are used as notices for display on a board. These should be particularly carefully designed so that the information is clearly displayed and very easy to read.

Memos are no longer merely reminders. The format may be used for quite lengthy documents, even for informal reports.

The principles of letter-writing apply: you need to plan what you are going to say and to say it clearly, concisely and in words which will be understood by the reader.

---

### FOCUS

There is one golden rule to bear in mind always: that we should try to put ourselves in the position of our correspondent, to imagine his feeling as he writes his letters and to gauge his reactions as he receives ours.

*Advice from the Board of Inland Revenue to its employees!*

---

## 1.3 ASSIGNMENTS

1  Look at the letter given in Figure 1.4. Sort the information out into a more suitable order and rewrite the letter, taking care to display the information clearly and attractively. (An answer is given in Appendix 1.)

2  Comment on the use of the letter in business communications. [IAA]

3  You work in the West Country office of an insurance company. One of your clients, Luxor Carpet Mills, has inadvertently failed to pay a premium by the due date and now faces a heavy fire loss. Your principal is at present in Aberdeen. He has telephoned you to say that he will visit the client next week. He asks you to write to Luxor to let them know. They are one of your firm's most important and reputable clients and he will do his best to see that the fire claim is met. You are to mention this in your letter without actually committing your firm to any legal obligation.

Meanwhile, it is essential that the outstanding premium is paid immediately so that the mill is covered against any further fire losses. A loss adjuster from your office will need to visit the mill at the earliest opportunity to make a detailed preliminary inspection. (He may also wish to question staff, examine documents and have on-site consultations with senior management.) You should make suitable tentative proposals in your letter.

Using as much of the foregoing data as you need, and inventing any additional minor details as appropriate, write the letter. [adapted from LCC PSD]

4  Your employer has recently been elected president of a professional association. He has planned to invite the twelve members of the

association's council (the governing body) to visit his factory. After being his guests at lunch, the council will hold a session in your employer's boardroom to conduct routine business. Your employer has prepared the necessary papers ready for circulation, and has even arranged the menu, but before he has been able to inform the council members of the invitation to visit his factory and hold a meeting there, he has had to fly to Australia for several days' urgent business.

On your employer's behalf, you need to prepare and send out a circular letter to the members of the council. You will need to explain the situation, briefly and without undue formality. At the same time, the letter will be a notice of meeting. Mention any further details which you think might be particularly important. (*Note*: there is no need to give the text of any 'enclosures' you may send.) [LCC PSC]

5   As Principal of a college write a letter to the Personnel Officer of a large firm inviting him or her to address a group of students who hope to join his organisation.

As the Personnel Officer, write a reply accepting the invitation. Outline the main points you will include in your talk.

# REPORTS

A business report is a document in which a given situation or problem is considered. It may state facts, give analyses and opinions, report progress, draw conclusions, and, perhaps, make proposals.

## 2.1 VARIETIES OF REPORT

Reports vary in length, degree of formality and format as much as they do in content. In some companies they are standardised, using a common house style and presentation. Forms often exist for accident and safety reports, progress reports or reporting the results of scientific investigation.

Whether written or oral, for internal or external use, standardised or specially written, reports do have certain elements in common. They must be precisely and concisely written and are a widespread method of informing management (and others) of persuading and of initiating change.

Many reports do not fit into the standard patterns, however. Discussion of these 'special' reports forms the greater part of this chapter as they demand a particular approach.

**Standard reports**

These use a pattern acceptable within an organisation. Certain formal headings may always be used, such as:

> Terms of reference
> Procedure
> Findings
> Conclusions and recommendations.

A specific numbering system may be common, together with such instruction as:

*Use note form,* OR
*Reports should not exceed X thousand words.*

Financial data may always have to be presented in a particular tabulated form. Also, a preliminary summary/synopsis may be required.

The application of a standard system depends on whether sufficient reports in the organisation are regularly repeated. Monthly sales and production reports, for instance, could suitably be standardised.

### Form reports

Further standardisation can take place with the use of pre-printed forms. These are commonly used for accident or progress reports (see Figure 2.1). The practice can usefully be extended to other areas as well, for instance to save the writer's time because he does not have to plan each one and to save the reader's time because the format is familiar.

The designing of forms is a specialist job on which advice is given in section 5.5. Here we are concerned with the completion of form reports, and so we shall assume that they are well designed and suitable for their purpose.

When you have to fill in a report form, start by asking yourself some questions, such as:

(a) *Who is going to use this?*
(b) *How will it be used?*
(c) *What information is essential?*

Most forms give relatively little space and demand very concise reporting. The combined arts of summarising and note-making (see Chapter 3) must be applied with precision. Ambiguity or missing out important facts are major dangers.

The example of the progress report shown in Figure 2.1 shows the care that needs to be taken. Section 2 of that report could easily have been ambiguous if worded thus:

*State the target hoped for this month.*

Sections 3, 4 and 5 have to be very concise as space allowed is very limited.

### Special reports

Each of these reports will in some ways be a one off, though they will sometimes follow, at least partly, the pattern of a previous report. They include:

## Fig 2.1 *progress report*

**MONTHLY PROGRESS REPORT**

MONTH.................... DESCRIPTION......................
JOB NO....................

---

1. STATUS OF JOB AT END OF PREVIOUS MONTH (Enter item 6.
   from previous report)

MOST URGENT      VERY URGENT       URGENT      NON-URGENT

    (delete whichever inapplicable)

---

2. TARGET THIS MONTH (Enter target stated in item 7. of
previous report)

..........................................................
..........................................................

---

3. HAS TARGET BEEN ACHIEVED?      YES/NO (delete whichever
                                                     inapplicable)
    IF NOT, STATE REASONS FOR DELAY

..........................................................
..........................................................
..........................................................

---

4. PROBLEMS ENCOUNTERED (other than in 3. above)

..........................................................
..........................................................
..........................................................

---

5. SOLUTIONS ACHIEVED

..........................................................
..........................................................
..........................................................

---

6. PRESENT STATUS OF JOB (delete if inapplicable)

MOST URGENT      VERY URGENT       URGENT      NON-URGENT

---

7. TARGET TO BE ACHIEVED BY END OF NEXT MONTH

..........................................................
..........................................................

---

8. FINAL COMPLETION DATE (if different from orginal estimate)

..........................................................

---

SIGNATURE............... DESIGNATION......................

DATE....................

(a) self-inaugurated reports
(b) investigative reports
(c) feasibility studies
(d) annual reports to shareholders and employees
(e) organisation and method studies
(f) work studies.

Some will be very short and informal, perhaps presented as memoranda. Others will be the result of long and intensive work by a team of researchers and will run into thousands of words. (Reports of Royal Commissions are published in book form and may fill several volumes.)

All will, however, have common elements and can be successfully written by following the same logical and methodical scheme of planning and writing.

## 2.2 COMPILING A REPORT

### The purpose
It is important to establish immediately the exact purpose of the report. Think of who is to read it, what it is intended to achieve and how it will be used. From this you can establish your 'terms of reference' — see section 2.4.

### Planning the report
The general method of planning communications as outlined in Chapter 11.5 is applicable to the compilation of reports but there are particular features about report writing.

## 2.3 SUMMARY

Although found at the beginning of some reports, the summary obviously cannot be completed until the whole report is written. It should be of not more than one page and should include a comment on the main areas of investigation, general conclusions and proposals. An example follows the sample report in section 2.16.

## 2.4 TERMS OF REFERENCE

Before starting to compile a report it is wise to write out the terms of reference so that you know precisely what you have been asked (or have decided) to do. They will also form the opening of the report. Terms of reference should include the following:

(a) By whom the report has been requested —
EXAMPLES
> *at the request of the Sales Director*
> *as directed by the Board*

(b) The precise area to be covered —
EXAMPLES
> *to enquire into present procedure of . . .*
> *to examine the documentation in the . . . department*
> *to carry out a feasibility study into . . .*

(c) What it is intended should be the outcome of the report — the objectives —
EXAMPLES
> *to establish the nature and extent of existing problems and make recommendations for their solution*
> *to inform shareholders of plans for rationalisation*
> *to make proposals for market development*

(d) Establishing the limits of the report, such as recognition of financial or economic constraints, company policy, union agreements or factors external to a department which partially determine the working method.

EXAMPLE OF TERMS OF REFERENCE
*This study, requested by the Sales Director, investigates the present Sales Order methods and documentation and presents proposals for reorganisation and improvement.*

*The report recognises that the requirements of other departments must be met in any reorganisation suggested.*

## 2.5 PROCEDURE

This element concerns the method of investigation to be adopted. There are several which may need to be mentioned in a section of the final report which immediately follows the terms of reference. Methods which might be mentioned include:

(a) experiment
(b) observation
(c) survey
(d) consultation
(e) research.

See also Figure 2.2.

People consulted should be identified and reference made to the place of experimental, survey or research material in the report. Any reference material separately listed in a bibliography should also be noted.

## Fig 2.2 *methods of investigation*

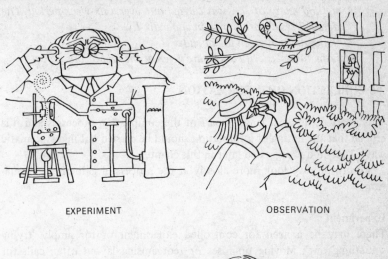

EXPERIMENT                    OBSERVATION

SURVEY

CONSULTATION                  RESEARCH

> *Departmental staff were consulted.*
> *A method study of . . . was carried out over a six-week period. The detailed results are shown in appendix I.*
> *A bibliography is given in appendix II.*
> *Manufacturers' specifications are given at the end of this report.*

## 2.6 COLLECTION OF INFORMATION

This is often the most lengthy part of the compilation processes and it is crucial that the noting of information should be carried out in a systematic way. A method is suggested later in this chapter.

Meanwhile, we look more closely at the process of gathering information.

### Experiment
There may be a need for controlled experiment or for simply 'trying something out'. Moving premises or reorganising layout often calls for scale floor plans and models of furniture, equipment, etc.

### Observation
This would include method studies, work measurement, observation of customer or staff behaviour, analysis of work flow, etc.

### Survey
Market surveys are familiar. Attitude surveys have also come into use and questionnaires of many kinds abound.

### Consultation
Discussions with both colleagues and outside experts are often helpful and necessary. The first draws on the expertise of colleagues and has the additional advantage of involving them in establishing proposals for change which they might otherwise resist. Second, our own knowledge may be limited in extent and restricted in outlook. Outside experts (or even contacts with experience of similar problems) can extend our information and give a more objective appraisal.

### Research
We may need to seek information from publications, whether these are books, specialist periodicals, trade literature, sales brochures, or previous in-company reports. If research is considerable, then the report should include a bibliography at the end which states the name of the publication, publication date, title of article (if appropriate) and author(s).

## 2.7 QUESTIONS TO BE ASKED

The method or methods chosen will be determined by the nature of the report. Some questions will, however, commonly arise and need detailed answers, such as.

(a)  What is the present position (or method)?
(b)  What are the problems?
(c)  What are the objectives of the report?

EXAMPLE OF DETAILS OF PRESENT POSITION

A report which seeks to reorganise the Sales Office must first establish.

(a)  What broad areas of work are carried out? For instance
     *accepting orders – by mail; by telephone*
     *completing order forms*
     *checking orders received from representatives*
     *processing orders to production department, etc.*
(b)  Within each area, what is the *exact* method of work which is prescribed?
(c)  What methods of work are actually followed?
(d)  Where (b) and (c) differ, what are the reasons for the variation?
(e)  Are there any aspects of the work for which there is no prescribed procedure?
(f)  What is the documentation and how is it used?
(g)  What about supervision and control?

And so on.

EXAMPLE OF PROBLEMS DISCOVERED

The following broad headings might apply and would have to be expanded to give detail:

> *organisation structure*
> *methods of work*
> *communication*
> *documentation*
> *layout and work flow*
> *equipment*
> *insufficient or ill-trained staff*
> *motivation*
> *management and supervision*
> *control systems*

And so on.

EXAMPLE OF THE REPORT OBJECTIVES

This area cannot be detailed until the first two questions have been answered. It might include improvement of some of the following:

*reduction of waste*
*co-ordination and control*
*simplification*
*cost reduction*
*quality control*
*communication and documentation*
*morale and job satisfaction*
*selection and training*

And so on.

## 2.8 RECORDING THE INFORMATION

There are four rules which, added to the planning techniques outlined in Chapter 11.5, simplify the work of a long report and reduce the amount of writing.

**Write in short note form**
Don't use full sentences or paragraphs until you come to write the final draft.

**Use a new page for each topic**
This is a method of keeping similar information together and distinct from dissimilar items. It also allows for the addition of new information.

**Write on one side of the paper only**
This allows for the re-ordering of material without rewriting. Your notes become a pack of cards to be shuffled into suits.

**Use A4 size paper**
Large sheets of paper are easier to cope with than small ones. With a long and complex document this method keeps rewriting down to the minimum.

## 2.9 ANALYSIS OF THE FINDINGS

Reverting to the three questions mentioned in Chapter 2.7, we can now examine the details of our answers. It may not be possible to tackle all the problems identified, but it is important to adopt a positive approach to them. Don't feel that:

(a) any problem is insoluble, even if it is a long-standing one
(b) you know in advance that some of the solutions which may be suggested will not work
(c) you do not know enough about the situation to be able to reach a satisfactory solution
(d) your proposals may not find favour with your manager and so are not worth presenting
(e) there is only going to be one possible solution to each problem.

Such negative approaches could prevent success. Instead, work through the details of each problem, analysing why and how it occurs and the consequences, but keeping an open mind on its solution.

### EXAMPLE OF PROBLEM-SOLVING APPROACH

In the report example IMPROVEMENT OF SAFETY RECORD given in section 2.16 mention is made of the safety problem in the offices of a company where there are cramped conditions and a proliferation of electrical equipment without sufficient suitably placed power points. The second appendix to that report might have been written from the following notes.

### *SURVEY OF PREMISES: SECTION 2 THE GENERAL OFFICE*

*EXISTING SITUATION*

>*Size of office − 6 × 4 metres*
>*Number of staff: 16*
>*Number and position of power points: 12 (see attached layout)*
>*Equipment needing mains electricity:*
>>*2 word processors*
>>*1 high-speed printer*
>>*6 electric typewriters*
>>*2 plain-paper copiers*
>>*1 collator*
>>*1 stapler*
>>*4 mains calculators*
>>*3 VDUs on-line to main computer*
>>*$\overline{20}$*
>*Positions of desks and equipment (see attached layout)*
>*Expansion planned*

*CONSEQUENCES*

>*(a) Insufficient power points*
>*(b) Lack of space*

(c) Poor positioning of equipment vis-à-vis points and lighting
(d) Trailing leads
(e) Possible accidents
(f) Inefficiency and low morale
(g) Effects on health

POSSIBLE SOLUTIONS

(a) Move into new building, planned specifically to cater for expansion (build if necessary)
(b) Take over the three managers' offices in same corridor
   (i) move them to another area (to be decided on)
   (ii) either open up the three offices and join to general offices, or move Wages, Sales and Purchasing sections respectively into the separate offices
(c) Move the three sections in b (ii) into another area
(d) Move all the typists/secretaries into another area
(e) Reorganise the existing space to use it more effectively
(f) Rewire and install 8 more power points or put in double points
(g) Sink leads in underfloor channels
(h) Invest in power packs to remove need for so much mains electricity
(i) Buy solar-powered calculators
(j) Install venetian blinds
(k) Improve artificial light
(l) Introduce more sophisticated and miniaturised microelectronics to reduce work force and release space
(m) Replace the two copiers and collator with one sophisticated high-speed copier with attached collator

ANALYSIS OF SOLUTIONS

(There would then have to be a close analysis of each suggestion, considering whether it is within the terms of reference of a report on safety, its practicality, desirability and cost effectiveness.)

As the detailed analysis proceeds, certain common threads will become apparent and will thus emerge as the major areas in which solutions must be sought.

## 2.10 SEARCHING FOR SOLUTIONS

Sometimes a possible solution springs to mind quickly. However, it is dangerous to accept it as the best approach without seeking more widely. Even unlikely approaches should be thoroughly examined.

The report should include all the solutions considered, even those which after analysis prove unsuitable. This will pre-empt the risk of criticism that the report is not thorough. Additionally it is not only the technical suitability of solutions that must be considered but also their cost effectiveness and impact on both management and employees.

## 2.11 CONCLUSIONS AND RECOMMENDATIONS

A final choice has to be made of the solutions to be recommended. The conclusions of a report should state clearly which of the solutions are most effective and why. The recommendations then follow automatically.

---

### FOCUS

Special reports will include a combination of some or all of the following elements:
    summary
    terms of reference
    procedure
    collection of information
    analysis of information
    consideration of solutions
    conclusions
    recommendations

---

## 2.12 ILLUSTRATIONS

Most reports benefit from relevant illustrative data or other material, such as plans. These illustrations should be numbered, referred to in the text and placed as near as possible to the point in the text where they are first mentioned. Bulky or complex illustrations might be placed in appendices.

## 2.13 APPENDICES

So that the main flow of argument is not interrupted by a mass of detail, information such as bibliographies, results of surveys, technical specifications, financial and other data can be summarised or referred to in the report but attached at the end. Appendices are to a report as enclosures are to a letter.

## 2.14 WRITING THE REPORT

Successful use of the method suggested in section 2.8 will mean that the report will only have to be written out once in full before it is typed.

### Title
When writing starts, the choice of title must come first, but this can often prove difficult. A simple, concise title can frequently be used.

EXAMPLES

> *Computerised Accounting – a Feasibility Study*
> *Survey of Sales Office Documentation*
> *Report on the October 19-- Sales Promotion Campaign*

Sometimes a short title merits expansion with a sub-title.

EXAMPLES

> *Computerised Accounting*
> *a feasibility study on the introduction of a micro-computer for sales and purchase accounting*
>
> *Sales Office Documentation*
> *a report investigating problems with existing documentation and proposing improvements*
>
> *Sales Promotion Campaign*
> *report on the October 19-- promotion prepared for the meeting of regional managers to be held on 16 December 19--*

You will note that these titles contain part of the terms of reference of each report.

### Language and style
Reports are generally written in formal language and often wholly in the third person. However it is not incorrect to use the first person, *I* or *We*, when the report is addressed to a person or persons known well. Indeed, a useful phrase with which to start a report to your manager would be.

> *As you requested, I have examined . . . ,* or
> *As you instructed, we . . . ,* or
> *According to your instruction, I . . .*

The report must be objective, based on facts rather than opinion. It must show clearly the distinction between the *facts* and the *inferences* drawn from the facts. It must seek to persuade by logical argument, not to be controversial or provocative. The wording should be concise and technicalities must be explained or limited to meet the reader's existing knowledge.

Tact must be used in presenting both information and recommendations. No manager likes to have his time wasted by having to read facts that he knows well, or to be criticised, or to be told what to do. So:

(a) Assess his knowledge and, if you have to remind him, do so discreetly —
    EXAMPLE

> *The profit margins have diminished by 1.32 per cent points from 3.6 to 2.28 per cent. This is causing concern.*
>
> might be better expressed thus:
>
> *Concern has been expressed at the 1.32 percentage point fall in profit margins. It is felt that, while a margin of 3.6 per cent was acceptable, one of only 2.28 per cent is very narrow.*

(b) Avoid obvious criticism if you wish your report to be successful, and use very great tact —
    EXAMPLE

> *Changes in the department since the present method of working was introduced would seem to make it appropriate to reappraise the procedure. The changes include: . . .*
>
> This might be more acceptable than the following:
>
> *The present method of working is unsatisfactory. There have been a number of changes in the department recently, including . . . . The procedure should be changed.*

(c) The wording of recommendations should avoid the use of the imperative or 'command' form. It is better to write:

> *I recommend that the equipment be purchased*
>
> rather than
>
> *Purchase the equipment.*

**Format**

Reports are documents which are not only to be read but also often to be used in the making of decisions and as a basis for action. They must therefore have a well-defined format which allows for easy reference.

Therefore, we use a system similar to that of a book. Each major section of a report is treated as a chapter, with its own number and heading.

EXAMPLE

Title Page

*Sales Promotion Campaign*
*report on the October 19–– promotion, prepared for the meeting of*
*regional managers to be held on 16 December 19––*
*by*
*J. R. Wilson, Sales Promotion Manager*
*4 December 19––*

Page 1

*CONTENTS*
(Details of contents)        (Page numbers)

.
.
.

Following pages

*(REPEAT OF TITLE)*
*1. TERMS OF REFERENCE*
.
.
.

*2. PROCEDURE*
.
.
.

*3. OUTLINE OF THE PROMOTION CAMPAIGN*
.
.
.

*4. DIFFICULTIES ENCOUNTERED*
.
.
.

*5. ANALYSIS OF IMPACT*
.
.
.

*6. ASSESSMENT OF SUCCESS*
.
.
.

*7. PROPOSALS FOR AMENDMENTS TO FUTURE CAMPAIGNS*
.
.
.

## 8. APPENDICES

.

.

.

No two reports will have the same range of section headings, of course. Short reports will have no title page, contents page or summary, but will start with a first page which includes the title, terms of reference, procedure and perhaps the start of the first main section. Also, the headings, 'Terms of Reference' and 'Procedure' are not always used, the first main section heading being merely preceded by a simple explanatory paragraph.

Flexibility is the keynote, but it is important that whatever headings are used should be definitive of the sections that follow them, as must be any headings for sub-sections.

### Numbering systems

There are two systems of numbering in common use. One follows a pattern similar to that used in this book. Arabic numbers are used and within each section the section number is repeated for each sub-section, followed by a further number.

EXAMPLE

Section Heading

   *3  Outline of Promotion Campaign*

   *3.1  The campaign commenced in the North of England with nightly 45-second television commercials at peak viewing times*
   *3.2  Supplementing this, commerical radio advertisements were broadcast as follows:*
      *3.2.1  on Station Northcoast every morning at 9 am*
      *3.2.2  on Radio Blackpool twice a week at midday.*

A second commonly used system alternates numbers and letters. The example just given could have been numbered like this:

Section Heading ·

   *III*

   *A*

   *B*

   *1*

   *2*

or

  *3*

   *(a)*

   *(b)*

    *(i)*

    *(ii)*

All five varieties of capital and small letters and numbers can, of course, be used if necessary, but it looks better if large Roman numerals and capital letters precede rather than follow the small ones.

### Order of writing

It is desirable that the sections of the full draft of the report should be written in the correct final order. In a short report this is usually possible. However, in a longer investigation sometimes information comes in fits and starts. Sections are therefore ready at different times and can be written in final form even though some of the preceding sections may not be complete.

## 2.15 REVISION AND EDITING

Once the report has been drafted and, preferably, typed, it is desirable to be able to put it aside for a while before revising it. This makes it easier to spot errors and inconsistencies.

It also helps if you can persuade someone else to read and criticise it. Your critic should be encouraged to point out errors of logic, fact, omissions, mistakes in grammar and syntax and also problems of tone and approach. It is often very difficult for the writer of the report to recognise his own errors, so take advantage of any help available from others.

---

### FOCUS

When writing the report consider:
- title
- sub-titles
- language
- style
- format
- section headings
- numbering system
- order of writing
- revisions and editing

## 2.16 EXAMPLE OF A REPORT AND REPORT SUMMARY

**Report on safety**

### IMPROVEMENT OF SAFETY RECORD

#### 1 TERMS OF REFERENCE

As requested by the Safety Committee at their meeting of 16 January 19--, an investigation has been undertaken into the causes of accidents in the company over the year ended 31 December 19--. The findings are given below and recommendations for improvement are contained in sections 5 and 6. These recommendations cover proposals for immediate implementation and areas for further long-term consideration.

#### 2 PROCEDURE

2.1 An analysis has been undertaken of all reported accidents during the period under review. Additionally a detailed survey of the premises has been undertaken by Safety Officers.

2.2 Consultations have been held with union representatives, all levels of management, the Safety Inspectorate and members of the Safety Committee.

#### 3 FINDINGS

3.1 Analysis of reported accidents

The details given in Appendix 1 show that accidents during the past year have had one or more of the following causes in common.

3.1.1 Unsafe equipment. There have been four accidents caused by faulty equipment, one of them very serious.

3.1.2 Failure to comply with safety regulations. Some employees are still reluctant to use safety equipment or follow regulations which they often consider reduce the speed of work and thus diminish bonus earnings.

3.1.3 Ignorance. Three accidents were caused because trainees were not fully conversant with safe working practice.

3.2 Survey of the premises

The information gathered through the Safety Officers' survey is shown in Appendix 2. It shows broadly that the company is complying with statutory health and safety requirements but that improvements are needed in the following areas.

3.2.1 Electric equipment in the offices. More power plugs are required to eradicate the problem of trailing leads. Also the increase in staff numbers has made conditions very cramped and additional space will be needed shortly, particularly with the introduction of more new equipment.

3.2.2 Gangways. Gangways in both the offices and factory are sometimes not kept clear and urgent attention should be paid to this problem.

3.2.3 Factory equipment. Three machines require attention to the guards and this is felt to be a priority.

## 4 OVERCOMING SAFETY PROBLEMS

There would seem to be numerous ways in which the company could seek to eliminate the problems:

4.1 improving the quality of equipment and safety guards

4.2 providing additional power points and resiting equipment in the offices

4.3 removing obstructions from gangways

4.4 providing additional office accommodation

4.5 increasing employee awareness of the availability of and need to use safety equipment

4.6 introducing a programme of training and publicity to improve knowledge of safety regulations and safe working practice

4.7 enquiring further into employee claims that bonus earnings are adversely affected by adhering to safety regulations.

LEEDS METROPOLITAN UNIVERSITY LIBRARY

## 5 RECOMMENDATIONS FOR IMMEDIATE IMPLEMENTATION

5.1 Improvements to equipment

The unsafe equipment and inadequate safety guards mentioned in 3.1.1 and 3.2.3 should receive immediate attention. Details of the work required, together with time/cost estimates, are given in Appendix 3.

It is anticipated that the total cost will not exceed £460 and that the work could be carried out by the Maintenance Department.

5.2 Gangways

All obstructions should be immediately cleared from gangways and Supervisors and Safety Officers instructed to ensure that gangways remain clear.

5.3 Safety equipment

Supervisors should ensure that each department has an adequate supply of goggles, etc., for its needs. They should both set an example by always using such equipment themselves and also reminding their staff to do so.

5.4 Publicity

The use of easily available safety posters should be increased. The Safety Officers should regularly change posters to ensure that their effect is not lost.

## 6 RECOMMENDATIONS FOR LONG-TERM IMPROVEMENT

6.1 Power points and office accommodation

The office accommodation position should be analysed more closely. Additional space should desirably be made available before any additional power points are installed so that an effective and safe office can be planned.

It is recommended that the Safety Committee should ask the Board of Directors to treat this problem as a priority.

6.2 Training and publicity

Plans for more effective training and publicity should be drawn up. It is recommended that the Safety Committee liaise with the Training Department, possibly setting up a small working party, to produce the following:

6.2.1 an improved safety training programme to cover the needs of all new employees

6.2.2 designs for refresher and retraining sessions for existing employees

6.2.3 a safety competition between departments

6.2.4 suggestions for improving awareness through effective publicity.

6.3 Bonus scheme

The Safety Committee should request the Board to discuss the problems of the bonus scheme with the union representative and the work study engineers to establish:

6.3.1 Whether there is a significant problem and its extent.

6.3.2 Whether standard times need revision.

6.3.3 What changes in the bonus scheme could be made.

Since the employees appear to have strong feelings about this problem it is suggested that its satisfactory solution is basic to the effective implementation of many of the other recommendations in this report.

It is hoped that the foregoing recommendations in this report will be endorsed by the Safety Committee and forwarded to the Board of Directors.

T. W. Williams
Chief Safety Officer

26 February 19--

(The appendices mentioned in the example would be attached but are not included here.)

## Summary of report

SUMMARY OF THE REPORT ON IMPROVEMENT OF SAFETY RECORD

The report, prepared at the request of the Safety Committee, investigated the previous year's accident record, commented on a premises survey and recommended action.

1 FINDINGS

The main findings were:
1.1 that unsafe equipment, failure to implement safety regulations and ignorance had been the main causes of accidents
1.2 that more power points, better office accommodation, clearance of gangways and repair of safety guards on machinery were needed.

2 ELIMINATION OF PROBLEMS

The major problems were identified and the following recommendations to solve them were made.
2.1 Recommendations for immediate improvement
    2.1.1 Improvements to factory machinery.
    2.1.2 Clearance of gangways.
    2.1.3 Increased availability and use of safety equipment.
    2.1.4 Increased publicity.
2.2 Recommendations for long-term improvement
    2.2.1 Improvements in office accommodation and installation of additional power points.
    2.2.2 Improved training and retraining programmes, a safety competition and more effective publicity.
    2.2.3 Enquiry into the bonus scheme and consideration of appropriate changes.

T. W. Williams
Safety Officer

26 February 19– –

## 2.17 ASSIGNMENTS

1  In what main sections would you set out a formal written report? What is the purpose of each of these sections?

What are the most important errors which should be avoided in the preparation of a formal written report? [ICSA]

2  What guidelines would you recommend to administrators who wish to ensure that their formal reports are examples of good communication?

Justify your recommendations in terms of underlying principles of communication (see also Chapter 17). [ICSA]

3  Comment on the value of reports as a tool of management. [IAA]

4  A 'bibliography' and/or an 'appendix' often appear in written reports. What is the difference between them?

5  You are assistant to a Sales Manager whose staff is soon to be increased. To accommodate the additional sales representatives and typists the office will require additional equipment and reorganisation. It is not in a good state of decoration. Report in a memorandum to your Manager, proposing the changes you think will be necessary. (Notes and a suggested answer are given in Appendix 1.)

6  You work for Arthur Rogers, a partner in the firm of Brown, Rogers & Clifton, industrial consultants. Your headquarters is in the capital city of your country but the firm is increasingly carrying out work in a growing industrial area some 250 kilometres away, near the town of Zero.

To reduce the amount of travelling, Mr Rogers feels that the firm should consider either moving to Zero or setting up a regional office there. Suitable premises would have to be sought, transport facilities, particularly air transport, investigated and hotel and entertainment facilities (for client and company use) considered.

You have recently spent a week with a client company in the neighbourhood of Zero. Mr Rogers asked you to stay on for a short while, investigate the town and its facilities and assess its suitability, either as the firm's new headquarters or as a regional office, and report to him.

If the former is decided upon, most staff will be asked to move, while in the latter case there would need to be some local recruitment.

Write a formal report on your investigation. The report will eventually be considered by the other partners.

7   You are a Section Manager in Juggs Department Store in a large town. The store's profits have been consistently falling over the last few years.

The Store Manager believes in encouraging his staff to look constructively at the store and, although he recognises that you lack experience in some areas of the business, he hopes that you will have a fresh approach. He does not expect you to consider profitability or costs directly, though these must obviously be borne in mind.

He has asked you to comment on the present position, outline the problems, make proposals for further investigation, suggest immediate areas for action and present ideas for promotions and advertising.

To help you, he has given you the following information, to which you should add only such detail as is necessary to explain your proposals.

1  *INFORMATION ABOUT JUGGS STORE*

The store is situated in the town centre on the main shopping street, now a pedestrian way – Marsh Street.

It was modernised in 1973 when small departments scrapped at that time included toys, stationery, cards, gift wrappings, cosmetics, cigarettes and confectionery. The store specialises in areas where it is felt it has an advantage over competitors in the town. Merchandise is generally well presented and of good quality.

The departments are:

| | |
|---|---|
| Leisure goods | Audio and TV equipment |
| Electrical goods | Records |
| DIY | Ladies' fashions |
| Kitchenware | Men's fashions |
| Gifts | Children's wear |
| China and glass | Fashion accessories |
| Haberdashery | Hosiery |
| Dress fabrics | Household linen |
| Beds and bedding | Furniture |
| Curtains and upholstery fabrics | |

Stock variety is limited. The store holds little more than basic stocks in the adjoining warehouse and its appeal, particularly in fashion, is to the more conservative and older end of the market. Generally stock is of good quality but high price.

The range in some departments is very limited because of lack of space, for example furniture, beds, gifts. The merchandising knowledge of some of the buyers is limited. There is a lack of communication and co-ordination between buyers from different departments and no central buying policy.

Profit margins are very low in leisure goods and electrical goods and local competition is very fierce.

The present advertising policy is to increase advertising in the local newspaper. The cost has recently gone up by 20 per cent per column cm. The paper is the only one in the district so has an effective monopoly. Other advertising considered has been a more effective, illuminated sign outside the store; mailshots at promotion times; posters; competitions, raffles or bingo games with vouchers as prizes.

## 2 PROMOTIONS NORMALLY HELD

| | |
|---|---|
| January | General Sale |
| 3rd week February | Stocktaking bargains – chiefly items left from sale. Coincides with schools half-term. |
| 3rd week March | Mother's Day week |
| 4th week March | Cookware demonstration – pressure cookers, non-stick ware, etc. |
| Two weeks in April | Fashion promotion to include Easter period. |
| 1st week in May | 6-day spectacular – all departments |
| Last two weeks May | Wedding gifts and bridal wear. |
| 3rd week June and first two weeks July | Sale – holiday specials. |
| Last week July | Sports and leisure promotion – linked when possible with international event, for example World Cup football, Olympic Games. |
| August | Schoolwear promotion. |
| Early October | Painting, sculpture, pottery and craft displays. |
| November/December | Christmas items and gifts. |

### Comments

Bargain sales have not been very successful in recent years. Items with big price reductions and some especially competitive bought-in lines sold well but end-of-line fashions were disappointing.

Cookware demonstrations attract attention but sales are often disappointing. Christmas and Mother's Day week have suffered because the store does not sell perfumery, toys, cards and gift wrappings, crackers or chocolates.

The sports and leisure promotions are often only really successful when they can be linked to very popular international events and boosted by sales of souvenir items.

New and imaginative ideas are very much needed.

### 3  EXTERNAL INFLUENCES

There has been a significant change in shopping patterns in the town over the last five years. Two new large shopping precincts with car parks have been opened and there has been a restriction of car access to the town centre with traffic-free roads and reduced road parking. The old bus station has been replaced with a new one near one of the outlying shopping precincts and two large stores in Marsh Street are now vacant because their occupants have moved to the new precincts. Four smaller shops have closed down because of the effects of national recession and the town in general has now got more shops than are needed by a population in which there is an unemployment rate of 15 per cent.

# SUMMARISING

Summarising exercises are very often set on business examination papers because they test our abilities to understand what we read and to express ourselves concisely — two essential work skills. Examination questions may ask for a summary, precis or abstract. Generally a *summary* or *precis* implies a condensed version of the original, while an *abstract* requires the extraction of selected ideas from the passage and often their rearrangement.

## 3.1 USES OF SUMMARISING TECHNIQUES

We use summarising skills in many different contexts at work, for example in the composition of:

> telex messages
> telegrams
> telephone messages
> synopses of reports
> minutes
> abstracts of information
> summaries of correspondence.

## 3.2 NOTE-MAKING

Note-making has value as a memory aid. Not only that, simply writing something down often helps us to understand it better — especially if we try to structure our notes by putting the most important points down in capitals and relating detail to these headings.

Note-making from the spoken word is more difficult than from the written word because one cannot always repeat or review, but the following guidelines will apply to note-making from speech or writing.

(a) Never write in complete sentences.
(b) But don't abbreviate so much that your notes are meaningless later!
(c) Use key words like *because, therefore, but, and* to indicate relationships between ideas. Sometimes it helps to put these in capitals.
(d) The dash – is the most useful punctuation mark in note-making.
(e) Use plenty of space. This allows for expansion later. Putting each idea on a new line allows you to rearrange the ideas by numbering them.
(f) Use the layout – paragraphs, headings, underlinings – to help make the meaning and the relationships of ideas clear. (See also Chapter 8 on writing notes for speeches.)

## 3.3 BRIEF SUMMARIES

### Telephone messages

Most firms use printed telephone message forms like that shown in Figure 3.1 which help to prompt the message-taker into obtaining the necessary information. You should always read back the message you have taken to check its accuracy before closing a telephone conversation.

Fig 3.1 *telephone message form*

TELEPHONE MESSAGE

DATE:_____          TIME:_____

FOR: _____

FROM: NAME _____

    (AND ADDRESS) _____

    TEL.NO. _____

    (AND EXTENSION)

MESSAGE _____

_____

_____

_____

_____

    TAKEN BY: _____

## Telex messages

The cost of telex messages is based on the transmitting time and the distance; hence they are expressed much more briefly than letters. The

### Fig 3.2  *from letter to telex*

```
Dear Mr Masters

There is now some urgency to finalise the Paish
Limited contract. I shall be at Heathrow airport
for a short while on Wednesday 16th November
during the stopover of my flight from Rome
to New York. Will you please meet me there
so that we can conclude this business? My
Alitalia flight 627 is due to arrive at 16.50
hours.

Please let me know whether or not you will
be able to meet me. I very much hope that
it will be possible.

Yours sincerely


Robert Walters
```

letter given in Figure 3.2 could be condensed into the following telex message:

URGENT WE FINALISE DETAILS PAISH LIMITED CONTRACT. ARRIVING HEATHROW ALITALIA FLIGHT 627 SIXTEEN FIFTY HOURS WEDNESDAY SIXTEENTH NOVEMBER. PLS CONFIRM THAT YOU CAN MEET ME THERE DURING STOPOVER ONLY.
REGARDS WALTERS.

This message could have been expressed more concisely still, as you can see below, but telex messages often contain 'unnecessary' words (like *Regards*) which help the tone of the message. At the same time, telex messages often use abbreviations like *PLS*, and people who communicate regularly with one another will develop their own contracted forms.

## Overseas telegrams

Such expensive messages need very careful condensation for economy's sake. The message above can be reduced as follows:

URGENT YOU MEET ME TO FINALISE PAISH CONTRACT DURING STOPOVER FLIGHT ALITALIA 627 HEATHROW SIXTEEN FIFTY HOURS SIXTEENTH NOVEMBER STOP PLEASE CONFIRM WALTERS

When you have to write abbreviated messages:

(a) select only essential points
(b) arrange them so that they are clear and convey the information accurately and as concisely as possible
(c) avoid very long words
(d) do not abbreviate where this could cause confusion
(e) use words rather than figures where there might be misunderstanding
(f) remember that parts of the address count in the number of words in a telegram
(g) avoid using 'stop' wherever possible in a telegram – it counts as a word – telexes use normal punctuation.


## 3.4 LONGER SUMMARIES

### Purpose
Decide *who* is going to use your summary, *what* it is they need to know and what will be the most suitable *format*, for example a memo, a list of numbered points, notes, and so on.

### Intrusion of your own ideas
The summary should be only of the information that has been presented in the original passage. No other ideas, digressions, illustrations or opinions of your own should be added. You are concerned solely with the writer's ideas. Therefore, be careful to follow these rules:

(a) do not let your own opinions colour your interpretation
(b) do not add examples of your own
(c) do not discuss the opinions given
(c) do not give additional information
(e) do not alter the balance of any arguments presented.

### Tenses and reported speech
Whereas it was once obligatory to write a formal summary in reported speech, i.e. using an impersonal tone and past tenses, this is now considered rather pedantic. The rules to follow are:

(a) the tense of the original may be retained in most cases
(b) personal pronouns must be avoided
(c) where the passage is written entirely in the first person it is often preferable to change it to reported speech
(d) where a quotation in direct speech is included in a passage for summary, this should be changed to reported speech.

If reported speech is being used, care is needed with pronouns, tenses and adverbial expressions. Look at the following example:

> *In his Annual Report the Chairman said, 'Our company has had a successful year but your Board of Directors hopes to have even better progress to report next year.'*

In reported speech, the passage reads as follows:

> *In his Annual Report the Chairman said that their company had had a successful year but that their Board of Directors hoped to have even better progress to report the following year.*

The present tense is retained if the stated facts are still true, for example

> *He said, 'Everyone dies sooner or later'.*
> *The author said that everyone dies sooner or later.*

Note that the word *that* should be used to introduce reported speech, as in the above examples.

Questions need particular care:

> DIRECT SPEECH      *Can we meet next week?*
> REPORTED SPEECH      *He asked whether they could meet the following week.*

But rhetorical questions need more rephrasing:

> *Shall we suffer such a trading loss again?*
> *The Chairman said that they could not suffer such a trading loss again.*

(You will find a list of forms of reported speech in Appendix 3.)

**Examples and illustrations**
These may often be omitted, or, if they are retained, be generalised. Consider the following passage:

> *I think people ought to be allowed a second crack at their names, re-registering at, say, eighteen. Indian tribes do this. No squaw leans into the birchbark cradle and names its contents 'Great Swift Buffalo Hunter': they probably wait until he's met a few buffalo first. Plenty of people do it already, of course. Justin de Villeneuve, Englebert Humperdinck II; John Wayne was christened Marion.*

> (Katherine Whitehorn, *The Observer*)

The illustrations in this passage should be treated by omission.

*She thought that people ought to be allowed to change their names, re-registering at, say, eighteen.*

Statistics may often be generalised, as the following example shows (the original precedes the generalisation).

*Some of the population-doubling times in the UDCs (underdeveloped countries) are as follows: Kenya, 24 years; Nigeria, 28; Turkey, 24; Indonesia, 31; Philippines, 20; Brazil, 22; Costa Rica, 20; and El Salvador, 19.*

*Population-doubling times in many underdeveloped countries are less than twenty-five years.*

In some summaries prepared for businessmen it will be right to retain some detail. For example, if a manager had asked for background information prior to visiting Brazil, it might be relevant to include for him the actual population-doubling time in that country.

### Quotations
Since these are frequently used as illustrations of a point, they may often be omitted. If they are retained, however, and turned into reported speech, care must be taken to attribute them to the correct author, not the author of the passage.

### Order
You should not gratuitously change the order of ideas in a summary of a passage. Indeed, you should never do so except when you are summarising parts of the passage, for example the arguments for or against the policy, or if there is repetition in the original. The safe rule is to stick to the original order wherever possible.

### Balance
An author will generally write at greatest length on his most important ideas. In summarising a writer's ideas you should aim at giving them the same weight in terms of comparative length as he has done, unless you are instructed to include only some of the information — otherwise you may distort the meaning. It is a common fault among the inexperienced to find that too many words have been used on the first part of the passage, leaving the temptation to compress the second half into a quarter of the words allowed.

**A method**

The flow chart shown in the **Focus** on page 56 gives a method of writing an examination summary.

**Summarising correspondence**

A summary of correspondence may be required, for example by management, for a decision, or to be presented at a meeting, or to be circulated to several departments whose managers can then ask for the original of any correspondence that is their concern. The general rules of summary-writing will apply and the following special points should also be observed:

*The heading*

A simple standard heading should be used.

> *Summary of correspondence between . . . and . . . on the subject of . . .*

*Dates*

If the dates of the letters in a series have no particular significance, the first and last letter dates may be incorporated in the heading after the second address and before the subject, for example

> *from 12 October to 17 December 19--*

However, the dates of the letters may be important and then they must appear at the beginning of each letter in the summary.

*Paragraphs*

Each letter in the series should be contained in a separate paragraph.

*Important details*

Such facts as delivery dates, specifications, quotations, numbers and sizes cannot be generalised but must be quoted in full.

*Acknowledgements*

Acknowledgements and complimentary phrases and conclusions can be omitted. Mention of a complete letter which is simply an acknowledgement may usually also be left out of the summary.

An example of a summary of correspondence is given in Appendix 1 as an answer to Assignment 2.

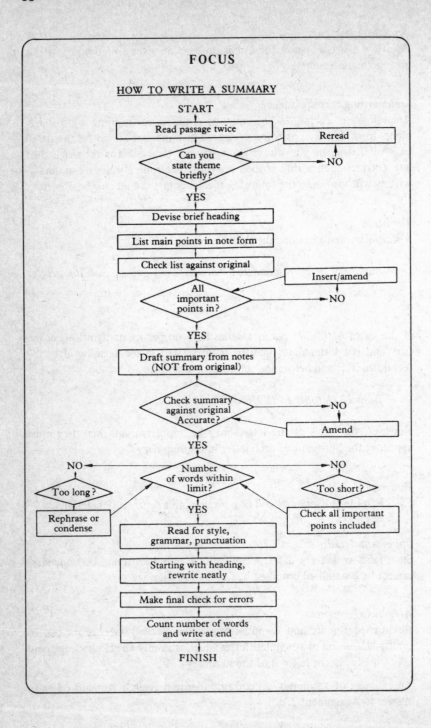

# FOCUS

## HOW TO WRITE A SUMMARY

START

Read passage twice

Can you state theme briefly? → NO → Reread

YES

Devise brief heading

List main points in note form

Check list against original

All important points in? → NO → Insert/amend

YES

Draft summary from notes (NOT from original)

Check summary against original Accurate? → NO / Amend

YES

Number of words within limit? → NO (Too long?) → Rephrase or condense

Too short? → NO → Check all important points included

YES

Read for style, grammar, punctuation

Starting with heading, rewrite neatly

Make final check for errors

Count number of words and write at end

FINISH

## 3.5 ASSIGNMENTS

1 Your employer is an official in a local government transport department. He is interested in trends affecting cars and driving habits. Summarise the following passage in not more than 160 words ready for placing in his 'in' tray. You will need to draft a brief explanatory memo because he has not heard of the article from which the passage is taken. The memo does not count as part of the 160 words. There are 494 words in the passage.

The most dramatic response to higher petrol prices is simply not to buy a car. Economist Intelligence Unit figures show that there has been a drop of nearly 10 per cent in new car registration over the past twelve months. But, again, this is complicated by factors like the imposition of credit controls — which make it less easy to buy through hire purchase. And the figures disguise the bustle of activity in the second-hand market. Here there is more conclusive evidence of petrol-related changes in behaviour. In this market, buyers are choosing cars with a smaller engine capacity. Yet in the same week that a pop star traded in his Rolls Corniche for a Mini, an American bought five Rolls-Royces, a dealer's entire stock, in one sale. So the dealers' returns, on which evidence of this shift is based, should be treated with caution.

Less drastic is the decision either to take the car off the road or to drive it a shorter distance down the road. With an alternative form of transport available, like the London Underground, it should be possible to gauge the change in habits from the increased use of station car parks. Most of London's are brimming already. The 35 per cent increase of tube fares on 23 March might even thin car park users out a little: people might drive on. Certainly property magazines like the *London Weekly Advertiser* seem to think that the recently increased British Rail fares are at least as powerful a factor in home-buying decisions as petrol prices.

Commuter traffic may well not be sensitive to petrol price increases. The Automobile Association reckons that 40 per cent of all car-owners either have cars provided by their employers or, at least, get help towards running them. If there are changes in behaviour, they will show in the remaining 60 per cent, and particularly in that sector's casual or pleasure driving.

The fuel crisis must have seemed to environmentalists a dream come true: higher petrol prices would cut unrestricted use of cars at a stroke. National parks would be relieved of nose-to-tail car queues. Spine roads to the south-west, like the M4/M5, would be freed of congestion. But the signs are that this hadn't happened and won't happen. For example, receipts at National Trust properties have not dropped. There are two explanations for this. One is that people are driving shorter distances. Where they might, pre-crisis, have driven down to Brighton, they will now stop short at Box Hill. Thus the number of visitors shows no signs of slackening but their origins have changed and they are visiting more local attractions. The second explanation is that higher petrol prices have had no discernible effect on weekend driving habits. The weather may have a far bigger effect. People going out to enjoy themselves will expect to have to pay for their pleasure.

[LCC PSC]

(Notes and an answer for this question are given in Appendix 1.)


2   Write a summary of the following correspondence in not more than 120 words.

LETTER 1

5 Maple Grove,
BINGLEY,
Wilts.
WB4 6LM
14 March, 19- -

The Reliable Insurance Co.,
Broadgate,
BRADFORD.
BD1 5CX

Dear Sirs,

Thank you for your letter dated 10th March, giving a quotation for insurance cover on my car. I note that your premium is £65 per annum.

My present insurance company allows me the maximum no-claim bonus on my premium and I wish to know whether you are willing to do the same. I see from your quotation that this allowance would reduce my premium by £18.50.

They also made a further deduction from my premium since I agreed to pay the first £25 costs on any damage incurred. What is your policy in this respect?

I look forward to your reply.

Yours faithfully
John Maggs

LETTER 2

The Reliable Insurance Co
Broadgate
BRADFORD
BD2 5CX

Ref EH/JW
16 March 19--

J Maggs Esq
5 Maple Grove
BINGLEY
Wilts
WB4 6LM

Dear Sir

We acknowledge receipt of your letter dated 14 March.

You will receive a full reply to the points you raised during the next few days.

Yours faithfully
E. Higginbottom
Motor Insurance Dept

LETTER 3

The Reliable Insurance Co
Broadgate
BRADFORD
BD1 5CX

Ref EH/JW
18 March 19--

J Maggs Esq
5 Maple Grove
BINGLEY
Wilts
WB4 6LM

Dear Sir
Further to our letter of 16 March, I note that you have received our quotation for a comprehensive motor insurance premium of £65. You ask whether we can allow you a no-claim bonus and a reduction for your agreement to pay the first £25 of any damage incurred.

If you can let us have evidence of your no-claim bonus by sending us a copy of the insurance schedule from your previous insurers, we shall be able to offer you a similar reduction in premium of £18.50.

We are pleased to be able to offer you a further reduction of £10 for your agreement to pay the first £25 of any damage. Your revised quotation with these two reductions will be £36.50.

I hope this answers your queries. If you require any further information I shall be pleased to help.

Yours faithfully
E Higginbottom
Motor Insurance Dept

LETTER 4

5 Maple Grove,
BINGLEY,
Wilts.
WB4 6LM
22nd March, 19- -

The Reliable Insurance Co.
Broadgate,
BRADFORD.
BD1 5CX

Dear Sirs,
    Thank you for your letter dated 18th March.
    I enclose my insurance schedule for the Apex Insurance Company which shows that they allow me the maximum no-claim bonus of £18.50. I hope you will find this satisfactory.
    If so, I shall be pleased to accept your revised quotation for £36.50 for comprehensive motor insurance.

Yours faithfully,
John Maggs

Enclosure

LETTER 5

The Reliable Insurance Co
Broadgate
BRADFORD
BD1 5CX

Ref EH/JW
25 March 19--

J Maggs Esq
5 Maple Grove
BINGLEY
Wilts
WB4 6LM

Dear Sir

Thank you for your letter dated 22 March.

We are pleased to enclose our revised quotation of £36.50 for comprehensive motor insurance.

We also enclose the proposal form for your signature and look forward to receiving your instructions.

Yours faithfully

E. Higginbottom
Motor Insurance Dept
Encs

LETTER 6

5 Maple Grove,
BINGLEY,
Wilts.
WB4 6LM
28 March, 19--

The Reliable Insurance Co.,
Broadgate,
BRADFORD.
BD1 5CX

Dear Sirs,
    Thank you for your letter dated 25th March.
    I am pleased to accept the revised quotation and return the signed proposal form.

I also enclose my cheque for £36.50 and wish you to arrange the commencement of cover as soon as possible.

Yours faithfully,

John Maggs

Enclosures

(An answer to this question is given in Appendix 1.)

3   Summarise the following passage on 'participation' in about 130 words:

> 'Participation' is a fashionable term, but too often it seems to imply an immediate involvement of shopfloor workers without any recourse to managers or office staff. Both these groups of employees have a contribution to make to company performance: furthermore, if they are ignored, at least cynicism and at worst active hostility will be the result. Despite the current spate of legislation, employee participation is not new.
>
> Participation is not a question of welfare, or of doing good in the world, but a way of helping to run a business more effectively. It is a style of management which permits employees — by some means or other — to have a say decision-making.
>
> Legislation which has recently been enacted, and membership of the EEC, will force British companies to become involved in participation. Many managers, however, consider that participation is not a positive approach to management, that it is a sign of weakness and an unproductive use of their time. It is our view that these attitudes spring partly from the formative educational processes which many managers in Britain have undergone. From the ages of five to eleven most children have gone to the neighbourhood school where the tendency nowadays is to encourage free expression and to avoid compulsion. At the age of eleven, about 20% of children have been 'creamed off' and have been subjected to a different form of education from the others. They have been encouraged to work hard so as to 'get on', to be competitive and to be individuals. Between fifteen and eighteen these children have been subjected to 'ordeal by examination'. Many of them have then gone on to further education and training. The rest of the children have been through a less individualistic experience, have left school at fifteen or sixteen and have then gone into factories and offices to work. They soon learn

to take a collective rather than an individualistic view of life and join a culture which is entirely different from that of management. They have not been subjected to the rigours of an intellectual discipline.

In a situation in which a participative style is being introduced managers are asked not to renounce the intellectual disciplines they acquired during their formal education, but to contribute these disciplines to joint problem-solving with the workpeople. In this way they will be able to run the enterprise more effectively with the help of the workpeople. From 'I know I am right', we proceed to 'let's try it this way'.

(extract from *Managing Human Resources* by Inbucon Consultants, published by Heinemann)

[LCC PSD]

4   Using your own words, condense this review of about 550 words, adapted from *The Times*, to not more than 150 words. Supply a title and state the number of words you have used.

It is fairly obvious that the first and most important reason for keeping accounting records is to provide up-to-date information about the workings of a business. Without this, many decisions about present operations or future plans become total guesswork. But the training of most accountants, and of auditors in particular, emphasises that there is another, almost equally important reason for having an accounting system: to provide a control device to protect the firm's assets. The system must ensure, for example, that money and bank accounts are guarded against theft: that debtors pay up (eventually if not immediately) for the goods they have bought; that stocks of materials (or even scrap products) are not surreptitiously removed from the premises, but are all accounted for. In spite of the attention given to these problems, they still occur. Cash is stolen or misappropriated; debtors abscond; stocks and materials disappear. To expect otherwise is, perhaps, to believe either that accountants have superhuman powers or that a benevolent deity has suddenly abolished original sin. There is however a danger that, when such events are discovered, the management may over-react. The accountant is summoned and agrees to set up even more rigid controls to prevent the recurrence of such a disaster. The auditors, hanging their heads in shame for not spotting the fraud or theft sooner, are admonished. In some cases this response by management may well be correct — but not necessarily. The auditor's prime concern is, after all, giving immediate protection to the shareholders' assets. But the manager's main interest is, or should be, the overall efficiency and productivity of the organisation.

It is not yet sufficiently recognised by some managers that there may well be conflict between the objectives of asset protection and that of optimum productivity. The effectiveness of a firm can undoubtedly be impaired if undue weight is placed on internal control procedures. Some employees may be dishonest, but what percentage? If it is the majority there may be some point in a total monitoring process. But the familiar description of mankind as being 5 per cent saints, 5 per cent sinners and the rest somewhere in between is probably nearer the mark. It cannot be emphasised too strongly that if employees believe that they are being treated as potential criminals, they are much more likely to behave like them. So if rigid controls are set up to prevent the possibility of minor frauds by the 5 per cent of sinners, it is quite possible that the rest may feel distrusted and that their loyalty and motivation towards the firm is correspondingly reduced. A company must beware of alienating its employees and even driving them towards collusion, by appearing over-suspicious of their honesty.

The message here, then, is essentially a simple one: excessive zeal in applying controls over all possible frauds and theft can lead to low employee loyalty and an atmosphere of distrust. This in turn is likely to bring about a reduced interest in the firm's work by employees and, paradoxically, can even result in a greater risk of loss through fraud than would have been the case without the increased controls.

[ICSA]

5 Your firm's main warehouse and records have been damaged by fire. Draft a telex to your suppliers asking them to:

(a) inform you of any orders delivered within the last week or en route
(b) hold any deliveries due to be made during the next ten days
(c) send a full list of all your orders
(d) be prepared to deliver to an alternative address.

# ADVERTISING AND

# PUBLICITY

Many companies use professional advertising agencies, news agencies and public relations consultants for the majority of their advertising and publicity needs. Others have public relations and/or advertising departments within their organisations.

However, there are occasions when you may need to prepare advertising and publicity, so this chapter looks briefly at some of the items with which you may be concerned.

## 4.1 DIRECT ADVERTISING

Direct advertisements will appear in local and national daily or weekly newspapers, magazines and journals, in mail shots and posters, leaflets and brochures.

Radio and television are also well-established forms.

The principles to be considered when designing an advertisement will include the following.

(a) The *type* of the advertisement, e.g. to publicise job vacancies, sell a luxury product, a public service.
(b) The *result* being sought, e.g. increased sales, job application, donations to charity, improving the organisation's image.
(c) The most *suitable medium* or combination of media, e.g. direct mail shots coupled with local radio.
(d) The possible *costs vis-à-vis* the anticipated results — the cost effectiveness of the exercise.
(e) The *minimum content necessary*, e.g. a job advertisement must state what the job is and where to apply for it.

(f) The importance of *layout, printing, use of colour, photographs*, etc., for each advertisement (the best possible within the cost limits).

(g) The *classes of market* (usually divided into six groups, ranging from 'upper management' to 'pensioners, widows and lowest-paid groups'; based on income).

## 4.2 CLASSIFIED ADVERTISEMENTS

Classified advertisements are the short, one-column wide verbal advertisements which appear grouped under main headings in newspapers and magazines. The information runs on from line to line, often in the same type face and with no special headings.

## 4.3 DISPLAY CLASSIFIED ADVERTISEMENTS

Within the confines of the classified advertisements, small display advertisements may be included. They allow for the use of larger, **bold** typefaces and for a more attractive layout (see Figure 4.1).

Fig 4.1 *display classified advertisement*

```
        BORROWED MONEY

         COSTS MONEY


        BORROWED MONEY

         COSTS LESS

       WHEN YOU DEAL WITH


     M O N E Y M A K E R S

         65 Ferry Road
       Witheridge   WT5 4DG
          019 423 6781

    We have lower overheads and
    lower margins.  You reap the
    benefit in many ways - by
    paying less or having extra
    money to spend.
```

## 4.4 DISPLAY ADVERTISEMENTS

Larger advertisements will run across several columns, or even fill a whole page of a newspaper. Considerable use will be made of more varied typefaces and sizes, of illustrations and perhaps of colour. Although the printer will set up the type, he must be given clear instructions, a sketch of the desired display and, of course, the full text. Photographs or print-quality illustrations will also have to be provided. Figures 4.2 and 4.3 are examples of effective display advertisements.

## 4.5 CONTENT AND STYLE OF ADVERTISEMENTS

Short and classified advertisements must be almost telegram-like, with an opening which attracts the reader's attention. Classified advertisements are charged for by the line, with a minimum charge for either a stated number of words or of lines. They are relatively cheap to insert and, to keep costs minimal, often have a very concise, even truncated form with common abbreviations being used, for example *o.n.o.* (*or near offer*).

EXAMPLE

> *HELP PEOPLE TO REMEMBER YOU*
> *Most attractive coloured*
> *personal business cards,*
> *printed with your name and*
> *business information in gold,*
> *silver and 4 other colours*
> *6 superior typefaces. Very*
> *competitive prices.*
> *Phone (01) 6792400*

Display–classified and display advertisements, although bigger than classified advertisements, will not necessarily contain more words, so space will be charged for, rather than the number of words used.

There are three main styles of advertisement display:

(a) the almost blank – designed to catch the eye and whet the appetite and usually followed later by more informative publicity
(b) the 'just enough' text approach with an imaginative display using much white space (see Figure 4.2)
(c) the very informative – with an attractive display but relying more heavily on the impact of the message itself (see Figure 4.3).

Fig 4.2 *display advertisement*

# ST. HILDA INDUSTRIAL ESTATE

## GREAT HARTLEMOUTH

★ In the fast-growing East Anglian Region

★ In the centre of the Town

★ Close to the Docks with good Port
facilities for Export/Import to/from Europe

★ Ample male and female labour

### Industrial and Warehouse Units
### Immediately Available

### From 3,000 to 60,000 square feet and upwards

Another project being undertaken by

United Building Enterprises Limited

Apply to Agents:  Barnes and Shacks
26 Fore Street
Great Hartlemouth GH3 4BR
Telephone: (061) 2233

Fig 4.3 *display advertisement*

---

## Woman living alone in a cold, wet flat

Mrs Thriscott is 68 years old. She used to live alone on the top floor of an old house. Her flat was cold, wet and full of draughts; there was no hot water, and it was virtually impossible for her to keep warm. When she wanted to go out, she faced climbing up and down a hundred steps in all.

Then she applied to Help the Aged for a new flat. Since she moved into the new place which Help the Aged have provided, Mrs Thriscott is a changed woman. "My great thrill, of course, is hot baths every day. I've never been cold since I've been here. My health is wonderful, perfect! People tell me I look years younger."

Help the Aged also help provide Day centres where old people find care and companionship.

Because of loans available to Help the Aged every £2 you give provides £40 of housing.

> £150 donation names a flat in memory of happy times with someone dear to you. £250 names a double flat. £450 names a common room.

Every day matters to old people in need. Tear out this advertisement and send with your gift as quickly as possible to:

Hon. Treasurer, Rt Hon. Lord Maybray-King
Help the Aged, Room G1,
8 Denman Street, London W1A 2AP

---

Each of these approaches has its merits. However, if the advertisement is designed to inform, then it will be more successful if it follows the approach in (c). Studies reveal that long copy outsells short copy by 90 per cent.

Look at Figure 4.3. It is far more effective than Figure 4.4 would be because it tells us far more about a *person* (and the personal touch is very important in advertisements). It also tells us what 'Help the Aged' can do and what even a small donation can mean, thus emphasising the value of your *personal* donation.

Good advertising copy must:

(a) follow the principles stated in section 4.1

Fig 4.4  *short display advertisement*

```
Woman living alone in cold wet flat

    Elderly People need
 companionship and good homes

Send your donation to:
  Hon. Treasurer,
  Rt Hon. Lord Maybray-King
  Help the Aged, Room G1,
  8 Denman Street,
  London W1A 2AP
```

(b) have an attention-catching heading which also, for those who will read no further, contains the essence of your message

(c) have correct copy progression:
  direct reader involvement
  development of 'selling' proposition
  suggesting reader action
  repeating the benefits
  indicating contact point (e.g. telephone number)

(d) be written in a language and style suitable to the type of product or service, the market and the publication.

## 4.6 DIRECT MAIL ADVERTISING

We are all familiar with the letters, leaflets, brochures and coupons which drop in a seemingly never-ending stream through our letterboxes. Many go straight into our wastepaper baskets, but at least some catch our attention. The sales letter, which with modern techniques can now be addressed directly to individuals by name and can even have their names in the body of the letter, is a favourite ploy of advertisers. Figure 4.5 shows an example (see also Chapter 1).

Apart from the letter form, direct mail shots are frequently colour leaflets, offering special discounts, reduced-price coupons and loans. Many have facilities for postage-free replies.

Additionally there are free newspapers and even regular magazines delivered to the doorstep by major companies such as supermarket chains.

Fig 4.5 *sales letter*

MAGNUM AND MAGNUM LTD

Steam House

Walsall Street

Manchester MN4 1BR

18 June 19--

Mrs K N Opus
16 Point Road
Beechwood
Cheshire   CH4 9AZ

Dear Mrs Opus

WE HAVE A 'MAGNUM' THAT REALLY BUBBLES!

No, we are not about to sell you a bottle of 1878
vintage champagne - the liquid we have in mind is
just plain, ordinary water; a liquid that combines
very well with our latest product. It is:

The MAGNUM Electric Kettle

made in stainless steel. The heat-resistant handle is
cool to the touch and a choice of fresh exciting colours
will enhance the decor of your kitchen.

It boils two pints of cold water in just ONE minute and
the automatic cut out means that you can be elsewhere
when the 'MAGNUM' bubbles!

That kind husband won't need a second mortgage in order
to buy it for you - - - - - - - - - - - - -

Do come and see it today in your local showroom.

Yours sincerely

J R Magnum
Sales Director

Many of these publications are of high print and display quality and require professional design. It is difficult for a small local firm to compete. An A4-sized leaflet printed on one side but using colour if possible and with a direct but imaginatively displayed message is probably the best answer.

## 4.7 RADIO AND TELEVISION

While lengthy commercials require professional design and are often very expensive, there are some simpler ways of using the broadcasting media.

For local or regional radio it is not too difficult to write a simple commercial which will either be presented by a broadcaster or which can be pre-taped for repeated use. You may find that you have suitably talented 'voices' within your organisation (but be careful not to infringe any of the rules of any entertainers' or journalists' union). A 'jingle' and some appropriate music (copyright laws being observed) can brighten even a short commercial.

You will need a script, written like a play, suitable speakers, a fairly sophisticated tape deck, good microphones, a sound-proof room and a lot of confidence!

If you can conquer the hills of the radio commercial, you might attempt to scale the giddy heights of television. A radio commercial, adapted and used as a voiceover for a static picture and lasting only ten to twenty seconds can become an effective TV slot, not too expensive if screened locally and at off-peak times. Many small organisations use both radio and TV commercials very successfully.

A complementary activity is the advertisement locally of products or services advertised nationally on TV, either by big companies or by national groups seeking to promote, for instance, the sales of indigenously produced cheeses or farm produce.

Radio and TV can be used for this purpose, as can local papers, direct mail, posters and 'as seen on TV' advertisements in local shops.

## 4.8 PRESS RELEASES

Any organisation welcomes the opportunity to obtain free publicity and the press release is one method of achieving this (see also Chapter 16.2). The firm prepares the release and sends it to the newspapers or magazines of its choice in the hope that it will be published with the minimum of editing. An example is given in Figure 4.6.

### Content of a press release
Since your article may have to be cut, it should be written so that it may be 'pruned' from the last sentence backwards. This makes it easy for the

Fig 4.6 *press release*

£55,000 WILL BRING IN THE STARS

The leading international figures in men's
tennis will return to Torquay this summer
for one of the world's leading competitions
- the £55,000 Torquay Tennis Tournament.
The Lawn Tennis Association have confirmed
that the tournament, the most valuable in
Britain after Wimbledon, will take place
from June 16th to 21st.

The event will be the only one in Britain
to be graded an AA men's competition in
the Commercial Union Grand Prix series.
The singles winner collects £9,000, the
runner-up £4,500 and the losing semi-
finalists £2,250 each. The winning doubles
pair share £2,400.

With the Wimbledon fortnight to follow, the
world's top men will be playing for three
weeks in front of British spectators.

Torquay made tennis history last year by
making a five-year agreement with the
Association of Tennis Professionals to
stage a major tournament annually. ATP
agreed not to support any other top-flight
competition anywhere in the world during
the same week as the Torquay event.

more

Fig 4.6 *cont.*

the Torquay event.

It was the first time such a long-term
arrangement had been made between a
sponsor and the ATP, with the full
approval of the LTA.

Ronald Lewis, Torquay's Special Events
Manager, said:

'With so many sponsors having to withdraw
their support from tennis, the borough is
particularly pleased to continue with such
a first-rate international event.  The
extra prize money should bring out the best
in the competitors.

'This is the tenth consecutive year in
which we've run a tournament in Torquay,'
added Mr Lewis.  'It's always been important in the British Calendar.  Now it's
one of the elite handful of the world's top
events.'

- ends -

11 February 19--

THE TORQUAY TENNIS TOURNAMENT
Contact: Brian Bryans, Martin Martins
0803 711111

sub-editor to fit it into the space available without having to rewrite. Thus the essence of the story should be contained in the first paragraph, with the next most important information in the second paragraph, and so on.

If you include photographs, you must write a condensed version of the article as a caption. The caption should be firmly attached to the photograph, preferably pasted on the reverse. Never send a photograph without this information.

Your article should be factual, without literary embellishments. A press release for the national press will be shorter and less detailed than for the local paper. Articles for technical and trade journals should be checked for accuracy by an expert.

If your release is sent to more than one newspaper, remember to alter the story slightly for each. No paper, literally or figuratively, likes to have a carbon-copy story.

People's names must be spelled correctly, and forenames, or at least initials, should be used, not just 'Mr'. For local papers it is helpful to give the addresses of persons mentioned and possibly some personal details, about their hobbies or children for example.

Finally, always include a name and telephone number of someone the press can contact for further information.

## Presentation
The following points should be observed.

(a) Leave plenty of space at the top of the first page (headlines are the editor's prerogative) but give a factual heading.
(b) Leave wide margins (for the sub-editor's use).
(c) Use double spacing (for ease of correction and alteration).
(d) Have it typed on one side of the paper only (this saves the type-setter's time).
(e) If you use more than one sheet of paper, write one of the following at the bottom of the sheet:

*more follows*
*m.f.*
*more*

(f) Each continuation sheet should have a catch line: that is, the last few words of the previous sheet should be repeated, for example:

*the Chairman spoke briefly about*

(g) Finish your release as follows:

*– ends –*

## 4.9 ARTICLES

Other indirect publicity can be obtained by getting published articles which refer to your organisation or its work. These might include articles of a specialist nature, written by you as an expert in the field, which identify where you work or even contain favourable comment on your experience in your organisation. Also, newspapers and journals run series on allied new developments in, for example, electronics, where your firm might be represented, or series on countries or regions where you again might be asked to contribute.

### Content of articles

Although the basic format is very similar to that of press releases, articles should be differently planned, particularly as they may have resulted from an approach by a publisher who may have a specific topic or approach in mind, for a readership that will be voluntary.

An article will normally be of a predetermined length, so it will not have to be 'pruned' by an editor. Thus it can be written in the form of a essay with the ordering of the content decided upon by the nature of the topic: for example, chronological for a historical review; in descending order of importance for the presentation of a series of facts; the statement of problems followed by solutions, or of each problem in turn followed immediately by a suggested solution.

### Style

The style and language must vary according to the readership; the article may be appearing in a technical journal, a woman's magazine, the company house magazine. It may have to entertain as well as to inform and, in a company magazine for instance, will include items about personalities, like a press release for a local paper.

An attention-riveting caption and opening sentence are crucial. From there the argument should flow logically and fluently to a concluding sentence which must also leave a favourable impression on the reader.

Publicity is sought by most organisations — good publicity, that is. Well-worded, attractive advertisements, good broadcast commercials and any 'free' publicity available help create a public image which in turn boosts sales.

---

## FOCUS

CHOOSE YOUR MEDIA
    direct advertising
    classified, display–classified, display advertisements
    direct mail advertising
    radio and television
    press releases and articles

CONSIDER CONTENT
    headline and sequencing
    display and presentation
    style

ESTIMATE COST EFFECTIVENESS

---

## 4.10 ASSIGNMENTS

1    Prepare a classified advertisement for the following and include all the detail that would appear in a real advertisement:

> *Sale of over 1000 items of office equipment including almost new items*

2    Prepare a display advertisement using a full side of A4 paper to advertise for funds for a local charity in your local paper.

3    Your company is trying to promote a range of inexpensive kitchen aids. Write a sales letter to housewives in your area informing them about the products and telling them about special displays and offers at local stores during the coming month.

4    On which important points would you give advice to someone drawing up a company's press release? [IAA]

5    Write a press release in about 300 words on *one* of the following:
   (a) a new company product which is to go on sale shortly and which is an important technological development
   (b) a fashion house's new autumn designs (this will be accompanied by sketches, which, however, you do not have to draw!)

6    As assistant to the Training Manager at Safeguard Insurance Plc, you are closely involved in the company's staff training and development programmes. As part of a plan to improve the induction of new

employees into the firm, you have been asked to liaise with the Personnel Manager and to write an article for the next edition of the company's house magazine.

The article is aimed at junior school-leavers joining Safeguard in the July–August period and is to be entitled:

> *'Making a Good Start – How to Handle Colleagues, Callers and Customers Successfully'*

Compose a suitable article of between 350 and 450 words. [RSA DPA] [See Appendix 1 for notes and an answer.]

# MANUALS, INSTRUCTIONS AND FORM DESIGN

Three further examples of written communication are considered in this chapter: the preparation of handbooks and manuals, the provision of written instructions, and the design of forms.

## 5.1 BOOKLETS AND HANDBOOKS

Companies produce a variety of short handbooks for potential employees and existing staff. There may well be one which gives the history of the company; one which sets out regulations and benefits, generally applicable to all staff; another which, produced annually, presents to staff and shareholders information on the company's financial and trading position for the past year and plans for the future.

All such booklets are attempts to provide information in a permanent, neat and concise form to which staff may refer quickly and easily. They range in size and format, as they do in subject-matter, from short, internally duplicated sets of rules to glossy, coloured and very well-illustrated annual reports.

**Content**
Before deciding to produce a handbook we should ask certain questions.

(a) What information do we need to convey?
(b) How will it best be communicated?
(c) Who are the intended readers?

Some information will not be suitable for inclusion. In an employee handbook, for instance, it would be inappropriate to include short-term information (the staff association football club's fixture list) or detail important only to a very few employees. Consideration of how best to communicate will quickly lead us to decide that such information should be communicated, in the former case via the notice-board, in the latter by individual contact with those staff concerned.

Identifying the readership will aid us in designing the handbook and deciding on the style of writing to be used. A handbook for new employees will need to be particularly clearly expressed as new staff will have no prior knowledge of the firm.

The content to be included might comprise the following.

(a) Introduction by the head of the organisation.
(b) General information about the whole company, perhaps with maps and pictures of products.
(c) Rules such as attendance, payment of wages, general conduct, health and safety regulations and discipline procedures.
(d) Benefits and schemes including canteen facilities, education and training, sports and social clubs, pensions and sick-pay arrangements, trade-union membership.

Similarly the annual general report of a company in the form presented to the Annual General Meeting is often difficult to understand, so a booklet for shareholders and staff would need to have the information in a simplified form, probably supported by well-drawn diagrams. It would also often be a prestige production, on glossy paper and in colour, and consequently expensive to produce.

### Choice of format
Cost is always a prime consideration, so further questions arise.

(a) How many copies will be needed?
(b) Is professional preparation and printing necessary?
(c) Is the proposed expenditure justified?

There is a wide variety of presentation that can be used. Type and size of paper (A5, A4, coloured?), the type of binding (spinebound or looseleaf?), typeface (can it be typed within the organisation?) and kind of covers must all be considered.

Within the document, decisions must also be made on, for example, the layout, use of headings, visual aids, contents page and index (whether to have one). Many such handbooks can follow a pattern similar to that suggested in Chapter 2 for reports.

### General style
The language will vary according to the readership, but any booklet for general reading, whether by staff or for external use, must be couched in the simplest possible language.

It is difficult to make such booklets easy to read and at the same time convey complex information, about pensions or health and safety regulations, which will often require legal terminology. A possible solution is to give only the broadest summary in the handbook, picking out major points and then referring the reader to another source of information for further detail.

Techniques that can be helpful are:

(a) the vertical listing of information which comes under one heading
(b) giving any numerical or financial data in tabular or graph form (see Chapter 14)
(c) using photographs and line drawings to either supplement, replace or enliven the text (see Figure 5.1)
(d) providing an index.

**Revision**
In either a general handbook or a booklet produced for one occasion, there is not likely to be much revision necessary. However, the use of a looseleaf presentation for general handbooks does make it possible to revise individual pages at will, rather than have to reprint the whole booklet following, say, a change in employment law.

There are some additional problems that can occur when revisions are made (see the next section).

## 5.2 PROCEDURE MANUALS

It is quite common, when procedures in an organisation are instituted or revised, to set them down in a manual, with flow charts, copies of forms, standard letters used, etc., also included. Such information is useful to staff for reference when they are implementing a new or replacement procedure and can also be invaluable to new staff.

**Format**
The manual will set down in great detail precisely what should be done, in what order, with what information and by whom. It will show the extent of and the flow of work with the new system. The extensive detail, plus copies of relevant documents, which must be included often means that the manuals will be bulky. Also, when procedures are changed, even if only in small details, new or replacement sheets, documents, new contents pages and amendments to any index will be required.

Procedure manuals should therefore be in loose-leaf form so that revised pages can be inserted and out-of-date ones removed. As it will often not be practical to provide each employee concerned with an individual copy, the copy or copies in any one department must be easily available and, in a workshop or production area, there must be a desk or table at which the manual can be consulted.

Two major problems that arise are.

Fig 5.1 *brighten up your booklet*

**HOLIDAY ENTITLEMENT**

| No. of yrs service | Statutory days | No. of days per annum | Total holidays |
|---|---|---|---|
| 0 – 1 | up to 8 depending on date joined | 1 per full month worked | maximum of 15 |
| 1 – 4 | 8 | 15 | 23 |
| 5 – 9 | 8 | 18 | 26 |
| 10 – 14 | 8 | 20 | 28 |
| 15 – 19 | 8 | 22 | 30 |
| 20 and over | 8 | 30 | 38 |

*The holiday year is calculated from 1 January to 31 December.

**SAFETY RULES**

Employees must wear suitable clothing, including protective clothing where necessary.

**PROTECTIVE CLOTHING**

Available to all employers are:

safety goggles
ear muffs
helmets
overalls
steel-tipped boots

(a) When amendments and additions are distributed, the old sheets are not removed and the new ones are put, out of order, at the beginning of the manual.
(b) The procedures are not regularly revised and thus the manual increasingly ceases to reflect current working practice and so is an irrelevance, never referred to. In consequence, individual staff may forget the correct procedures, never learn them or amend them, and take short cuts to ease their own work burdens, causing problems elsewhere in the system.

**Preparing a procedures manual**
Simple rules which will help you to compile such a manual include the following.

(a) Make certain, before you start, that there *is* an agreed procedure.
(b) Familiarise yourself with it.
(c) Collect together all the relevant documentation.
(d) Devise a suitable format, e.g. flow charts (see Figure 14.26 on p. 217) or a tabular presentation such as Figure 5.2, which is the beginning of the procedure for the weekly payroll.
(e) Use major steps in the procedure as numbered section divisions.

Fig 5.2 *extract from procedure handbook*

| STEP | TIME | PROCEDURE | DOCUMENTATION | RESPONSIBLE MEMBER OF STAFF |
|---|---|---|---|---|
| 1. Collection of Clock Cards | Wednesdays between 11 am and noon | a) collect Clock Cards from clocking-in board<br>b) Take cards to Wages Clerk | CLOCK CARDS (Document 1.) | Works Foreman |
| 2. Total each Clock Card | Wednesdays pm | Calculate:<br>a) basic pay<br>b) overtime<br>c) deductions for bad timekeeping, absence. | a) CLOCK CARDS (Document 2. shows totalled card)<br>b) OVERTIME RATES<br>c) DEDUCTION - REGULATIONS | Wages Clerk |
| | | | | |

(f)  Take each section and amplify it in a series of very short steps, thinking all the time about keeping the information as simply and concisely expressed as possible.

(g)  Number documents to link with appropriate sections.

(h)  On completion of the draft, pass it to appropriate colleagues for constructive criticism, then edit accordingly.

(i)  Prepare a contents page, list of documents and index if necessary.

(j)  Distribute with explanatory covering memo or, if it would be more helpful, distribute it to be read and then hold a meeting/series of meetings to deal with queries.

(k)  Ensure that all staff use the manual by regular checks and supervison.

(l)  Set up the mechanism for regular revision including consultation, amendment, distribution insertion/removal of sheets in manuals, informing staff of revisions, any retraining needed as a result of revised procedures.

## 5.3 INSTRUCTIONS FOR EQUIPMENT USE

These can also be somewhat bulky but need much less frequent revision. They may have to be written to supplement any available instructions from the manufacturer, which are often less than helpful, or when the manufacturer does not supply any.

In many ways such manuals will follow the pattern of procedure manuals. There should be charts to show the various parts of the equipment, switches, etc. A faults diagnosis and instructions for action should also be included.

The **focus** on dictating practice in Chapter 8 may give you some ideas on how occasionally to express such instructions in light-hearted terms, and this may have more impact than the general 'dry-as-dust' approach.

## 5.4 JOB INSTRUCTORS' MANUALS

These manuals  set out the details of succeeding tasks to be carried out by trainees, much in the format described in section 5.2. They include, however, detailed descriptions of how the trainee will be instructed phrased in language such as 'tell', 'tell and show', 'demonstrate'. Flow charts may be included to remind the instructor of the steps he must follow.

The compilation of such a manual requires very close-co-operation between the instructors and the writer, and it should be tried on a representative sample of trainees or relatively new employees before being finalised.

More general instruction and training manuals can also be prepared, without as much detail either of the tasks or of the instruction method.

```
┌─────────────────────────────────────┐
│              FOCUS                   │
│                                      │
│  HANDBOOKS AND MANUALS MUST:         │
│    afford easy reference             │
│    be clearly and succinctly written │
│    have carefully chosen content     │
│    be cost effective                 │
│    be capable of frequent revision   │
└─────────────────────────────────────┘
```

## 5.5 WRITTEN INSTRUCTIONS

In an instruction manual, direct commands can happily be used and accepted. However, when we send a memo to a subordinate, 'ordering' him to execute a particular task, such imperatives will frequently be resented unless they are more tactfully phrased. You would be wise to write

> *Will you please give me sales figures by 5 p.m.?*

rather than the bald *Give me . . .*

At the same time, the manager must maintain authority and control over subordinates. He is, after all, responsible for ensuring that tasks are carried out. Thus commands must not be reduced to mere suggestions.

> *Perhaps you might like to give me the sales figures – if you have time, of course.*

Such a weak approach indicates no urgency, nor will it necessarily be interpreted as a directive.

*Toujours la politesse* is the order of the day. It is a symptom of the growing awareness that people have of their individual status, and their need to have their position recognised that the direct command has largely been removed from both written and oral communication, except in the armed forces.

## 5.6 FORM DESIGN

In large organisations it is frequently the specialist *organisation and methods* staff who design the forms needed. Elsewhere, managers and administrators frequently design their own forms and need therefore to be familiar with both the principles and practice that, if correctly applied, will result in a form which is easy to complete and which elicits the information required.

The principles of form design are to:

(a) establish that a form is needed
(b) determine what information is required
(c) decide on the logical order in which information will be requested
(d) word the form in concise and unambiguous language
(e) choose a layout which allows an appropriate space for each item
(f) assess the handling, filing and use requirements (this will affect size and choice of paper or card)
(g) decide on the number and quality of forms needed and consider the duplicating or printing costs.

What can go wrong? It all seems straightforward, but we already know that our first principle is to ask whether or not a form is needed, and this question often goes unanswered. Thus useless forms proliferate.

Another major problem is that forms often seem designed to confuse and frighten those who have to complete them. C. Northcote Parkinson, of 'Parkinson's law' fame, wrote, tongue in cheek: 'The art of devising forms to be filled in depends on three elements: obscurity, lack of space, and the heaviest penalties for failure. . . obscurity is ensured by. . . ambiguity, irrelevance and jargon.'

Determine the information required. Consider *why* you want each item of information, *what* it will be used for and *in what form* it needs to be supplied. Then you may avoid the following pitfalls.

**Irrelevancies**
Resist the temptation to ask for information that is not needed, on the basis that 'it is interesting' or 'might come in useful sometime'. Thus you will avoid irrelevance. For instance, on a job-application form, do you really need to know all the detail listed in Figure 5.3? Most of it could be covered by a simple section, such as

> *Please list any serious illnesses or disabilities from which you suffer, or have suffered.*

A more detailed investigation of an applicant's health could be better sought through a medical examination.

**Omissions**
There can be omissions of words or of space (see section 5.6e). It is easy to leave a question out entirely and equally possible to leave out a crucial word or phrase so that the reply is not what you expect (see Figure 5.4). The omission is that the word 'delete' needs to read 'delete forms of domicile that do not apply to you'. But how much simpler it would have been to say *'Tick the appropriate reply'*!

Fig 5.3  *extract from job-application form*

| | |
|---|---|
| **HEALTH**<br><br>Have you ever suffered from any of the following? Answer YES or NO.<br><br>Nerves, mental illness, schizophrenia, paranoia | |
| Epilepsy, blackouts, fainting fits | |
| Migraine, headaches | |
| Dyspepsia, hiatus hernia, duodenal ulcer, indigestion | |
| Rheumatism, osteo-arthritis, rheumatoid arthritis | |

Fig 5.4  *extract from ambiguous form*

| |
|---|
| **DOMICILE** (delete)<br><br>Owner of freehold property<br><br>Owner of leasehold property<br><br>Tenant of whole property<br><br>Tenant of shared property<br><br>Lodger<br><br>Living with parents<br><br>No present permanent domicile |

## Ambiguities of expression

Careless phrasing of the questions or instructions leads to nonsense answers. Look again at Figure 5.3. Many people would have to admit that at some time in their lives they had been nervous, fainted, had backache, a headache, indigestion or some twinges of muscular rheumatism. Thus they might have answered 'yes' to all those questions and unwittingly given the idea that they are epileptic, paranoid paraplegics with migraine, duodenal ulcers and rheumatoid arthritis!

You may feel that this example is so far-fetched as to be ridiculous. It is, however, based on a section in a similar and widely used application form.

## Complexity

Legal documents are very complex, full of long and technically difficult language. This, or other specialist terminology, can also be found in forms (see the use of 'Domicile' in Figure 5.4). Instead of:

> *'Give brief details of your career to date'*

followed by a clearly designed tabulated space for the answers, there may appear something like:

> *Furnish a synopsis of your employment particulars in chronological order indicating length of tenure of each employment . . .*

When forms are both long and filled with obscure and confusing language it is no wonder that they do not elicit adequate replies. Many people will give up the attempt altogether. Also, the language may serve not only to confuse but to frighten people.

## Space

Allowing sufficient space for the reply to each question – not too much, not too little – calls for experience or some experiment. Inappropriate space is often allocated for:

(a) names and addresses
(b) qualifications
(c) employment details
(d) names of people attending a course or conference.

## Inappropriate printing/paper

A form for purely internal use, to be used on one occasion only and requesting information from about fifty people, scarcely needs to be professionally printed on stout cards. Conversely personnel record forms would not be very useful if spirit-duplicated on to thin paper, with a very limited shelf-life.

The quality of the printing and of the material must be directly related to the amount of handling expected, the impression it is desired to give (is it for external use?), the number of copies likely to be needed before the form has to be revised or ceases to be used, internal reprographic facilities or external printing estimates.

> ## FOCUS
>
> FORM DESIGN REQUIRES CLARITY OF:
> thought about information required
> expression and use of language
> layout and design

## 5.7 ASSIGNMENTS

1 Draft a booklet which will give information on your organisation's training schemes to applicants for employment.

2 Obtain copies of company annual reports and accounts and information booklets for staff and shareholders on the same subject. What differences do you note and in what ways has the information been simplified in the booklets?

3 What are the principal considerations to be borne in mind, having established that a form is essential, when one comes to design the form itself? [IAA]

4 When considering the design of forms, the mode of entry has a considerable effect on the spacing required for answering questions and the kind of paper used for the form itself. What points should therefore be borne in mind under these headings? [IAA]

5 The Association of Training and Personnel Officers is holding a one-day conference on recent developments in industrial training on 16 February 19-- at their headquarters. Details of the conference are being sent out all over the country. Delegates are expected to come from some distance and some will have to stay overnight. Some will bring their husbands or wives and many will wish to attend the annual dinner on the evening of the conference. A complete list of delegates and their organisations will be compiled for distribution at the conference. Payment of the conference fee plus accommodation and the annual dinner must be made on enrolment, by cheque or by credit card. As only 200 places are available, they will be allocated on the basis of 'first-come, first-served'.

Design a suitable form. (See Appendix 1 for an outline answer.)

# MEETINGS DOCUMENTATION

The widely recognised conventions applying to meetings documents make them fairly standardised and straightforward. So the papers you prepare for a monthly production meeting will probably differ only in the degree of formality from those of a company board meeting. (For types of meeting see Chapter 7.2.)

Despite the undoubted advantages of face-to-face communication, meetings are time-consuming and, thus, expensive. Efficiently drafted documents which prepare and inform people beforehand will help save discussion and explanation at the meeting.

All documents must be drafted and circulated in accordance with the 'rules', otherwise the meeting could be invalid. The 'rules' see (Chapter 7.2) are to be found in your club's Constitution, or in the Memorandum and Articles of Association of a company, or in the meeting's Standing Orders. At less formal meetings you will simply observe the conventions your manager imposes.

There are three basic documents which we need to be able to prepare, and two supplementary ones.

(a) *The notice* – to inform people when and where the meeting will take place.
(b) *The agenda* – to brief people on what will be discussed.
(c) *The minutes/report* – to record the discussions and decisions of a meeting.
(d) *Agenda papers* – additional material to supplement what appears on the agenda if necessary.
(e) *Chairman's agenda* – an extended version of the agenda to ensure that the chairman is particularly well briefed.

## 6.1 NOTICE OF MEETINGS

The notice must be sent out at a suitable time before the meeting and to everyone whose presence is needed. Additionally, others who are not attending may need to be notified — for example, so that they can brief their representatives beforehand.

There may be statutory requirements (to be found in the rules) and naturally these must be observed. It is both common sense and courtesy to give busy people ample notice if we expect them to attend; about two weeks is advisable. Of course, you will already have checked that the date is suitable. If the date were fixed at the previous meeting, then the reminder notice may be sent perhaps a week before the meeting. In practice many meetings at work are held at very short notice, as the need arises, while others are held at a regular time and day each week or month, so that a written notice may not be necessary.

The contents of a formal notice of meeting are as follows:

(a)  name of the organisation or meeting
(b)  place of meeting
(c)  date and time of meeting
(d)  date of notice
(e)  signature of person convening the meeting, with title
(f)  type of meeting, if applicable, e.g. committee, AGM.

These items can often be drafted as a simple memo (see Figure 6.1) or, for a more formal meeting, as in Figure 6.2.

Fig 6.1  *notice of meeting — informal*

Traders Limited

MEMORANDUM

TO:  Production Manager        FROM:  Managing Director
     Maintenance Manager
     Sales Manager
     R & D Manager
     Personnel Officer         DATE:  4 May 19--

LIAISON COMMITTEE

The next meeting of the Committee will take place at 1400 hours on 10 May in Committee Room A.

P Foster

Fig 6.2  *notice of meeting — formal*

TRADERS LIMITED
BURNTHOUSE ROAD
LONDON WC4 3BJ

26th May 19--

ANNUAL GENERAL MEETING

NOTICE IS HEREBY GIVEN that the Annual General
Meeting of the Company will be held in the
Burnthouse Rooms, Burnthouse Road, London
WC4 3BJ on Thursday, 30th May, 19-- at 12
noon to transact the following business:

1.  To receive the report of the directors
    and the accounts for the year ended
    31st March, 19-- and the report of
    the auditors.

(The remainder of the agenda would then follow)

By order of the Board

K Brown
Secretary

## 6.2 AGENDA

This is the programme of items to be discussed at the meeting, in the order
in which they will be taken. Each item needs a heading and a number. You
might use the following sources for your agenda items:

(a)  minutes of the previous meeting
(b)  items received from members
(c)  correspondence
(d)  action and events since the last meeting
(e)  the chairman and other officers.

In addition there are standard items which appear regularly on formal
agendas. The first three items on such an agenda will be:

1. *Apologies for absence.*
2. *Minutes of previous meeting.*
3. *Matters arising.*

Then follow the special items of business derived from (a) to (e) above and
numbered 4, 5, 6, and so on. The final items on the agenda are:

*Correspondence (optional).*
*Date of next meeting.*
*Any other business (AOB).*

The order in which special items are listed on the agenda is important. Urgent matters must obviously appear early. The position of controversial items, where long discussion is likely, needs more thought!

It is useless to overload an agenda with more items than can be covered in the time available. Either the members, in an attempt to complete the business, may make hasty or unwise decisions, or they may continue the meeting so long that tiredness and frustration lead to the same result. Much better to be realistic and hold matters over to the next meeting.

Some agendas are mere skeletons, but a list of headings like *The Paish Contract, Proposed Extension* or *Improving Company Communication* is likely to be meaningless to members. For example, the Office Services Manager might interpret *Improving Company Communication* as implying that the meeting was at last going to consider installing a new automated switchboard. He might even prepare himself by obtaining prices. On the other hand, the Public Relations Officer might prepare himself to talk about the advantages of introducing a company newspaper. (See Figure 6.3.)

Members need to be sufficiently informed beforehand to be able to prepare for the discussions by thinking, forming and seeking opinions or collecting information. If they have done this, the discussion and decision-taking at the meeting will be speeded up. So it is important for the agenda to amplify headings sufficiently (see Figure 6.3). Sometimes supplementary documents, agenda papers, are needed.

An agenda is sometimes combined with the notice of meeting, which is both economical and ensures that people *do* have the opportunity to consider the business prior to the meeting.

Finally, an AGM agenda has its own series of standard items which have to be included. The most common are given below:

### ANNUAL GENERAL MEETINGS – AGENDA ITEMS

| *A Limited Liability Company* | *A Club or Society* |
| --- | --- |
| Directors' Report | Chairman's and Secretary's Reports |
| Annual Accounts | Annual Accounts |
| Auditor's Reports | Auditor's Report |
| Appointment of Auditors | Appointment of Auditors |
| Remuneration of Auditors | |
| Declaration of Dividend | Subscriptions |
| Election of Directors | Election of Officers and Committee |

Fig 6.3 *designing an agenda*

## TRADERS LIMITED

Liaison Committee Meeting to be held on
Friday, 10 May, at 1400 in Committee Room A

**AGENDA**

| Skeleton Agenda | More Informative Agenda |
|---|---|
| 1. Apologies for absence | 1. Apologies for absence |
| 2. Minutes of previous meeting | 2. Minutes of meeting held on 12 March 19-- |
| 3. Matters arising | 3. Matters arising |
| 4. Paish Contract | 4. Paish Contract |
| | The meeting must agree on a completion date. |
| 5. Proposed extension | 5. Proposed extension |
| | Decision to be made on Maintenance Workshop location (Area A or Area B on attached plan, Agenda Paper 1.) |
| 6. Improving Company Communication | 6. Improving Company Communication |
| | It has been proposed that a series of regular briefing meetings chaired by a director and attended by representatives from each department should be considered. |
| 7. Date of next meeting | 7. Date of next meeting |
| 8. Any other business | 8. Any other business |

## 6.3 AGENDA PAPERS

These are any documents sent out with the agenda to supplement its information. They could be statistics, like copies of the balance-sheet, or copies of correspondence. Complicated reports, if given orally during the meeting, are difficult to absorb and are more usefully sent out in advance; so are diagrams, the plan of the proposed extension or whatever. Agenda papers should be clearly labelled and cross-referenced to the relevant agenda item (see Figure 6.3).

## 6.4 CHAIRMAN'S AGENDA

The Chairman has the leading role at the meeting (see Chapter 7.6) and thus needs to be particularly well informed if he is to lead members carefully and speedily through the business. Therefore, if there is a meetings secretary who briefs the chairman he or she should provide information (and perhaps advice) additional to that provided for the others. Compare Figures 6.3 and 6.4 to see how this may be done.

**Fig 6.4**  *a chairman's agenda*

TRADERS LIMITED

Liaison Committee meeting to be held on
Friday, 10 May, at 1400 in Committee Room A

CHAIRMAN'S AGENDA

NOTES

1. Apologies for absence  J Brown will be away at
             a conference

2. Minutes of meeting   Copy attached
 held on 12 March 19--

3. Matters Arising    Item 5.
            Mr Tomkins will report
            approval confirmed.

4. Paish Contract    Sales Manager will press
            for end of month. Main-
 The meeting must agree tenance and Production
 on a completion date. Managers will propose end
            of July. Overtime problem.

5. Proposed extension  Manager prefers Area A
            but this will cause pro-
 Decision to be made  duction problems.
 on Maintenance Work- Possible ad hoc committee
 shop location (Area A to consider and report?
 or Area B on attached
 plan, Agenda Paper 1.)

6. Improving Company  This is the proposal you
 Communication    discussed with the
            Personnel Manager who
 It has been pro-   will propose.
 posed that a series of
 regular briefing
 meetings chaired by a
 director and attended
 by representatives from
 each department should
 be considered.

7. Date of next meeting Friday 4 June?

8. Any other business  Bonus scheme. Should
            invite union rep.

(A chairman who does not have the help of a meetings secretary will find it helpful to annotate his own copy of the agenda with reminders before the meeting.)

It is usual to set out his agenda in a way which distinguishes the information given to him only and leaves a space for his own notes (see Figure 6.4).

The chairman will need his agenda in advance of the meeting, so that he may plan ahead (see section 7.6), but it should be compiled as late as possible so as to include last-minute information. The meetings secretary should have his or her own copy of this document — it will help in taking notes for the minutes.

## 6.5 RECORDING MEETINGS

A record should be made of almost every meeting and this record circulated among those present to ensure that everyone is aware of, and agreed upon, what took place — something that cannot be taken for granted, however obvious it might seem. This record can also be used to inform others who were not at the meeting of what took place. Such a record may be in the form of notes (see Chapter 3.2), a report (see Chapter 2), or minutes.

Minutes are always used for formal meetings and may be legally required (for example, at directors' meetings). They, like less formal records, are the basis for action by the organisation and its members. Since they record past decisions and activities, they also provide precedents and a basis for evolving future policy.

**Contents** (see Figure 6.5)
(a) *Heading.* The name of the body which held the meeting (this is not needed in a bound minute book, of course): kind of meeting, place of meeting, date (and, optional, time) of meeting.
(b) *Names of those present.* Alphabetical order is the least invidious, but as a courtesy the chairman's name comes first. If the meeting is very large, record the names of officers and committee members, and then the numbers present. Those 'in attendance', i.e. present by invitation, should be listed separately.
(c) *Apologies.* Record names only, not reasons.
(d) *Minutes of previous meeting.* Minutes are usually 'taken as read', having been circulated previously. (It is time-consuming to read then aloud.) They have to be approved as a correct record by the meeting before the chairman signs the copy in the minutes book. If corrections are necessary, they should be made formally by a motion (see Chapter 7.5).

Fig 6.5  *minutes*

**TRADERS LIMITED**

Minutes of the Liaison Committee meeting held at 1400 hours
on Friday 10 May, 19-- in Committee Room A.

PRESENT:   P Foster   Managing Director (Chairman)
           D Brown    Production Manager
           F Roberts  Maintenance Manager
           E Rumble   Sales Manager
           A Tomkins  Research & Development Manager
           V Williams Personnel Manager


           P Jones, Union Organiser, in attendance

ACTION

1.   Apologies for absence

     An apology was received from J Smith.

2.   Minutes

     The minutes of the meeting held on 12 March
     were taken as read, approved as a correct
     record and signed by the Chairman.

3.   Matters arising

     It was confirmed that final planning approval
     for the extension had been received,

4.   Paish Contract

     The Sales Manager reported that unless the
     contract could be completed by the end of the
     month there was a danger that Paish PLC would
     not offer a renewal of contract without a
     heavy penalty clause.  The Production Manager
     said that this date could not be met without
     excessive overtime working.  The extra cost
     could be £4500.

     It was agreed that the Sales Manager should       SALES
     visit Paish PLC and seek their agreement to       MANAGER
     a completion date in mid June.  Meanwhile
     overtime working at the rate of £500 per week
     would begin immediately.

                        et cetera

(e)  *Matters arising.* Only minor items should appear under this heading.
     Any important 'matters arising' topic from a previous meeting will
     have its own heading on the agenda and hence its own separate
     record in the minutes.

(f)  *Special items.* The recording of these items is described by two tech-
     nical terms, *minutes of resolution* and *minutes of narration.*

     Minutes of resolution are the essential content of minutes. They
     are the record of decisions taken and resolutions passed. They are
     usually introduced thus:

> *It was therefore resolved*
> *THAT* ... or
> *RESOLVED* ...

But decisions are not taken in a vacuum. They have a context of events, facts and opinions. Minutes of narration are that part of the record which describes the circumstances in which the decision was taken. In the following example the narration, typically, precedes the resolution:

> *The Secretary reported several recent instances of the diffi-*
> *culties arising from shared club premises and reminded members*
> *that similar problems had been experienced for the past two*
> *years.*
>
> *It was therefore resolved*
> *THAT a sub-committee be formed, chaired by Mr Tomkins, to*
> *investigate alternative premises for the club.*

(g) *Correspondence.* This is an optional item which does not appear on all agendas and, therefore, not in all minutes. Many meetings secretaries sensibly take the view that correspondence should be related to particular items of business, rather than have all letters miscellaneously put together under this general heading.

If the heading *is* used, the minutes will be drafted as in this example:

> *The Secretary reported that the following letters had been*
> *received:*
>
> *Letter No. 1234  Messrs J. Jones had quoted a price of*
> *£5534 for redecoration and the Secretary was asked to obtain*
> *further estimates and report back to the meeting.*
>
> *Letter No. 1235   A letter of resignation from B. Brown was*
> *accepted and the Secretary was requested to acknowledge it.*

(h) *Date of next meeting.* It is very sensible for members to choose the date convenient to the greatest number when they are all present to agree on it.

(i) *Any other business.* This open end to the agenda gives members the chance, if time allows, to settle minor details and to discuss matters arising since the agenda was compiled. If no such items are raised, the topic is omitted from the minutes. Any discussion will be given separate headings and minute numbers. The following shows how a secretary's notes on AOB might look when turned into minutes:

| | **SECRETARY'S NOTES**<br>**8 OB** | **MINUTES**<br>**8 INSTALLATION OF NEW**<br>**XX100 COMPUTER** |
|---|---|---|
| ROBERTS | *New XX100 computer being installed next month. Est. pay-roll transfer 3 wks. Running in conjunction with XX99 for 3 mths. Transfer Sales Ledg, Bought Ledg. Stock Contr. etc. by Xmas.* | The Computer Manager stated that the new XX100 system would be installed within a month. The payroll should be transferred from the XX99 computer within three weeks, and Sales and Bought Ledger and Stock Control by Christmas. |
| M.D. | *Dreadful hiccup last time. What about now?* | |
| ROBERTS | *No problem. All ironed out before get rid of XX99.* | No problems were envisaged on this occasion as the experience of the first installation had been profited from. |
| SMITH | *Believe that when see it.* | |
| ROBERTS | *Really will be OK. Learnt from last time. Made sure.* | |
| M.D. | *OK — let's get on. Jones wants to talk about bonus. Ask him to come in.* (Enter Jones — Union Rep) | |

**9. NEW BONUS SCHEME**

| | | |
|---|---|---|
| SMITH | *New rates offer gd incentive.* | The meeting was joined by Mr P. Jones, Union Representative. Following discussion it was agreed that the new bonus should be introduced for a trial period of two months followed by review, with no commitments by either side. |
| JONES | *Times too tight. Union not happy.* | |
| M.D. | *Will you give it try?* | |
| JONES | *How long?* | |
| M.D. | *Three months.* | |
| JONES | *NO! 1 month.* | |
| SMITH | *Not enough — 2 at least.* | |
| JONES | *Review without commitment.* | |
| M.D. | *AGREED.*<br>(Exit Jones) | |

**10. CHRISTMAS SHOPPING TIME**

| | | |
|---|---|---|
| M.D. | *Anything else?* | The allowance for Christmas shopping for female staff was agreed at one half day each, without pay. |
| SMITH | *Yes. Time out for Xmas for women to shop?* | |
| ROBERTS | *Farce. Use it to slope off.* | |
| SMITH | *Tradition.* | |
| M.D. | *Not from now on. No!* | |
| SMITH | *Trouble!* | There being no further business, the Chairman declared the meeting closed at 1550 hours. |
| ROBERTS | *True — strike.* | |
| M.D. | *OK — one $\frac{1}{2}$ day without pay. Can't do more. AGREED.*<br>Closure 3.50 pm | |

(j) *Closure of the meeting.* Note how this is recorded in the above example.

(k) *Action column* (see Figure 6.5). This is simply a wide right-hand margin to the minutes in which the names of those asked to do something are noted, opposite to the relevant minute. It is a very useful visual prompt to ensure that those concerned read the relevant minute.

**Taking notes for minutes** (see also Chapter 3.2)

(a) Summarise as you record what is being said. Leave out any irrelevant discussion.

(b) Keep your notes as short as possible — but you will need to be able to read them later!

(c) Use your copy of the agenda as the framework.

(d) Record the names of persons speaking. They are usually omitted from the minute but make a useful reference point.

(e) Make a careful record of those present, possibly either by passing round a sheet for signature *or* recording numbers present.

(f) Distinguish between items under AOB.

(g) Use a device such as capitals or underlining so that essential notes and records of decisions stand out.

(h) Make a careful record of essential detail, dates, numbers, amounts, quantities and the names of those receiving instructions (to be put in the ACTION column).

(i) If a vote is taken, make sure you note the numbers for the minute thus:

> *RESOLVED by x votes in favour, y against, with z abstentions, THAT* . . .

## 6.6 WRITING MINUTES

### Style

Formal minutes must be concise but give sufficient detail to enable someone not present at the meeting to understand fully what took place. They must be factual and written in complete sentences. They must be orderly, and it is often necessary to rearrange the material in one's notes so as to produce a logical account without repetition.

Look back through the minutes book and match your style with that of the previous minutes so as to give consistent reporting. Use the precedent of earlier minutes to decide how much detail is needed and whether or not to include, for example, the names of proposers and seconders and the numbers voting.

Use the past tense and the other conventions of reported speech (see Appendix 3).

### Format

Minutes must be suitably titled and have appropriate headings to individual items (see Figure 6.5). They must also be numbered. There are three methods.

(a) The minutes are numbered consecutively, starting with number 1 for the first item of each set of minutes.

(b) The first set of minutes is numbered as described above. If the last item in this set is number 9, then the first item of the minutes of the next meeting becomes number 10, and so on. Thus no two minutes of the meetings would bear the same number.

(c) A similar system to (ii) but the numbers run through one year. At the beginning of the new year the minutes once again start with number 1.

### Indexing

As minutes accumulate from year to year it can be useful to have an index to show when subjects were previously discussed and what decisions were made. A convenient method is to give each minute sheet a title and number to which a separate list of topics refers.

## 6.7 THE MINUTE BOOK

Minutes may either be kept in a loose-leaf binder or may be written in a bound minutes book. The loose-leaf book has several advantages:

(a) minutes may be typed and duplicated easily for circulation
(b) copies of past minutes may be made quickly
(c) reports and other documents can be filed with the minutes
(d) corrections may easily be inserted.

It is important to take suitable security precautions such as having numbered pages, lockable binders and fireproof filing cabinets for minutes.

## 6.8 WRITING MEETINGS REPORTS

These are usually much more concise than minutes. Often they are used for display on a bulletin board. The notes given as an example of the AOB discussions earlier might appear in a report as follows:

> 1.  *The new XX100 computer is to be installed in the next month. The payroll, Sales and Bought ledgers and stock control will be transferred to it in that order by Christmas.*
> 2.  *The new bonus scheme will be introduced for a trial period of two months followed by review with no commitment by either side.*
> 3.  *Female staff will be allowed one half day without pay for Christmas shopping.*

Such a report would of course need a clear heading to identify which meeting was reported and when it had been held.

Finally, remember to get your minutes and reports circulated as soon as possible after the meeting.

> ## FOCUS
>
> Use documentation to make meetings more cost effective.
>
> NOTICE to warn members
> AGENDA to inform them
> AGENDA PAPERS to brief them
> CHAIRMAN'S AGENDA to prompt him
> MINUTES to record and to remind members

## 6.9 ASSIGNMENTS

1  A works consultative committee has been organised in your firm and you are appointed Secretary. Describe the correct procedure for calling a meeting, the duties of the Secretary before and after the meeting and state the points you would bear in mind in writing up the minutes afterwards. [RSA DPA]

2  Prepare minutes for the first meeting of a sub-committee comprising management and staff representatives set up to advise the firm on the possible production (for issue to all new employees) of a handbook covering conditions of service, company rules, remuneration, absence and sickness procedures, fringe benefits and other matters. The meeting dealt with (favourable) staff reactions to the proposal and with ways and means of implementing it. [RSA DPA]

3  How would you minute the following?

   (a) a resolution
   (b) an amendment to the minutes of the previous meeting
   (c) a request by one committee member that his dissent be recorded
   (d) the taking of the chair by the vice-chairman when the chairman was called away during the meeting.

   (An answer to this question is given in Appendix 1.)

4  Part of your duties as assistant to Mrs Joy Lawson, Office Administration Manager of Sherwood Furniture Limited, is to assist her generally in her capacity as Secretary to the firm's Management Committee.

   The Committee meets monthly and acts in an advisory capacity to Mr Stephen Watkins, Managing Director, and his board of directors. It is mainly concerned with internal company matters.

   The Committee is made up as follows:

| | |
|---|---|
| Mr John Howard (Chairman) | *Deputy Managing Director* |
| Mrs Joy Lawson (Secretary) | *Office Administration Manager* |
| Mr. Jack Barton | *Production Manager* |
| Mrs Lesley Chesterton | *Sales Manager* |
| Mr Richard French | *Chief Purchasing Officer* |
| Mr Gordon Prince | *Assistant Accounts Manager* |
| Mrs Pamela Trenton | *Senior Secretarial Supervisor* |
| Miss Naomi Watson | *Assistant Personnel Manager* |

Earlier today, Mrs Lawson raised the work of the Committee in this context:

*'Look, I'm sorry to have to burden you with this, but if I'm to get out to see Mr Perkins this afternoon, I simply won't have time to draw up the Agenda and Chairman's Agenda for the Management Committee's meeting next Wednesday week at 4.30 in the Conference Room. If I leave you the essential information later this morning, I'm sure you could manage them for me to submit to Mr Howard.'*

As promised, Mrs Lawson left you the following hurried notes:

### MANAGEMENT COMMITTEE AGENDA NOTES

Sorry about these random jottings — had to note in haste:

Mrs Benson just resigned from Restaurant Manageress post — agreed to work notice 2 weeks.

Recv'd following today:

THAT consideration be given by the Management Committee to requesting the Board of Directors to examine the possibility of establishing a Training Department to co-ordinate current and future training needs.

It's been proposed by Mrs Chesterton with Miss Watson as seconder.

Letter (attached) arrived yestd. — H.O.D. Marford Coll. Techn. Mgt and Bus. St. Dept. Wants to know if we can help with wk experience placements. Rang Peter Kent, Personnel Mgr — in favour if enough time given — N.B. MD on Coll. Gov. Body as I recall.

Have recv'd 10 copies of Marford Coll. Techn. Mgt. and Bus. Studies Prospectus — ought to explore day-release possibilities.

Mrs Bately to retire next month — 22 yrs as Co. Sec. MD keen on approp ceremony and present — C'tee to decide.

Have note from Gordon Prince — re item 6 last mtg mins: figure for micro-ovens shd read £1540 and not £1940 in estimates.

N.B. Jack Barton rang today — he's away for next fortnight on course — 'Robotics, Friend or Foe?' (sounds very foe to me!).

Mrs Trenton stopped me in corridor — still on about cost of vending machine drinks (again!) — likely to raise but fully debated about two months ago — Co. already selling at cost.

Almost forgot — Jack Barton offered his wife's help with Restaurant — apparently Inst. Catering quals — cd be delicate situation.

Hope you can make sense of this — if not ring me tonight as out all day tomorrow.

Many thanks.

J. L.

Using Mrs Lawson's notes as a guide, compose a CHAIRMAN'S AGENDA *only,* for Mr Howard's use at the next Management Meeting. [RSA DPA]

# MEETINGS

No excuse is offered for discussing this aspect of oral communication in some detail. Indeed, as everyone in business spends so much of his time in meetings of one kind or another, it would be wrong not to cover it as thoroughly as possible. However, it is still not possible to include in this book all the intricacies of meetings' procedure and practice. Students requiring this are advised to consult a specialist book on meetings (one or more is usually to be found in any good library).

One of the difficulties in discussing meetings is that they are often separated into two types: formal and informal. What is meant by a *formal* meeting? Usually it means a meeting where there is/are:

(a)  a Chairman
(b)  a set of rules which govern how the meeting is constituted, business recorded, etc.
(c)  conventions applied to the way in which the business of the meeting is conducted.

Yet anyone who has been to a number of different meetings will know that the degree of formality or informality can be very different between two meetings which might be thought to be similar in character: that the size of a meeting or the diversity of membership can affect the formality; that within one meeting, dependent on the item under discussion, there can be changes in the degree of formality. For instance

(a)  Some union negotiation meetings are very formal but others, where a very good relationship exists between management and unions, will be much more relaxed and easy, with fewer procedural devices needed or used.
(b)  A small meeting often requires less formal control than a very large meeting might do.

(c) Within a meeting, a formal motion, which is to be debated and voted upon, may be put to the meeting at the beginning of discussion of the agenda item, and thus a very formal procedure may be followed. The next item, however, might be a preliminary discussion of a problem where it is not envisaged that any decision will be reached immediately. The discussion will probably be much more informal.

What we can deduce from these examples is that different meetings and different topics require different approaches.

## 7.1 THE MAIN TYPES OF MEETINGS

The following are examples of meetings which follow rules and conventions to varying degrees.

(a) *Very formal meetings*, e.g. the deliberations of government assemblies such as parliaments, executive councils and local authorities; meetings of shareholders of companies; meetings of boards of directors or governors of companies and other organisations; management/union negotiations.
(b) *Intermediate meetings*, e.g. committees of various kinds, including management committees and voluntary organisations; general meetings of voluntary organisations; management meetings, advisory groups, briefing sessions.
(c) *Informal meetings*, e.g. *ad hoc* gatherings of small groups; brainstorming meetings (deliberately structured attempts to produce a wide range of ideas in a very short time — used in commerce and industry; see also Chapter 11.2c).

Meetings can be classified in other ways than formal and informal and these classifications refer to the type of business being discussed. It should be remembered that in any one meeting there might be a combination of several types of business considered and that, within a generally accepted procedure, the formality of a meeting should be changed to allow for effective discussion and decision-making as required.

### Executive meetings
The people at these meetings will be discussing and deciding matters but will have the additional task of implementing decisions. A board of directors is an example of an executive committee.

### Decision-making
Some meetings have the power to make collective decisions on action to be taken. Such authority will have been given to them by a parent body or

electorate and, as long as the meeting acts within its powers, its decisions are absolute. All true committees hold decision-making meetings. (A true committee is one where the members are collectively bound by their decisions and actions to a higher authority and are authorised to take decisions, for instance a board of directors or an elected local authority.)

## Discussion and advice

Discussion takes place in most meetings but there are many where it is the function of members to discuss and proffer advice to other people or bodies. Joint consultation meetings come within this category.

Many of these meetings, when held on a regular basis, are called (mistakenly) committee meetings. The members do not have any decision-making powers except in deciding what advice to give. An 'advisory committee' is a contradiction in terms.

## Problem-solving

Any item of special business on an agenda may be a problem which the meeting has to solve. Also, special meetings may be held for the purpose of solving one specific problem only.

## Information-giving

Meetings held for the purpose of providing information are frequently called 'briefings'. The prepared brief will be read to the meeting, and it is common for questions to be answered. The meeting is not intended as a forum for discussion and debate. That would take place on another occasion.

Briefings are given by companies and official bodies to the press, and also many organisations now hold regular briefing sessions for their employees, from senior executives to the office junior or production worker. At each level of the organisation, the staff will be split into groups of up to twenty, each to be briefed by the immediate manager. This can be a valuable addition to the formal systems of communcation.

## Negotiation

Trade-union representatives and employers most commonly form the two sides in the battle that is joined in these meetings, where details of pay rises, fringe benefits and other changes in conditions of work, or redundancy payments and arrangements, are working out.

Such groups hope to reach agreement, even if only after a series of meetings, but their agreements will then have to be ratified by the bodies that they represent.

Meetings between one person and another, or one person and a group of other people, for purposes such as employment, performance appraisal, reprimands and discussion of grievances are covered in Chapter 8.

## 7.2 RULES GOVERNING MEETINGS

The procedure adopted for calling a meeting, conducting its business and recording it is often determined not just by the wishes of the chairman, officers and members but by *rules* – which may be legally binding or which may have been drawn up by the members themselves.

For instance, company law will state certain requirements about the conduct of company business which will affect meetings of shareholders and boards of directors. In the UK these rules are specified in the Companies Acts and/or in the individual Memorandum and Articles of Association of each individual company.

Sometimes the rules are very specific, sometimes not, but in any case companies have to fulfil certain requirements, such as giving statutory length of notice of annual general meetings (AGMs) and keeping proper written records of meetings.

Other organisations have Standing Orders which serve the same purpose. These are found in organisations where there are Standing Committees (they do not always bear this name). Such committees are always in existence even though their membership may change, as in local government after an election. Other meetings, such as those of clubs, societies and political parties, have constitutions, some very detailed, which govern their activities.

The purpose of all these documents is to ensure, first, that business is transacted in an open and correct way, and second, that business is conducted in a controlled and effective manner.

## 7.3 WHAT THE RULES COVER

Generally speaking, the rules governing meetings include the following:

(a) membership, namely those people entitled to attend the meeting and vote
(b) proxies, i.e. the procedure when a member cannot attend and wishes another person to speak and vote in his place
(c) arrangements for election of officers and members of committees
(d) arrangements for ballots
(e) remuneration of, for example, directors or trustees
(f) the frequency with which meetings must be held
(g) the length of notice required for meetings
(h) regulations regarding the submission of motions
(i) the duties, powers and privileges of officers
(j) the rules governing the recording of proceedings, e.g. minutes.

Even when there are no written rules, it is advisable to work out sensible procedures covering the above items and make sure that everyone knows about them. Thus it is usually helpful if they are written down.

## 7.4 GENERAL PROCEDURE

Written rules are generally found only where there are general meetings of members or where there are committees of elected or appointed representatives. However, there are also many conventions which are used in a whole range of meetings. Most of these cover the procedure in the meeting and are aimed at furthering the smooth conduct of the business. Many of the conventions use a rather specialised language and thus a glossary of meetings terms is given in Appendix 2.

The pattern followed is a well-established one. It comes from rules and conventions that have been codified, considered, adjudged in courts of law and generally accepted as fair and reasonable. Many of the procedures are old and not only are traditional ways still followed but traditional terms are still used. Some of these are English words and phrases used in a special way, such as *rider*, others are Latin terms, e.g. *sine die*.

## 7.5 PROCEDURES AND CONVENTIONS

### The agenda
Agendas for meetings are more fully discussed in Chapter 6.2. Suffice it to say here that it is always advisable to have a written agenda and to distribute it to members before the meeting, with any relevant papers. Occasionally special meetings may be held with the sole purpose of drawing up the agenda. It is essential to have clear agendas if meetings are to be effective.

### The chair
It seems obvious that one person should control the meeting. Thus either an elected chairman or, in most business meetings, the senior manager becomes responsible for the control and direction of the meeting. Details of the chairman's duties and responsibilities are discussed in the next section.

### The minutes and the secretary
Some record of the meeting is always desirable, whether it be formal minutes, a report or just notes (see also Chapter 6.5). Thus there also has to be someone responsible for taking notes in the meeting and writing the record. This person may be the official secretary, or it may be a minutes secretary, or it may be a member of the meeting who is taking part in the discussion but who has also been asked to take notes.

## The decision-making

When a decision has to be taken formal procedures can be very useful. For instance, it is always advisable to state clearly what the proposed decision should be — that becomes the *motion* or *proposition*. Any changes to that motion should also be stated — and become the *amendments* or *addenda*. The final decision is the expressed *resolution* of the meeting and will be so recorded in the minutes.

## The debate

As is shown in Figure 7.1, the debate on a formal motion follows a very precise procedure. For some meetings, motions must be submitted in writing by a specified time before the meeting takes place, and must be duly proposed and seconded.

Motions may be changed, before they are voted upon, by amendment or addendum. An *amendment* alters a motion by inserting, deleting or changing words of the original, but it is not permitted to negate the motion or completely change it. Amendments may be submitted before the meeting or, commonly, will be raised during the course of discussion. They must also be formally proposed and seconded and the chairman should call for all amendments to the motion before allowing discussion and voting on any single one. The amendments should then be taken in the order in which they affect the words of the original motion. An *addendum* is simply an addition of words to the end of a motion and is treated in the same way as an amendment.

The motion, if amended and/or added to, becomes the *substantive* motion. When voted upon and carried it then becomes the *final resolution*. This can be further altered by a *rider*, yet another phrase or clause.

It is the final resolution (including any rider) that appears in minutes and it is the decision upon which action is based. See the following example:

ORIGINAL MOTION
*THAT there shall be a promise of an additional three days' holiday made to all salaried staff.*

PROPOSED AMENDMENT 1
*That the word 'not' be inserted between 'shall' and 'be'*
    NOT ACCEPTABLE — negates the proposal
PROPOSED AMENDMENT 2
*That the words 'an additional three days' holiday' be deleted and 'a bonus payment of 2 per cent of salary' be inserted.*
    NOT ACCEPTABLE — changes the nature of the proposal

Fig 7.1 *from motion to resolution*

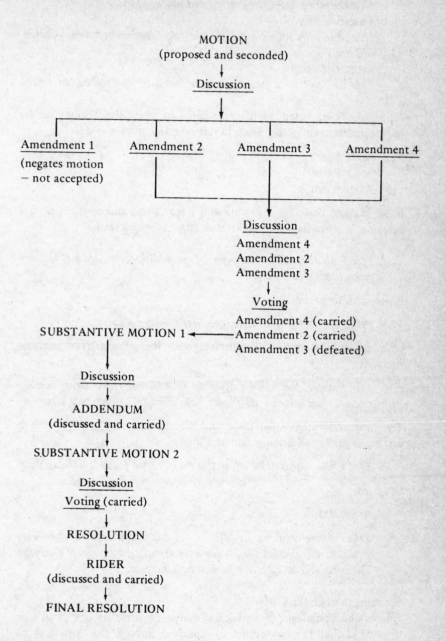

AMENDMENT 1
*That the word 'three' be deleted and the word 'two' inserted.*

AMENDMENT 2.
*That the words 'and weekly paid' be inserted between 'salaried' and 'staff'.*

AMENDMENT 3
*That the words 'a promise' be replaced by the words 'an offer'.*

Amendments are voted upon in the order in which the wording of the original motion is affected. Thus, in this case, the order would be:

Amendment 3
Amendment 1
Amendment 2

If we suppose that amendments 3 and 1 are carried and amendment 2 is defeated, we then have a SUBSTANTIVE MOTION which reads:

*THAT there shall be an offer of an additional two days' holiday made to all salaried staff.*

It may now be proposed:

*THAT the words 'who have completed one year's service'*

be added to the motion. If this is agreed, the SUBSTANTIVE MOTION becomes:

*THAT there shall be an offer of an additional two days' holiday made to all salaried staff who have completed one year's service.*

The motion is then voted upon and becomes the RESOLUTION if it is carried. A further addition would be a RIDER:

*THAT the words 'The offer will be effective for this holiday year'*

be added.

RESOLUTION

*THAT there shall be an offer of an additional two days' holiday made to all salaried staff who have completed one year's service. The offer will be effective for this holiday year.*

### Speaking through the Chair
One of the advantages of having a chairman (whether he bears that title or not) is that the convention of 'speaking through the Chair' can be enforced. This means that all remarks are addressed through the chairman to the meeting (which means that only one person will be speaking at any

moment) rather than there being a criss-crossing of talk which not every-one hears, or several conversations taking place simultaneously.

## Procedural motions

Sometimes discussion goes on too long, or is ineffective. There are certain motions which are deliberately aimed at making the meeting effective. The main ones are

(a) *That the question be now put* (often referred to as the *closure* and with the intention of ending the discussion on the motion).
(b) *That the question be not now put* (this may mean that it is desired to give more time for discussion at this or a subsequent meeting, or it may be the intention not to take a decision at all but to return to discussion of an earlier motion or *previous question*).
(c) *That the meeting leave the matter on the table* or *let it lie* (i.e. take note but not discuss it).
(d) *That the discussion* (or *the meeting*) *be adjourned.*
(e) *That the meeting proceed to the next item* of business.
(f) *That the meeting be adjourned sine die* (i.e. indefinitely).

## Points of order

Opportunities need to be given for interruptions to the debate. There are certain interruptions which are called *points of order* because they are connected with the correct procedure of the meeting. They include

(a) *The meeting is not quorate* (that there is not a sufficient number present for the meeting to be authorised to conduct its business — it is not a quorum).
(b) *The item being discussed is not on the agenda.*
(c) *The speaker is not speaking to the agenda.*
(d) *The speaker is not speaking to the subject.*
(e) *The subject is ultra vires* (i.e. outside the authority of the meeting; outside its terms of reference).
(f) *The speaker is using unseemly language.* (One of the memorable examples of this occurred in the UK House of Commons when Winston Churchill called another MP a liar. When called upon, on a point of order, to withdraw the accusation, he substituted for it the phrase 'terminological inexactitude' — no less accusatory, but more polite.)

Rulings on points of order are given by the chairman.

## The ballot

At many meetings, decisions are reached when the chairman 'assesses the sense of the meeting', i.e. gauges whether or not most of those present are in favour of the proposition. However, when there is a formal motion (and sometimes when there is not) there may be a vote, either by show of hands or by a secret ballot. Resolutions at meetings are usually carried by a simple majority, i.e. the number of votes in favour being more than the number against. Abstentions are ignored.

**The casting vote**
If there is a dead heat in the voting, the chairman may have a casting vote. This is not his own vote, but an extra one which must be expressly given to him to break the deadlock.

It is customary for the chairman to vote to keep the status quo, i.e. the existing situation, until there is a clear majority in favour of change.

All the conventions and procedures mentioned are designed to make discussion and decision-taking more efficient and purposeful. Meetings are expensive, costs including not only the wages and overheads of members, accommodation, secretarial assistance, etc., but also the 'opportunity cost' of taking people away from their work, and the possible reduction in efficiency of other staff left unsupervised.

Meetings should have very limited agendas and specific purposes, such as to identify problems, generate ideas, plan, review past actions and make decisions.

---

### FOCUS

**PROCEDURES AND CONVENTIONS**

written agenda
chairman
written record
secretary
from motion to resolution
speaking through the chair
procedural motions
points of order
voting

---

## 7.6 CHAIRMANSHIP

Meetings are also about persuasion: obtaining a consensus. The chairman needs to pre-plan and establish priorities, to be able to state clearly at the commencement of the meeting the purpose of the discussion and to allocate tasks. He needs to have strength of character, without being dogmatic or wishing to impress his own views on the meeting. He must have the ability to express himself fluently without making speeches. He must be able to maintain control over the meeting, but should not prevent useful exchanges of views. He must earn the respect of the members but respect the opinions of others. He must ensure that he is always impartial in his conduct of the meeting even when he strongly disagrees with the decisions taken. He will need to restate problems from time to time and summarise discussion before decisions are taken.

His duties include the following:

(a) ensuring that his own appointment and that of other officers is in accordance with the rules
(b) making certain that the meeting has been properly convened, is correctly constituted and that a quorum is present
(c) maintaining order and ensuring that the meeting is conducted correctly
(d) taking items of business in the correct order
(e) preventing irrelevant discussion and allowing adequate opportunity for those who wish to speak to do so
(f) ascertaining the 'sense of the meeting' when a vote is not taken, or putting motions and amendments to the meeting in proper order
(g) making, or having made, a record of the proceedings
(h) communicating decisions to other people who will be affected by them.

The chairman usually has certain powers to assist him in the performance of his duties. They include the power to:

(a) maintain order and have disorderly persons removed from the meeting
(b) give rulings on points of order
(c) decide points of procedure
(d) adjourn the meeting if it is impossible to maintain order
(e) conduct the business so that results and decisions are made known to the meeting
(f) use a casting vote when the meeting is deadlocked (*note*: the chairman has an additional vote only if it has been conferred by the rules of the organisation — there is no casting vote in Common Law).

The chairman can help the meeting by careful study of the agenda and any accompanying papers. He will then be briefed before he attends the meeting. His approach to the meeting may well follow a pattern similar to the following:

(a) welcome members, particularly new ones

(b) state the purpose of the meeting (if members do not already know this)

(c) promote discussion (this can be done by addressing general statements or questions to the group or by addressing more specific enquiries to an individual)

(d) sum up at various stages

(e) reiterate the arguments for and against any proposal just before any decision is taken

(f) state the conclusion and action decided upon

(g) bring the meeting to a close at an appropriate time.

## 7.7 THE ROLE OF THE SECRETARY

The secretary is the servant of the meeting. The extent of his role will depend on the meeting, but normally he is responsible for the following:

(a) convening the meeting and preparing the requisite documents

(b) all correspondence

(c) general administrative work

(d) any legal business (the secretary to a large organisation will have considerable responsibilities in this field, for instance all the legal work connected with the transfer of shares)

(e) the financial work of the organisation (except where there is an officer separately appointed to carry out this work, for example a treasurer of a society or a chief accountant of a company).

In many voluntary concerns the secretary is often the workhorse of the committee structure and sometimes carries a disporportionate share of the work burden.

## 7.8 COMMITTEE MEMBERS

Members of committees are often recognisable types. Figure 7.2 shows some who are attending the Board meeting of Noah's Ark Plc:

MR HARRY HIPPOPOTAMUS. He came up the hard way and covers his insecurity with roaring ill-temper when crossed, particularly if by the young upstart on his left.

MR CHESHIRE CAT. A keen young director with high-level paper qualifications. Thinks he knows it all.

LORD THOROUGH-BRED EQUINE. Sits on a multitude of boards – his title lends prestige. Covers his ignorance with irrelevant social chatter. Anxious for the meeting to finish (going to the races?).

**Fig 7.2** *the board of Noah's Ark meets*

Committee members

SIR LEO LION. Chairman and Managing Director. Autocratic figure who wants to maintain his sovereign power.

MR D. O. Z. DORMOUSE. Not really interested. It's all 'a bit of a bore'. He's much too tired anyway.

MR BASKERVILLE BLOODHOUND. A thorough, tenacious type with a good nose for trouble and a direct approach to problems.

MR SILAS SHEEP. Follows the crowd — afraid of expressing his own opinions. The perfect 'yes man'.

One feels that this firm is not going to have too much useful direction of its activities from the directors.

People's relationships with one another change according to the group they may be in at any one time. Nowhere does this show up more clearly than in meetings.

In *The Social Psychology of Industry*, J. A. C. Brown states: 'Reason, however important a part it may play in society, does not play a major part in most people's lives.' Thus much of the time spent in meetings will be concerned with the expression of feelings and emotions.

This is not to say that in every meeting the discussion will be accompanied by fierce argument, displays of petulance or by a dozy dormouse falling asleep, though each of these things can happen. What frequently occurs is time-wasting or, in a belated attempt to save time, hurried and unsuitable decision-making.

Since the complexities of most organisations demand that meetings be held and because there is often a genuine desire to inform, consult and involve as many people as possible, it is increasingly important that all those who attend meetings develop a positive attitude to them and a determination to make them work. The attitude that a meeting will be a waste of time 'because we always spend hours talking about stupid things and don't get anything done', or 'because there's never an agenda and we don't know what we're supposed to discuss', must go.

It is the responsibility of the chairman to encourage useful contributions from all attending the meeting, but he cannot always choose members for their usefulness and co-operativeness. Members should take certain responsibilities. They should, for example, make themselves familiar with the work of the committee and make sure they have read the information provided for them by the secretary. They have a duty to take a full part in the working of the group and to assist the chairman in the performance of his duties. They must make their contributions pertinent, clear, correct and courteous.

They should not expect the secretary to take on duties that are outside his normal responsibilities and should be willing to accept such other duties as the committee sees fit to give them, always provided that they have the time and capacity to perform them.

Just as the chairman and secretary should not use a meeting as a forum for their own views, so should the members avoid this also, remembering that other people deserve the opportunity to express their opinions. Finally, the views having been expressed and a majority decision arrived at, the member either should be prepared to help carry this decision into effect or he should seriously consider his position as a member of the committee.

## 7.9 PRESENTING A CASE

The chart in Figure 7.3 shows the main steps to be followed in preparing and presenting a case to a meeting. As usual we need considerable pre-planning and preparation.

**Fig 7.3** *presenting a case*

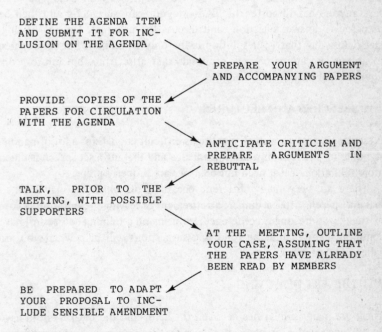

PRESENTING A CASE

DEFINE THE AGENDA ITEM AND SUBMIT IT FOR INCLUSION ON THE AGENDA

PREPARE YOUR ARGUMENT AND ACCOMPANYING PAPERS

PROVIDE COPIES OF THE PAPERS FOR CIRCULATION WITH THE AGENDA

ANTICIPATE CRITICISM AND PREPARE ARGUMENTS IN REBUTTAL

TALK, PRIOR TO THE MEETING, WITH POSSIBLE SUPPORTERS

AT THE MEETING, OUTLINE YOUR CASE, ASSUMING THAT THE PAPERS HAVE ALREADY BEEN READ BY MEMBERS

BE PREPARED TO ADAPT YOUR PROPOSAL TO INCLUDE SENSIBLE AMENDMENT

First, of course, we have to ensure that the item is on the agenda. For this purpose it is desirable to write out exactly what the agenda should show and then give it to whoever is responsible for preparing it.

With the agenda should go all the details of the item, which you would hope that members would read before the meeting. Thus your main argument will need to be written.

Both when you are writing the agenda paper and when you are thinking about what you want to say at the meeting, you must anticipate criticism of your proposals, questions and argument, and must, within your agenda paper and any notes taken to the meeting, prepare rebuttals of the criticisms. A single unanswered criticism can be enough to destroy the whole case, so it must be meticulously prepared. You must also know your facts very thoroughly in order to be able to answer questions that you have not anticipated.

Before the meeting it is often useful to lobby support and explain your proposals carefully to members who might be inclined to favour them. Also before the meeting you should prepare a careful summary of the argument. Remember that there will only be a limited time in which to present your case, so not only write suitable notes but if possible try out your presentation to assess the time you will need and adjust it if necessary (see also Chapter 3).

When you go to the meeting, take extra copies of your agenda paper in case anyone has forgotten his. Present your case succinctly and then be prepared to answer questions and discuss the proposal. Do not be dogmatic, insisting that your solution is the only possibility, but be prepared to accept alterations or new proposals that arise from, but improve on, your original ideas.

## 7.10 SPEECHES AND LECTURES

Presenting a case to a small meeting is difficult enough for a lot of people; standing up in front of a larger audience and making a set speech is much more inhibiting. Yet it need not be, if we are properly prepared.

There are very many different occasions on which we may have to make a speech: after a dinner; a retirement or leaving presentation; a vote of thanks; addressing a conference; lecturing on a training course. All have common features and the following suggestions will help when you are called upon to speak.

## 7.11 THE ART OF ACTING

There are many similarities between the actor and the speaker. Both have an audience and a prepared part to play. Both wish to appear confident and at ease; both are nervous and tense before starting.

The skill is to make people believe in your outward appearance of relaxed authority which may hide shyness, hesitancy or tension. This is, of course, not easy and often only comes with experience and practice. It can be helped, however, by careful preparation, both of the speech and of minor matters, such as arriving for the occasion with time to spare, having a last look at the speech, etc.

## 7.12 PREPARING THE SPEECH

### The audience

Before you put down your ideas on paper, think about your potential audience. Age, sex, background, numbers: all these will affect the choice of what you will say and how you will say it.

### Content

The content of any speech or lecture will be restricted by the proposed length of the talk, the declared topic(s), the occasion, the audience and any external restriction such as the lack of visual-aid facilities.

Some speeches will be released to the press or circulated as conference papers and are therefore written in full and read. However, it is very difficult to *read* a speech well. Even great orators find that practice is needed so that the final delivery will be fluent and easy, but practice can, if carried to extremes, result in a speech losing its freshness. So you may do better to read through the speech until you are familiar with it, limiting your practice in reading it aloud. If you do not have to release the full text of a speech, then you will achieve more immediate impact if you speak from notes, prepared as suggested in Chapter 3.

When you do have a rehearsal, time it, to ensure that it is of the desired length. Be mindful of passages that could be omitted should the occasion require it, as well as of some extra points that can be added should the need arise. Plan the content in the same way that you would plan any other communication (see Chapter 11).

### Format

A full-text speech should be typed in double-line spacing and in a fairly large typeface. Key points can be put in as side headings or underlined in red. Stresses and emphasis can also be marked.

A talk given from notes allows greater variety of choice of layout. If you use paper for your notes, you could merely have a series of headings and keypoints listed, or divide the page in half, putting the main points on the left, the supplementary detail on the right.

Postcard-sized cards can be used very effectively. They have advantages over paper if there is no lectern available. Being held in the hand, they do not give away how nervous you are. They also facilitate movement away from the lectern or desk to a chart, overhead projector, blackboard or model. On each card should go not more than three headings, fewer if supplementary information must also be included.

Colour can be helpful in achieving a good format. Main headings in red, sub-headings or keypoints in green, with other notes in black; all this makes it easy to glance at the notes and quickly establish what comes next.

Remember that, even with a full-text speech, the object is to seem to *talk* rather than *read*. An effective format can be a great help.

## 7.13 VISUAL AIDS

Chapter 10 gives detailed information and suggestions on visual-aid material which you can use to enliven a speech, present detailed information and help in attracting and keeping attention.

Such visual aids are very valuable but must be an integral part of the content, not merely added on as frills without particular purpose. A dull talk will still be dull even if there are attractive visuals.

## 7.14 DELIVERY

Good speech begins with good breathing. Tension, which shows in tight neck and shoulder muscles or clenched fingers, also affects the diaphragm, the muscle just below the ribs with which we control our breathing. It also tightens the vocal cords in the larynx, raising the pitch of the voice. If you are a very tense person, then some exercises in relaxation, even yoga, might help.

Clear, relaxed and varied speech commands attention, engages the audience's interest straight away and can be easily understood. The style of speaking should suit the context, making it more effective. Thus a light humorous tone would suit a witty after-dinner speech, a more solemn, serious approach being more appropriate to an address to a professional association.

To vary your style of speech you need to be in command of your voice and aware of the variations in volume, pitch, speed, rhythm and texture. Resonance (carrying power), clear articulation of vowels and consonants and use of pauses are also important.

You can learn how to use your voice by attending elocution classes, but if you do not wish to go to such lengths you can raise your awareness of the use of the voice both by listening to others and by taping your own voice.

Try to lose recurrent mannerisms such as *'Er'* or *'Um'* and any accent (if too 'thick') which will make it difficult for the audience to understand you.

One aspect that actors consider is that of stress or emphasis on words.

First, stress whould be placed on the correct syllable of a word (usually, in English, the first syllable) for example:

*ea*rly; *ne*cessary; *ma*rry

Some words have alternative stresses, for example:

*a*dult (or) ad*ult*

and the stress can change from noun to verb, for example:

a *com*pound (but) to com*pound*

Emphasis, coupled with pitch and use of pause, can change the sense, as this example from Shakespeare shows:

ORIGINAL '    '*Who* is Sylvia? *What* is she?'
RESTRESSED   'Who *is* Sylvia? *What! Is* she?'

The great music hall artiste Marie Lloyd is reputed to have been brought before a north of England Watch Committee (supposedly safeguarding local morals) following a complaint that she was singing very suggestive songs. Saying that any song could sound rude if sung in a suggestive way, she gave the committee a rendition of Lord Tennyson's impeccably respectable Victorian ballad, which begins *Come into the garden, Maud*, that left them speechless!

## 7.15 STANCE

*'What shall I do with my hand and feet?'* Achieve a degree of relaxation and hands will take care of themselves. Meanwhile avoid holding fluttering papers, clenching the lectern or twiddling a pen. If necessary put them behind your back for a few moments. Movements of the feet should be purposeful, not involuntary shuffling.

## 7.16 ANSWERING QUESTIONS

Take your time when phrasing your answers. It is always useful to remember that no one is infallible, and sometimes the only answer is to say that you do not know.

Questions should always be answered, not avoided.

---

**FOCUS**

Acting a part
Preparation
Content
Format
Visual aids
Presentation

---

## 7.17 ASSIGNMENTS

1  The camel has been described as a 'horse designed by a committee.' State the advantages and disadvantages of committee organisation and give an example, with reasons, of the circumstances in which:

(i)  a committee would be well-employed
(ii) it would be unsuitable. [LCC PSC]

(An outline answer is given in Appendix 1.)

2  Most, though not all, of the responsibility for the effectiveness of a board or committee meeting can depend on the chairman. What can an individual member do to help make the meeting as effective as possible? [IAA]

3  Meetings can be an exciting and rewarding element in business life. Why then is frustration, boredom and a low level of accomplishment the outcome of many meetings? [LCC PSD]

4  How can a speaker maintain contact with his audience throughout his presentation? [IAA]

5  What advice would you give to someone who, for the first time in his life, had been invited to give a lecture? Your advice should include both how to prepare and how to deliver a talk. [ICSA]

6  You have been asked to make a short presentation to top management on the application of a new administrative technique. What principles of communication would you bear in mind in preparing and delivering your talk? [ICSA]

# SPOKEN COMMUNICATION

The importance of planning has been stressed throughout the chapters on written communication (see also Chapter 11) and most people would agree that it is certainly very helpful in achieving effective communication. However, because so much of our talking is casual and spontaneous, we do not easily recognise that planning and preparation can be equally applicable to this area of communication.

Planning a spoken communication involves considering:

(a) the content of the communication
(b) the accessibility of supporting documents
(c) the recipient/audience
(d) clarity of speech
(e) appropriate language and style (see Chapter 12).

There are four main occasions, apart from general conversation, when we talk to another individual. Two of these, telephoning and dictating, involve using equipment, and in the others, radio and TV interviews, while you may be talking to a single interviewer, you have to bear in mind a mass audience.

## 8.1 TELEPHONE TECHNIQUES

### Outgoing calls

Planning telephone calls is simple and takes little time. Yet it can save much of the actual speaking time and thus much of the cost of calls. All that is necessary is to note briefly, in order, the items to be discussed during the call and have all relevant papers to hand before making the call (see also Chapter 11).

## The dos and don'ts of telephoning

(a) **do**

answer calls promptly

always have pen and message pad handy

answer with the appropriate information, e.g.,

*Extension 340. John Smith speaking.*

speak into the mouthpiece

speak pleasantly and distinctly

try to recognise the voices of people you should know and use their names

obtain the caller's name

assure people who may have to wait for information that they have not been forgotten

give callers the chance to ring back rather than wait

take messages correctly, write them out so that the recipient will be able to read them easily and put them where they will be seen

exercise self-control when callers are annoyed or impatient

know enough about your organisation, e.g., to re-route calls that have been put through to you in error

exercise discretion

have the same courtesy and consideration for everyone, from your most senior executive to the caller making a frivolous complaint

admit it when you do not know the answer to query

leave instructions when you are expecting a call and have to go out of the office

(b) **don't**

misuse the instrument

use slang or jargon

sound curt or rude

ask first 'Who is speaking?' before saying that the person required is out

carry on a conversation with someone else in the room

call across the room to someone who is wanted on the telephone without covering the mouthpiece

lose your temper

## Taking messages

Messages must be taken fully and correctly, in writing. It is sensible to use a message pad such as the one shown in Figure 3.1. This provides a prompt to ensure that relevant information is not forgotten.

It is rarely possible to take down all the words spoken by a caller.

Summarising techniques should be used (see Chapter 3.3). Do, however, read back your notes to the caller to make sure that they are accurate.

## 8.2 DICTATING

### Planning
Planning a letter or some other document is necessary when you are going to write it in longhand. The same technique helps very much when you are going to dictate, whether to a secretary or to a dictating machine.

It is also sensible to have accessible any documents to which you may be replying or papers which have to accompany what you are dictating.

### Equipment use
If you are using a machine, make sure that you know how to use it properly. As the analysis of common faults given later in the chapter indicates, several of the problems that occur in dictation, such as inaudibility, result from inefficient machine use.

### Execution

#### Speed
If you are dictating to a secretary, remember that you must suit your speed of dictating to the speed of his or her shorthand. On a machine, it is advisable not to speak very fast, but neither is it necessary to dictate very slowly, as the audiotypist can control the replay.

Choose a speed which is a little slower than your normal conversation speed.

#### Diction
Most dictation machines distort the voice a little. Speak at the correct distance from the microphone (usually about 15 cm but consult the instructions for your particular machine) and enunciate clearly.

Your secretary will also appreciate it if you speak clearly when dictating.

#### Instructions to the typist
It is surprisingly common for typists to reach the end of a piece of dictation and only then find instructions such as:

*Type this in double-line spacing.*

Remember that the typist should not have to listen to the complete dictation before commencing to type. All instructions should be given at the beginning of the dictation, for example:

> *Memo to Company Secretary, copy to: Chairman, MD and Sales Director. Enclose the next piece of dictation – the report on the reorganisation.*

Send the typist any relevant notes or accompanying papers. Give your secretary similar instructions or documents.

## Punctuation

If your organisation has house rules about what punctuation and indication of paragraphs should be given, do follow the instructions. If there are no such rules, make it clear at the beginning of the dictation what punctuation you intend to dictate. (Obviously you will only need to do this once if you are constantly dictating material for the same person to type.)

It is normal to expect any competent secretary to be able to insert all punctuation but some audiotypists and junior secretaries may be less experienced and you may need to indicate some of the punctuation and paragraphing during the dictation.

## Spelling

Spell names of people, organisations, addresses and any technical or difficult words which the secretary or audiotypist may not know.

### Analysis of common faults

| FAULTS | CAUSES | |
| --- | --- | --- |
| | *The dictator has not* | *The typist has not* |
| (a) The recording was poor | . . . checked the dictating machine before use . . . pronounced each word clearly . . . spoken directly into the microphone . . . dictated in a quiet place | |
| (b) Words or punctuation incorrect or missing | . . . dictated slowly enough . . . dictated all the words . . . spelt out names, technical terms, etc. . . . given clear instructions on punctuation | . . . used common sense and checked that the meaning is clear . . . used the transcription machine correctly . . . checked the work after completion |
| (c) Incorrect format, number of copies, etc. | . . . given clear instructions at the beginning of the tape . . . given clear instructions to the typist | . . . taken note of the instructions |

This analysis shows that many common causes of error are likely to be the responsibility of the dictator.

---

### FOCUS

HOW TO BE A DISTINGUISHED DICTATOR

Always commence dictation before planning the communication
Never have the relevant documents to hand
Don't check that your dictating machine is in good working order
Wander around so that you are not at a consistent distance from the microphone (or your secretary)
Speak with a pipe/cigar/gum/boiled sweet in your mouth
Rattle off some of the dictation very fast and then have long pauses while you stop to think
Change every other sentence
Avoid giving any instructions, punctuation clues, spellings
Mispronounce words
Fail to hand over necessary documents
Always dictate in a rush late in the day and expect the typed copy before you leave
Continually interrupt the typing to check progress
Refuse to check the finished result carefully *or* check it, change it considerably and demand retyping before the end of the day.

*IF YOU DISOBEY EACH AND EVERY ONE OF THE ABOVE RULES, YOU MAY BECOME A SUCCESSFUL DICTATOR!*

---

## 8.3 INTERVIEWS

All managers have to interview staff for one reason or another. Many of these interviews are informal conversations arising directly from day-to-day work but others require careful preparation.

In this latter category come interviews with prospective employees, with employees seeking promotion, appraisal interviews within a formal company performance-appraisal or management-by-objectives system, reward, grievance and counselling interviews, and discussions with employees who are leaving the organisation.

## 8.4 SELECTION INTERVIEWS

Certain preparatory work should be carried out before selection interviews are held.

## Job specification

To decide on whom to appoint it is first necessary to know exactly what the job will involve and what skills and attributes the most suitable applicant should possess. Thus a job specification should be drawn up following a careful analysis of the job itself and of the requirements of skills, qualifications and experience. An example of a job specification is given in Figure 8.1.

The efficient firm will already have job specifications for all its employees. All that is then necessary before a job advertisement is drafted is for you to look at the specification for the particular job and decide whether the specification is current, and what needs deleting, amending or adding.

## The advertisement

Suggestions about the writing of effective advertisements were given in Chapter 4. To secure applications from candidates who have suitable qualifications and background it is essential to be as informative as possible or, at least, to offer further details on request.

Care must also be taken in choosing the newspapers or journals in which the advertisement is to be placed so that you may attract the best applicants.

## Method of application

There are three methods commonly used for obtaining the applications.

### By telephone

It is common practice today for a telephone number to be given in the advertisement. Candidates may be specifically asked to telephone a named person or merely given the opportunity to ask for further details and an application form.

In the former case, there may be a degree of interviewing during the telephone call. Thus the person whose name is given in the advertisement should be thoroughly briefed and should have an interview check-list, copy of the advertisement and job specification to hand.

Alternatively, the applicant may be asked straightaway to come to the firm and fill in an application form. In this case the interview(s) will probably follow immediately.

### By letter

Many advertisements ask for application by letter, either because the organisation does not have suitable application forms for the job in question or because it is felt that more can be learnt about the applicant's personality from a letter than from the often restrictive form.

Fig 8.1 *job specification*

JOB SPECIFICATION

**TITLE:** DEPUTY DIRECTOR, OPERATIONAL RESEARCH UNIT

**ACCOUNTABLE TO:** OPERATIONAL RESEARCH DIRECTOR

**FUNCTION:** Assist the Director in control of all OR projects;
co-ordinate and communicate with clients at all levels;
supervize the implementation of research recommendations;
deputize for the Director.

**RESPONSIBLE FOR AND WITH AUTHORITY OVER:**

| | |
|---|---|
| 4 operational researchers | 2 statistics/clerical assistants |
| 2 shorthand/audio typists | 1 computer operator |

**DUTIES/RESPONSIBILITIES**

1. Achieve the stated objectives of the OR programme.

2. Instigate investigations and co-ordinate projects.

3. Conduct project studies and supervise the work
   of the researchers.

4. Supervize the work of the junior staff.

5. Maintain good relations with clients and other
   departments.

6. Deputize for the Director in day-to-day work during
   his absence.

7. Write research proposals and reports.

8. Carry out any other duties required by the Director.

**QUALIFICATIONS AND EXPERIENCE:** Honours graduate in mathematics,
statistics, OR, economics or related discipline.

At least three years OR experience with some managerial
content.

**PERSONAL QUALITIES:** Self-reliant and self-motivated; able
to work under pressure; initiative; practical problem-
solving ability.

**SALARY:** Commensurate with qualifications/experience.

**CONDITIONS OF WORK:** 37½ hour week; 22 days holiday; contributor
pension scheme; free life assurance; car.

You will frequently find *curriculum vitae* specifically requested but even when this is not so stated fairly short letters of application, accompanied by detailed *curriculum vitae*, are preferable (see Chapter 1).

## Application form

There is a further variation in practice here. Sometimes an initial telephone call or letter of application is requested and then the application form and further details are sent. This practice is acceptable when the first approach is by a telephone call, but it does seem somewhat unfair on applicants to expect them to send in a letter and *curriculum vitae* (CV), which has probably taken them some hours to prepare, and then ask for an application form to be completed, with almost identical information having to be repeated, albeit in a slightly different format.

It is more satisfactory to ask candidates simply to telephone or write in for the application form and further details.

The choice of which method to use will usually be dependent on the selection policy of the firm. There are many advantages and disadvantages in each method. Many applicants for higher-level posts prefer the letter plus CV approach as they will already have CVs prepared and thus can concentrate on writing a good letter of application to accompany the details. Application forms for such posts should in any case have sufficient space on them for a letter to be included or should encourage applicants to enclose a separate letter. This reduces the restrictions imposed by a standard form (see also Chapter 5.6).

## References

Candidates should be asked to state the names of two, sometimes three, referees. In commercial and industrial circles the name of the applicant's present employer is not usually expected, as most candidates will not wish their present employers to know that they are seeking another post. A candidate may be asked if his present employer may be approached in the event of an offer being made.

References should be taken up before interview and are properly part of the process of shortlisting for interview and of obtaining the maximum information about the candidate before interviewing him.

## Selection testing

Candidates may be asked to take tests to establish, for instance, their level of intelligence, personality traits, verbal and numerical abilities or special skills. Such tests should not be used in place of the interview, merely as extra information to assist in the final choice.

**The interviewer(s)**

Who conducts the interview varies considerably from organisation to organisation. Companies with specialist Personnel Departments will use a member of that department (trained in interviewing techniques) for at least part of the interviewing process, though the employing manager should interview his prospective staff also. For some jobs several people will interview the applicant together as a panel.

**Preparing to interview**

The aim of any selection interview is to obtain the maximum information about each candidate in the minimum time. To do this it is essential to put candidates at their ease and establish *rapport* quickly.

The interview must elicit information from the candidate to allow the interviewer to build up a composite picture, to compare it with the job specification, references and the assessment of other candidates, and make some prediction of likely future performance and capabilities. This can be done in a variety of ways depending on the nature of the post. Three common ways are

(a) *In depth*, with the interviewer having working out in advance what main areas must be covered in questioning.
(b) *Standardised*, often with a very comprehensive questionnaire, which the interviewer will go through with the candidate.
(c) *Under stress*, where the interviewer will deliberately seek to put the candidate on the defensive, to embarrass or annoy him, in order to discover how he can stand up to working under strain. This technique should only be used by a well-trained interviewer and for posts where it is essential, otherwise it is both unfair and counterproductive (see Figure 8.2).

Whichever technique is adopted, it is essential to plan the general areas of questioning at least, to study and make notes on each short-listed application and to have some kind of check list to make sure that you do not omit any important points.

The venue for the interview also deserves some thought. Is it to be very formal, or informal, with you and the interviewee seated side by side in easy chairs, talking over a cup of coffee? A positive decision on choice of venue and informality should be made.

## 8.5 INTERVIEW TECHNIQUES

To a considerable extent the techniques adopted will depend on the decisions made in preparing for the interview. Many attempts have been

Fig 8.2 *the stress interview*

made, however, to try to help interviewers to make the interview effective. One of the most widely accepted has been the Seven-Point Plan of the British National Institute of Industrial Psychology. This plan has been amended over the years, as with the following modification, which was developed by Elizabeth Sidney and Margaret Brown:

(a) *personal data*: age, sex, home circumstances, marital status
(b) *physique*: health, speech, manner and appearance
(c) *education and technical qualifications and experience*
(d) *work or other experience*
(e) *mental abilities*: intelligence, verbal ability, speech and writing, mathematical ability
(f) *social roles*: gregarious/solitary, leader/follower, persuasive/organising
(g) *initiative*: self-starter/dependent, ability to work without supervision
(h) *emotional stability*: ability to tolerate stress, maturity
(i) *motivation*: goals and objectives, strength (drive).

The information under (a), (b) and (c) can be partly obtained from the letter or form of application and item (e) can be partially assessed through selection tests. Items (g), (h) and (i) are the most difficult to assess and it is here that the interviewer must be most skilful.

## 8.6 ASSESSMENT

When the interview is completed the interviewer will make a written assessment of the candidate so that he can eventually make his choice. Assessment forms are frequently used for this purpose, with the interviewer either filling in spaces with short comments or ranking candidates on a scale, such as that shown in Figure 8.3.

---

### FOCUS

SELECTION PROCEDURE
Current job specification
Informative advertisement
Choice of method of application
Referees
Selection tests
Choice of interviewer(s)
Preparing to interview
The interview
Assessment

---

## 8.7 APPLYING FOR EMPLOYMENT

We have now looked at the purpose of the interview and how it may be conducted. You will also be involved in selection interviews as candidates for employment, so let us look more closely at this area.

### The application

There are several routes that can be taken in applying for employment. In addition to those mentioned in section 8.4 you may obtain details of available posts from government employment centres or from private agencies. Also it is possible to telephone or write to firms in which you may be interested, to enquire whether or not they have, or are likely to have in the near future, any suitable vacancies.

If you have to telephone a firm, have with you a copy of your *curriculum vitae* in case you are asked detailed questions, and a pencil and paper to note details given to you. The writing of letters and CVs is covered in Chapter 1.

You must consider carefully before making your application. It takes a few hours to write suitable letters and fill in the forms, so it is worth while

Fig 8.3 *interview assessment form*

## CANDIDATES FOR SECRETARIAL POST

Grade candidates on the following scale:

A. highly suitable for the post
B. suitable
C. suitable only if she receives, for example, further training or is relieved of some responsibility (please specify any reservations in the section headed 'Comments')
D. unsuitable

| | A | B | C | D |
|---|---|---|---|---|
| **EDUCATION** <br> 1. General Education <br> e.g. 'O' and 'A' levels, PSC, OND <br> 2. Skills | | | | |
| **JOB EXPERIENCE** <br> 1. General Secretarial experience <br> 2. Other relevant experience | | | | |
| **BACKGROUND AND INTERESTS** <br> 1. Stable personal background <br> 2. Interests and pursuits | | | | |
| **PERSONALITY** <br> 1. Stable and mature <br> 2. Shows qualities of leadership <br> 3. Shows qualities of initiative <br> 4. Integrity and loyalty <br> 5. A warm and friendly personality | | | | |
| **MOTIVATION** <br> 1. Ambition <br> 2. Realism of goal <br> 3. Degree of determination | | | | |
| **PHYSICAL IMPRESSION** <br> 1. Health <br> 2. Physical appearance <br> 3. Dress and turnout <br> 4. Speech and manner | | | | |
| **COMMENTS** | | | | |

choosing posts which offer you some chance of an interview, rather than wasting your time and that of prospective employers.

## Preparing for the interview

Assuming that you have been offered an interview for a job, you should then make careful preparation for the interview. Such preparation should include the following.

(a) Try to find out additional information about the organisation.
(b) Study this information, the advertisement and further information, such as the job specification, thoroughly.
(c) Look again at your copy of your letter of application or the details that you have put on the application form.
(d) Think about the interview and the questions that you may be asked.
(e) Be prepared to answer fully any questions about yourself, your past and your ambitions for the future (the interviewer will certainly not be impressed with monosyllabic answers).
(f) In particular, be clear about why you want that particular post with that particular organisation. Employers are always more interested in people who can express definite views on why they are seeking to work for them in that specific post rather than simply 'needing a job'.
(g) Be ready with queries. You will almost certainly be asked if you have any questions and you will not create a good impression if you have none. In particular, think about what you wish to know about the post, about conditions of service and about prospects.
(h) Remember that the initial impact is of importance, so wear clothes in which you feel smart but comfortable and which are impeccably clean and tidy.
(i) Remember other 'little things' about your appearance such as clean and shining hair, hands and fingernails, and shoes.

Realise that, if you are good enough to be called for interview, then you are already a possible choice for the post. So have confidence in yourself and your ability.

## The interview

Although we would all like to think that it is the overall impact that we create in interviews that gains us the jobs, it is unfortunately true that the first few minutes are of disproportionate importance. The interview starts as soon as you walk through the door. The interviewer will notice how you walk, shake hands, sit down, and answer the first few questions. You will inevitably feel somewhat selfconscious but should attempt to seem confident and relaxed and to answer clearly and distinctly the first points. After this you will probably relax a little anyway.

The first few questions will probably be intended to put you at your ease, though some interviewers do deliberately put a difficult question first, such as:

*What makes you think that you are suitable for this job?*

Such a question is designed to put you under some stress before you have had a chance to relax. Do not rush into an answer. Take a momentary pause and answer calmly and deliberately. If you have prepared effectively for the interview, the answer should not cause too much trouble. Remember that interviewers are more impressed with positive answers than with temporising.

During the interview the interviewer will be judging your reactions and answers to his questions; in turn you must judge his reactions to your answers and try to give the length and detail required, in clear and precise speech. You should also be attempting to assess your future employer so that if you are offered the post you will know whether or not to accept it.

## 8.8 OTHER INTERVIEWS

Employment interviews have been considered in detail because of their importance to every student. There are other formal interviews which you are likely to encounter at work. They will be concerned with performance, pay, difficulties and grievances. Sometimes, inevitably, you will have to reprimand people and there are occasions when people must be dismissed. Others move from job to job and are interviewed before they leave your organisation, to establish the reasons for their departure.

The various kinds of interviews are discussed in the remainder of this chapter.

## 8.9 APPRAISAL

Employee-performance appraisal is the systematic evaluation of the individual employee related to his performance in his job and his potential for development. Such systems will allow provision for appraisal interviews at least once a year, preferably more often.

You may have to complete a written appraisal of an employee and then discuss it with the person, or you may talk to the individual and, with him, complete the appraisal form during the interview.

The interview will have several aims, including the following:

(a)  informing the employee of his present position in the working group
(b)  recognising good and efficient work
(c)  telling the employee where improvement is needed
(d)  developing the employee's capability in the existing job and training him for promotion or change
(e)  acting as a record of assessment.

Such an interview ought to be an exercise with the employee in solving any problems, encouraging the employee to think constructively and to work out the way in which improvement and development can be best achieved. The employee must have standards at which to aim and objectives to achieve. The interviewer must help in setting realistic targets. He must discuss rather than judge, listen rather than lecture, and use questions skilfully to help the employee.

## 8.10 REWARD REVIEW

Sometimes organisations use a rather similar system to the appraisal one but link it directly to rewards, usually bonuses or increments, which the employee may receive.

In this case you must judge how well the individual has worked during the review period compared with others with whom the reward must be shared. You must discuss with the individual what is likely to be given by way of reward and the reasons, and obtain acceptance of these, without making the employee feel disgruntled and dissatisfied.

## 8.11 COUNSELLING

It is now recognised that people's problems outside work or with their work and work-mates can have a significant adverse effect on efficiency and productivity. There is also a genuine desire to make working life as pleasant as possible and to help people with problems.

In some large organisations there are now professionally trained counsellors who spend all or part of their time helping and advising staff. Very often, however, individual managers try to assist their staff and will arrange confidential interviews with any employee who has a personal problem. The problem may have a direct connection with work, in which case you may have enough information to be able to discuss the matter in depth, but there are many other problems on which you will not be competent to give advice. You should seek to help the employee to find someone better qualified to give constructive advice.

Suppose that a member of your staff has a problem at home, say with a sick relative, which is adversely affecting his work. Perhaps he will approach you; perhaps you have noticed his diminishing efficiency and call him into your office to discuss it.

What sort of an interview will it turn out to be? It is to be hoped that you will be sympathetic; certainly you should listen to what he has to say. However, you will be conscious that you have other work to do. Also, while his major concern may be the solving of the problem of his sick relative, your primary purpose is to obtain efficient work from your staff. These two things may seem to go hand in hand but this is not always true.

The best that can happen is that you will help him to obtain practical advice by referring him elsewhere (to the firm's personnel department, the social services or other relevant agencies) and will give him time in which to settle the problem and become better and more reliable in his work again.

## 8.12 GRIEVANCES

Most organisations now have well-established procedures for handling grievances. Some of the interviews which may be held will be formal, even with union representatives accompanying the employee. There will be a well-planned routine for the interview and the interviewers will have thought carefully about what is to be discussed.

The informal interview with a manager, however, is likely to be largely unplanned. The manager has to remember that there is a problem to be solved and that the aggrieved employee is possibly annoyed, frustrated, resentful or suspicious. The best technique is to listen carefully, show that you understand and ask questions designed to encourage the employee to think about the problem and suggest possible solutions. Most of all you must try to 'defuse' the situation by discussing it in a quiet, rational way. You should not allow yourself to argue, criticise or be sidetracked by irrelevancies.

## 8.13 REPRIMANDS

As far as is humanly possible reprimands should never be an impatient response to carelessness, stupidity or dangerous actions. Reprimand (or disciplinary) interviews have a purpose: to improve performance, prevent repetition of errors and protect the member of staff and others against hazards.

You should make sure of the facts, taking whatever time is necessary to investigate, plan the reprimand so that it will be effective (thinking about the member of staff who will respond in an individual way), give the reprimand in private, refuse to argue and be exact about the error committed. The employee must be given the opportunity to explain and discussion should take place on improvements possible.

You must not show antagonism towards the individual either in the interview or afterwards.

## 8.14 DISMISSAL

The growth of employment law has led in some countries (such as the UK) to employees being able to claim compensation in cases where they have been dismissed unfairly. Thus formal procedures have been initiated, which include warning letters and interviews, leading to the final act of dismissal.

Of course, there are occasions where staff can be instantly dismissed, for example for flagrant breaches of their contracts of employment or of safety regulations. More often, however, it is the inefficient worker (often absent, late or careless) or the member of staff whose personality disrupts the working group whom we have to consider dismissing. The use of formal procedures, over a considerable period of time, can enable us to identify problems at an early stage. Through early interviews with the employee we may establish what is wrong and whether it can be remedied. At the very least staff can be made aware of their deficiencies and why we might seek to terminate their employment. A good employer will tell the employee concerned the reasons for dismissal.

If you are going to do this, then you must make sure that you have an irrefutable case, backed up by previous warnings and discussion. Too often people lose their jobs because their 'faces do not fit'. They never know why. The reputation of your firm will suffer if you dismiss people either for the wrong reasons or without telling them the reasons.

## 8.15 TERMINATION

This section started with the interview for a job. Now we have moved to the other end of the time-span of a job — when the employee is leaving the company: to retire, start a new job, start a family.

It is important to know what makes people leave a place of employment or a particular job. Sometimes it can give helpful insight into changes that should be made in organisation, management, working relationships, work content and conditions. Firms cannot afford to change staff too often. It makes for discontinuity and is costly and inefficient. Moreover, if labour turnover is high, the firm's reputation is hurt and future recruitment can be adversely affected.

When people leave a job because they are dissatisfied, bored or unhappy in their working relationships, they may be reluctant to discuss this with an immediate superior, or even a departmental manager. There is a fear that their references from the firm might be adversely affected if they really said what they thought about the people and the job.

The termination interview is therefore difficult to conduct if a positive result is to be achieved. It may be somewhat more useful if conducted by a person outside the job-leaver's own department (Usually a member of the personnel department) but even here it is often the judgement of what has been left unsaid that is important.

## 8.16 THE EFFECTIVENESS OF INTERVIEWS

Interviews take place between people: people are fallible. However well trained the interviewer and however carefully planned the interview is, the judgements made by the interviewer and interviewee will be subjective. Instinctive and emotional reactions will sometimes cloud rational thought, while lack of knowledge will lead to faulty conclusions or wrong advice. Time is rarely freely available for full discussion. Also records of interview are often incomplete or non-existent so that interviewer and interviewee, at a later date, may mistakenly rely on inaccurate memories.

It must be added that many people who have to conduct interviews still may not have been trained in the appropriate skills, may have given little or no thought to the interview beforehand, may lack innate sympathy with the people they are interviewing or with the difficulties of the situation, or may have far from sufficient knowledge to make a successful interview possible. Bearing this in mind it is surprising that the results of interviews are not more disastrous than seems to be the case (although it has been suggested that faulty interviewing is the major reason for up to 30 per cent of the working population being in jobs where they are not as happy, useful or well rewarded as they might be).

There are suggestions that computers may take over the interviewing process, at least for more routine and less important job interviews. Science fiction becomes science fact very fast but there are those of us who believe that relationships between people cannot be replaced by machines, however complex and clever, without losing something which is important. The various interviews at work are of consequence to management and to staff and form part of the basic pattern of social relationships and communication.

---

### FOCUS

#### OTHER INTERVIEWS

| | | |
|---|---|---|
| Appraisal | Reward | Counselling |
| Grievance | Reprimand | |
| Dismissal | Termination | |

## 8.17 RADIO AND TELEVISION INTERVIEWS

It might be that you become a senior manager and are asked to talk about a company development, or to give expert technical views, or give reactions to events affecting your organisation.

What must you bear in mind? Often your views will be taken as being the views of your organisation, so great care and discretion is needed especially not to commit your organisation to any course of action or to disclose confidential information. For a studio interview you should have time to prepare, making yourself thoroughly familiar with whatever the subject-matter of the interview will be. You may be able to ask for the main questions to be submitted to you in advance so that you can take advice on the answers. But even then there will be supplementary questions which will need 'off-the-cuff' answers, so your total familiarity with the subject is of the utmost importance. Try to anticipate areas of criticism and awkward questions.

It is important also to seem relaxed and confident. On the radio your voice can give you away if there are hesitations and long pauses in your speech or if there is a perceptible difference in volume or tone when difficult questions are asked (women, in particular, having voices which are generally higher-pitched than men's, can become very shrill when annoyed or anxious). On television, as in any face-to-face interview, your whole appearance can detract from the confident image which you wish to convey. You have to think of yourself somewhat as an actor, portraying the role your organisation would wish should be shown, yet at the same time being sincere and truthful. It sounds intimidating but if you have spoken at meetings and conferences and are used to interviewing staff, you will probably not find it as difficult as you think (see also Chapter 7).

Always answer the questions you are asked as directly as you can. Watching and listening to some politicians giving evasive answers is illuminating. It reflects little credit on them or on their political organisations. Avoid technicalities and, above all, too many figures, which tend to confuse rather than enlighten. Many sets of statistics, also, can be too easily challenged by different interpretations.

You should speak directly to the interviewer, not try to make a speech to the wider listening or viewing audience, but try not to forget them entirely. The interviewer may have specialist knowledge that matches your own; not all the wider audience will have. Without 'talking down' to them, you must try to put your points clearly and simply.

Interviewers are human beings after all, even if they do sometimes adopt a hectoring or unpleasant tone in their search for information. They should be firmly but courteously dealt with, without allowing their approach to upset you. After all, they are rarely trying to insult you, merely attempting to obtain facts which you may seem to be unwilling to give.

Some interviews will not be just between you and an interviewer but with one or more other people who will be putting views which conflict with your own. On such occasions, tempers can easily fray. Time is short and everyone is trying to emphasise the rightness of his own argument and the wrongness of yours. It is essential to remain unruffled and courteous but firm, adjusting your tone and delivery to contrast favourably with any bombast, sarcasm, outright accusation or anger expressed by your opponents. Refute their arguments with facts and give balance by putting your own case effectively. Righteous indignation is sometimes effective, as is the appeal to emotion, but generally these should be avoided in favour of logical argument.

---

### FOCUS

ACTING AS THE MOUTHPIECE OF YOUR ORGANISATION
  thorough preparation
  appear relaxed and confident
  remember the wider audience
  answer questions asked directly
  keep calm when conflict arises

---

## 8.18 ASSIGNMENTS

1  'The administrator should be aware of the fundamental differences between face-to-face and telephone communication.' Outline these differences and analyse their implications for communication.

   On the basis of your analysis present recommendations for the appropriate use of the telephone as a means of communication for the professional administrator.[ICSA]

   (See also Chapter 13.)

2  Draft a set of notes to be used by staff who will be dictating correspondence *either* to shorthand writers *or* into dictating machines.

3  Prepare a check-list for an employment interview with a candidate applying for the post specified in Figure 8.1.

4  What are the main characteristics of a properly organised and well-conducted interview? How can an interviewer apply these characteristics in order to monitor and improve his/her performance? [ICSA]

5  In response to an advertisement placed in *The Daily Courier* you recently applied for details of the post of Personal Assistant to the Personnel Manager of Prestige Office Furniture Plc, 14 Lennox Road, Middleton, Midshire ML6 4AQ. In addition to receiving the forms of application you were also sent the following job description for the appointment:

## JOB DESCRIPTION

| | |
|---|---|
| TITLE | Personal Assistant to Personnel Manager |
| DEPARTMENT | Personnel |
| FUNCTION | To assist the Personnel Manager in the discharge of his duties by providing administrative support; to maintain effective communication with the Personnel Manager and all members of staff and people in contact with his office; to supervise the work of three junior clerical/typewriting staff. |
| HOURS OF WORK | 8.50 a.m.–5.20 p.m. Mondays–Fridays (1-hour lunch) $37\frac{1}{2}$ hours weekly, plus overtime as required |
| ACCOUNTABLE TO | Personnel Manager |
| RESPONSIBLE FOR | 1 shorthand typist, 1 audio copy typist, 1 clerical assistant |
| AUTHORITY OVER | 3 staff members as indicated above. |

DUTIES/RESPONSIBILITIES

(a)  Work within company rules, regulations and procedures.

(b)  Assist the Personnel Manager in all aspects of his work, utilising appropriate administrative skills.

(c)  Maintain the efficient operation of the Personnel Manager's office and its systems.

(d)  Act on behalf of the Personnel Manager in his absence as required.

(e)  Supervise the work of the three junior staff in the Personnel Manager's office so as to maintain efficient standards of work and productive staff relations.

(f)  Co-ordinate and attend meetings and conferences and take minutes, notes, etc., as required.

(g)  Receive visitors and company personnel and maintain a favourable company image.

(h)  Employ initiative, resourcefulness and discretion in contacts with all company personnel and people outside the organisation.

You were asked in a covering letter sent with the details of the appointment to submit your application to the Personnel Manager, Mr G. A. Johnson, quoting reference PM/PA 26.

Compose a suitable letter of application to support your application for the above post. The body of your letter should comprise between 300 and 350 words. (See also Chapter 1; and Appendix 1 for notes towards an answer.) [adapted from RSA DPA]

# LISTENING AND READING

Listening has been cynically defined as 'what you do while awaiting your turn to talk'. *Hearing* is easy, but listening, like reading, is not a passive process through which the mind absorbs information as a sponge soaks up water. Listening and reading require positive effort.

## 9.1 LISTENING

The first requisite is a willingness to make an effort, and the techniques described below depend upon this.

### Positive interest

It must be a rare subject which holds no interest at all. An active listener has the positive attitude that *something* of interest or value is likely to reward his attention to even the least promising topic.

### Preparation

Any background knowledge or briefing will help you to be a better listener. If you know that a particular topic is to be discussed, look it up, read the file, or at the very least review the matter in your mind and remind yourself of what you know about the speaker.

### Silence

Eye contact, a physical stillness expressive of concentration, a posture and facial expression indicative of attention, will all help the speaker to express himself more effectively, and consequently the listener will benefit. Silence is a positive part of the communication process. (Remember that a glazed look and frozen posture quickly reveal to the speaker that he has 'lost' you!)

### Listening to the message

You should recognise that it is the contents, not the packaging, that matter. Listen to what is being said and refuse to be distracted by the speaker's voice, idiosyncracies, or clumsy use of visual aids.

But at the same time don't ignore the body language, the facial expressions, gestures and tone of voice which are also part of the communication.

Concentrate on the main ideas: don't be too distracted by amusing illustrative anecdotes, the examples and illustrations which should merely reinforce the main theme.

### Allow the speaker to finish

People speak at about 125 words per minute. We can probably think four times as fast as that. Therefore, we can often guess the end of a sentence or remark. The best of intentions can tempt us to interrupt the speaker to express our approval and agreement. It is possibly even more tempting to interrupt when we disagree: to ask the embarrassing question, to make a devastating aside. Quite apart from the discourtesy of such actions, we are not hearing the speaker when we are planning our replies.

### Avoid prejudice

Having a prior opinion about what is being said can close our minds to the speaker's arguments. The fact that we disagree should really make us listen even harder. Could we be wrong? What are the flaws in his argument?

Emotive words are a problem. A speaker may inadvertently use words which trigger emotions and arouse antagonism. For example, a speaker at a distributive trades conference used the expression 'shop assistant' and thereby offended his audience of 'salespersons'. At that point listening and thinking stop and attention may be drowned in feelings and prejudice.

### Time and place

Managers spend some two-thirds of their time with other people. To ensure that such a large proportion of their time is well spent, it is wise to plan when to be available, where and to whom. Planned 'interview' time makes for better listening, and the planning should include appropriate surroundings (offering privacy, for example, or informality, if that is desirable) and also the removal of interruptions, especially that of the telephone.

At the same time, a spontaneous two-minute conversation can be valuable communication and careful listening will make the most of the briefest chat.

### Integrity

People who are listeners by profession — doctors, priests and journalists — have their own code. A good listener is a person who can respect a confidence and help maintain the trust which is essential to communication.

## FOCUS

Good listeners are active not passive
They are interested
    prepare themselves
    demonstrate interest by the quality of their silence
    are neither distracted nor prejudiced
    allow the speaker to finish
    plan ahead
    have integrity

## 9.2 READING

Information technology and the mass media are already multiplying the number of words we need to read daily. Newspapers are growing bulkier and word processors are producing more and more business information which has to be read before it can be put to use.

To avoid spending a disproportionate amount of time simply reading things, rather than *taking action*, we need to find techniques for reading faster and more effectively.

Many readers waste a great deal of time for two reasons:

(a) they read everything at the same, often slow pace
(b) they do not understand or retain what they have read.

Reading more efficiently is not merely a matter of saving time by reading faster. This can lead to even less understanding or retention. First and foremost it is a matter of being able to vary your reading speed and adjust it to the purpose of your reading and the difficulty of the subject-matter.

### Skimming techniques

Skimming is glancing at speed over the printed words on a page. Words are not noted individually but an impression is gained. Far from being a superficial process, it demands great concentration.

Many of us find skimming difficult because of the way we learned to read, paying careful attention to each separate word, enunciating it aloud or mentally, noting the spelling and probably being reprimanded for laziness if words were glossed over.

People who do not develop reading skills beyond these early, and necessary, stages become reluctant readers. They naturally are very soon bored by the slow process of translating the symbols they are inspecting into meaning and, in fact, in the maze of individual words the meaning is lost; they cannot see the wood for the trees.

However, almost all of us have developed already some skill at skimming. When we look down a column in the telephone directory for a name, we do not read all the words we glance over; we skim.

This search for a particular piece of information by a process of recognition is much easier than skimming for general information. Then, as our eyes move so rapidly from left to right as to seem simultaneously to be travelling down the page, we have to learn to look for clues. Significant words are often repeated and this draws them to our attention. With experience we can identify expressions like *in conclusion, the most important feature, the result is*, which will direct our attention to particularly important parts of the passage. These we will read more slowly.

Thus a more flexible approach to reading is developed and we can vary our speed from the searching skim to a slower pace for careful assimilation of vital or complex information.

---

### FOCUS

USE SKIMMING
   to preview
   to identify priorities — where to read more slowly
   to find a required piece of information
   to help memory, by immediate review of what we have just read

---

## Anticipation

Moving our eyes over a series of symbols is not necessarily *reading*. If we are to derive meaning from the symbols, and not simply identify words, an intellectual effort is required. One way of achieving this more active and beneficial role is by anticipation.

As we read, we should be aiming to understand the whole content by seeing the complete picture rather than the separate bits of the jig-saw puzzle. Try to relate the meaning of what you read to your existing knowledge. You can think faster than you read and you should try to think a little ahead. Constantly make small predictions of what you expect to read next. If a problem has been described, you may well anticipate a solution, for example.

Such anticipation, especially if you have already previewed the passage by skimming, helps the reader to keep a firm grasp on the thread, i.e. the author's train of thought, and also helps memory.

## Organisation

Any piece of writing has a structure, the pattern into which the writer has organised his ideas.

Sometimes this skeleton is an external and obvious framework. This textbook is organised into chapters and sub-sections which are numbered and headed in an easily recognisable structure. Business reports have a similar structure which helps the reader to grasp the content and to distinguish readily those parts of it which are of most interest to him, possibly the report's purpose and recommendations.

The skeleton may be an internal one. The introductory comment may outline what is to follow. The author may summarise or emphasise as he writes. He may summarise what has gone before in his conclusion. Narrative structure is usually chronological . . . *and then, and then* . . . ; a description of a procedure or process runs . . . *do this, then this*; argument will be organised . . . *because of this, therefore this*.

If we develop the ability to recognise the structure of what we are reading, we shall find our way more speedily through it, and we shall also understand it more easily. A poorly planned piece of communication which lacks a recognisable skeleton or identifiable signposts will take up much more of the reader's time.

### Faster reading

The reading speeds of the general public have been measured as follows:

> below 200 words per minute – very slow
> 230–250 words per minute – average
> over 450 words per minute – very fast.

You can work out your own reading speed and make conscious efforts to increase it. But since reading efficiency is ultimately measured in terms of assimilation, the best method of all is to use skimming, to vary your reading speed, to read actively by anticipation and by recognition of the structure.

### A method

When you have a book (though not a novel) to read, make use of all the clues it offers before you actually begin reading it. Read the 'blurb', inspect the contents page (the skeleton), read the preface (the author's signposting) and check the subject index, which will give you some idea of the relative importance of topics and help your skimming and anticipation. Sample, by skimming, the first and last chapters, or a representative chapter on a familiar topic. You should already have a very good idea whether the book is worth reading at all, and if so, what it is all about. Familiarity with the subject makes for much easier understanding.

While you are reading, look for the internal skeleton, for synopses and summaries, for topic sentences in paragraphs, for headings and italics which may emphasise key points. As you read, identify vital sections by marking the book (only if it is yours!), or by note-taking, and skim these, once you have finished reading, for immediate revision and memorising.

> ## FOCUS
>
> ### ACTIVE READING REQUIRES
>
> a motive: *'Why am I reading this?'*
> conscious variation of the reading speed
> identifying the whole meaning
> relating the meaning to existing knowledge
> anticipation
> recognition of the structure
> That is, PARTICIPATION

## 9.3 ASSIGNMENTS

1   What do you understand by the words 'effective listening'? What are the main features that are needed in a good listener? [ICSA]
    (Notes for the answer are given in Appendix 1.)

2   Listen to a radio talk for ten minutes, recording it at the same time. Without playing it again, list immediately as many of the main points made by the speaker as you can. Two weeks later make a fresh list. Compare the two lists with the original talk.

3   How is listening related to management skills such as leadership and motivation?

4   Using only the contents page, list of illustrations and index, find the following in this book: *flow charts; making notes; lateral thinking; 'Parkinson's law'.*

# THE ROLE OF AUDIO-VISUAL AIDS

Simply listening to someone speaking is not a very effective way of learning. We remember only about 20 per cent of what we hear. But we remember 30 per cent of what we *see* and 50 per cent of what we *see* and *hear* (see Figure 10.1 on p. 154). Hence the value of using visual aids to enhance our lectures and presentations.

'Audio-visual aids' is the generic term for the various equipment, from the simplest blackboard sketch to the most sophisticated video equipment, that we use to help us to communicate more effectively.

The audio-visual equipment – the hardware – can be used in conjunction with 'audio-visual learning packages' – software – to provide self-instructional material. Such packages have a particular value when people need to learn or train as individuals rather than as part of a group. Thus a business recruiting very small numbers of people at any one time may perhaps find it valuable to put their induction training, or parts of it, into a slide/tape package from which the individuals can learn on their own. Such a package, once produced, can be used many times over and will save a trainer's valuable time.

When we are speaking to an audience the key word to remember is 'aid'. Too many speakers either become intoxicated by the technological possibilities of the equipment that they allow it to take over, or they are such nervous speakers that they are relieved to hide behind it. Neither approach promotes effective oral presentation. An 'aid' should not dominate but complement, illustrate and reinforce what we say (see Figure 10.1).

Any tool may be dangerous in unskilled hands and the most elaborate equipment will not help communication and might even distract the audience's attention, and thus be counter-productive, unless it is properly used.

The aid is not given merely to the audience but also to the lecturer. It is difficult to use notes unobtrusively while one is speaking; it is more

Fig 10.1 *audio-visual aids?*

difficult still to speak at length without any prompt. Pre-prepared visual aids, such as overhead transparencies, can guide the speaker most effectively and discreetly while helping the listeners to understand and memorise.

The guidelines for the effective use of audio-visual aids are simple; you need

(a) a basic non-technical knowledge of how to operate the equipment and what it will and will not do
(b) a little planning and forethought.

## 10.1 CHOOSING YOUR MEDIA

Ideally you will choose the aids most suitable to the content of what you wish to present.

In the teaching of languages, simple recording equipment such as a basic cassette recorder with microphone and headset would suffice. For teaching music, when quality of sound reproduction is very important, much more sophisticated equipment would be needed. Simple mathematical formulae might well be adequately conveyed with the help of a piece of chalk and a blackboard, but technical drawing is more likely, because of the need for accurate drawing, to be best presented by means of prepared overhead projector transparencies.

A sales presentation to introduce a new product could perhaps be done with the help of a blackboard or overhead projector. But the need to impress one's audience with the prestige and sophistication of the product is likely to lead to the choice of more sophisticated techniques, such as automatic slide presentation or video.

In practice the choice is often limited by more practical constraints, of which the most obvious is availability. If we have only a blackboard available, it will be adequate for presenting spontaneously prepared rather than pre-prepared material, like words or simple sketches — though we might have preferred a white board, flip chart or overhead projector.

Cost and convenience are other constraints. Chalk costs virtually nothing, but it is messy, work cannot usually be prepared on the board in advance or retained for future use and one loses time and contact with the audience while writing on the board. An overhead projector will need a much larger capital investment than a blackboard but it is more portable, transparencies are cheaply and easily prepared (except photographic ones) and may be used many times. Flip charts are relatively cheap and disposable, but they also can be used for retaining and re-using material.

Yet another constraint is the environment. If at least partial blackout is not available, then slide projectors and film cannot be used — but overhead projectors and video tape may well be usable. The size of room and audience is another factor. A television screen will be too small for a large room and large audience, but a film can be projected to suitable dimensions, whether the audience be large or small.

## 10.2 BASIC TECHNIQUES

(a) First plan the content of what you wish to say and put it in a suitable sequence (see Chapter 11).
(b) Remember that you need to establish a rapport with your audience and that this must be done before you switch its attention from yourself to the audio-visual element.
(c) Choose your medium or media.
(d) Design your software to complement your words.
(e) Make sure that you know how to handle the equipment you will use. Even writing on a blackboard demands practice. Fumbling distracts the audience and is counter-productive. The more sophisticated equipment always seems to attract gremlins at the most inopportune moments. They can be defeated by attention to detail. Make yourself familiar with the equipment beforehand. Where are the switches?

Where is the power supply? Do you need an extension lead? Have spares like bulbs, duplicate equipment or technical help available if possible.

(f) Visual material should never be overloaded. Short films are often more effective than long ones. A few words on the blackboard or overhead projector will have more impact than masses of them. It is best to present several short simple graphics than one overloaded one.

(g) Prepared material like slides or overhead projector transparencies need to be numbered so that if you drop your materials they can be quickly put back in order.

## 10.3 THE MEDIA

The audio-visual aids most commonly used are now described.

### Film

Since the earliest days of Hollywood, film has had tremendous audience impact and this impact has been enrolled as a valuable teaching/training aid for many years. Film is available in three sizes, 8 mm, 16 mm and 32 mm. The 32 mm format is used for commercial cinema projection, since it gives the largest image potential; most professionally made training films for purchase or hire are on 16 mm format, while the 8 mm size can only be projected to a maximum screen size of 4 ft square and therefore is only suitable for small audiences. It is the size used for home movies, which is not to say that it is unsuitable for some training purposes.

There are many professionally made training films available, some of them excellent. Very often they can be used to provide a starting-point for discussion on, for example, management techniques. A key feature of all teaching is repetition and the use of a film to reinforce and dramatise what has been said can be a valuable way of ending a lecture.

Technically film projection is somewhat demanding and you will need a suitable darkened room and some training in loading and operating the equipment – or a technician to do this for you. Of course, you will already have run the film through beforehand to check its content.

You can project films on a rear projection unit – though this will give a much smaller image than is possible using a screen. This method projects the image from *behind* the screen, making it visible from in front of the translucent screen. This method uses much less space between projector and screen (making it useful when space is limited, as on an exhibition stand) and the image is brilliant so that little darkening of the room is needed.

It is quite possible to produce your own film aids, usually using 8 mm film, but it is time-consuming and some skill and experience are needed for success. Sometimes, however, a custom-built product is the only way to obtain the material you need and, if you do not wish to make your own, there are professional firms to produce them for you.

## Video equipment

Technical developments in video equipment over the last few years are making video-recorders almost as commonplace as the television set, and the television camera almost as widespread as the home-movie camera. Their sheer familiarity adds to their value as a teaching and learning aid.

Currently there are three formats available, the most popular is the VHS system, followed by the Sony and Philips 2000. Regrettably these formats are incompatible, which means that cassettes designed for one system cannot (at the moment) be played on any other. The pre-recorded video disc is already beginning to provide yet another possible format.

The video recorder and monitor television set have some advantages over film. They are easier to operate and need no blackout, but the smaller screen limits the size of audience. (It is possible, though expensive, to have a larger screen.) Video presentations for briefings and sales have all the advantages of film but they require only a relatively small amount of space and can conveniently be used on an exhibition stand.

Most organisations which hire and sell educational and training films will also supply them in video format.

Colour television cameras are now relatively cheap and easy to operate. Many are easily portable, can carry their own power supply and require no special lighting conditions. They have the great advantage over film that material filmed is instantly replayable; this makes them a most valuable training aid in any situation where people can learn from observing their own performance. Thus closed-circuit television (CCTV) is an effective tool, for example in training people in interview or presentation techniques.

## Strip and slide projectors

Most film-strip projectors are also equipped to show slides. Although using a film strip limits one, in that the sequence of information cannot be varied, it has the advantage of being easily handled. Most of those commercially produced include valuable lecture notes.

Slides can also be bought, or made oneself using a 35 mm camera. They are perhaps most conveniently projected by using a carousel-type projector which can be loaded in advance with up to eighty slides. It is of course essential to load them in the correct sequence and the right way up, and you will do this more easily if the slides are carefully marked and stored. Generally both slide and strip projection on to a screen require a darkened room, but this makes it difficult to retain contact with the audience and for the audience to make notes. Rear projection units can be used, as described earlier.

Modern slide projectors can often be operated by remote control, which allows the lecturer to stand before his audience, beside the screen, and change the slides at will.

They can also be operated automatically on a timed sequence or synchronised with a sound track played on a cassette recorder, which changes slides by a pre-set pulse on the tape. Such a slide–tape package can provide self-instructional material for training or a sales programme which is left automatically playing and releases the salesman free to talk to potential customers and clients.

## Tape-recorders

Reel-to-reel tape-recorders give the highest quality sound reproduction, though the cassette type, because they are more easily handled and more portable (many are battery-operated), is more popular.

They can be used to make a record of conversations, or as telephone-answering machines, or in the form of a dictating machine they can save a business people valuable time.

In the context of training they have obvious value in language and speech training where instant playback speedily improves the speaker's performance. They can also be used to give instructions, for example to a trainee learning to operate a piece of equipment. A headset will leave his hands free, and listening will make it easy for him to keep his eyes on the process without the need to constantly stop and look at a manual.

## The overhead projector

This is the most versatile aid to the speaker. It projects images through transparent material (acetate film) on to a screen behind the operator. No blackout is required, though in brightly lit rooms the image will lose definition.

It gives the lecturer the great advantage of facing his audience whilst writing, or showing a transparency and thus retaining his rapport with them.

He has the advantage of being able to prepare his transparencies beforehand, by one of several methods. The simplest is to write or draw on inexpensive squares of acetate film, using special pens or markers, in colour if required. Transparencies may also be photocopied from any printed material. It is possible, though rather expensive, to reproduce them in colour from photographs or slides. Finally, transparencies on many subjects are available commercially or they may be specially commissioned and prepared, if the most professional results are needed.

No special skill is required to design and prepare transparencies, though since what you write is going to be considerably magnified by projection, it helps to be able to write or print very neatly. It is also important not to overload transparencies. Too many words projected at one time will lead the audience to stop listening whilst they are reading (or even writing down) what they see.

It is possible to 'build up' the information projected by means of 'overlays'. Thus one might start with a basic outline diagram and add information by laying over it a second transparency containing more detail. These overlays need to be 'registered' so that they fit exactly over one another, and up to four overlays can be added before light and image clarity are lost.

Another useful technique is 'revelation'. Parts of the transparency are initially masked by card which is removed in sequence to reveal the content bit by bit.

Various devices like the 'Opasym' make it possible to simulate animation, for example a flow of liquid through pipes, on the overhead projector.

Most overhead projectors are bulky, though not heavy to transport, but at least one model is available which folds neatly into a briefcase.

## Boards: black, white, magnetic and flip

The chief advantage of the various types of board available to the lecturer is that they are cheap and require a minimum of expertise to use.

A lecturer would be ill-advised though to use even a blackboard before an audience without a little prior practice. The blackboard is at its most effective when used for very simple visuals, a few key words or simple diagrams built up spontaneously during a discussion, for example. You need to remember, if speaking whilst writing, that you will need to raise your voice, since your back is to the audience. You should aim to keep the board uncluttered by erasing unneeded material and not leaving it as a distraction from new topics.

White boards, on which coloured felt tip type markers are used, are less messy than chalkboards and more vivid colour can be used.

Magnetic boards allow the user to attach prepared material to the board to built up a display. They are particularly effective for exhibition or foyer-type displays and are easily changed and readjusted or re-used.

A flip board or chart is in effect a large writing-pad on sheets of paper supported on an easel. It can be used like a blackboard and the used sheets flipped over to reveal clean ones or pages that contain prepared material.

## Visual control boards

The term covers a range of planning devices from the simple printed poster like 'calendar planner' to elaborate and expensive boards, often magnetic so that symbols may be attached and rearranged. Most commonly they are used for a range of planning and projecting tasks, and the larger sizes can both contain a great amount of detail and also display it to a large number of people.

For example, a supermarket is open for long hours each week (which entails shift work), has a large number of different departments (check out, delicatessen counter, off-licence, etc.) and a large number of part-time employees. Employees' shifts will change each week and job rotation and needs of different departments will vary. Management can use a large visual control board divided vertically into time periods (probably hours/days over a working week) and horizontally into departments. Bars with employees' names can then be slotted into the appropriate divisions and employees can see at a glance when and what hours they will be working during the forthcoming week.

---

**FOCUS**

AUDIO VISUAL AIDS
promote learning
help the speaker
need a little practice
some planning
careful choice

---

## 10.4 ASSIGNMENTS

1  A young O and M (organisation and methods) officer had produced his written report and was then asked to make an oral presentation to management.

A week beforehand he contacted the company and reserved a conference room and asked for an overhead projector to be put there for his use.

His subject-matter was complex so he carefully prepared a score of transparencies, including diagrams, tables of costings, etc., for his fifteen-minute presentation.

After the preliminary introduction he opened his briefcase, took out the transparencies and walked over to the overhead projector. He realised it was an unfamiliar model, and when he switched it on nothing happened. He quickly grabbed a plug and put it in the nearest outlet. He then ran through his presentation using the transparencies in order without further complications. He had even remembered to bring his pointer to indicate on the projector screen the vital features of his diagram.

What mistakes, if any, did the young man make in his use of the overhead projector? (An answer is given in Appendix 1.)

2  Analyse how audio-visual aids can affect

(a)  communication in business organisations;
(b)  the role of the professional administrator.

(See also Chapter 17.)

3  What are the main forms of audio-visual aids now available to the professional administrator? What are the relative advantages and disadvantages of each form as a means of communication? [ICSA]

4  If you were asked to give a lecture to employees of your company on the work done in its accounting department, what visual aids would be useful to you in your task? [IAA]

5  What would you say are the principal advantages of using a projector and slides in any business presentation? [IAA]

# THINKING AND PLANNING

Effective communication is the basis of success in many tasks: effective thought, reasoning, analysis and planning are essential for successful communication.

## 11.1 THE THINKING PROCESS

Most people think a little, some do much more, before writing an important communication, such as a letter of application for a job. However, we all give other communications, particularly oral ones, very little forethought. After all we have been communicating with other people since birth, so we often fail to see any necessity to give such a natural and easy process any special consideration.

There are, however, many good reasons for the suggestion that we should 'stop and think'. You can probably suggest a number of them — here are some examples.

(a) Reflection and reasoning will calm any emotion (such as anger or fear) which would make our communication less effective.
(b) A little consideration can often help us to avoid incomplete or incorrect communication.
(c) Without logical thought, our ideas are often expressed in a somewhat muddled, imprecise way.
(d) Without forethought we may present information in unsuitable language.
(e) Unless we spend some time reasoning out a complex communication, the end-product is rarely, whether spoken or written, in the most logical order.

## 11.2 THINKING TECHNIQUES

**Deduction**
Deductive, or analytical, logic is a method of vertical thinking. It is a form of reasoning which moves in precise steps from a generalisation to a particular case.

Analytical reasoning always starts with a statement, or premise, such as:

(a) *All computers can calculate.*

A second statement is then added:

(b) *This machine is a computer.*

From this we can conclude that:

(c) *This machine can calculate.*

For (c) to be a valid conclusion, statements (a) and (b) must be true. For instance, if (a) had stated:

*All computers can walk,*

the conclusion would have been:

*This machine can walk.*

which is obviously false.

It is also possible to disprove a statement, for example:

*No computers can walk.*
*This animal can walk.*
*This animal is not a computer.*

It is very easy to reason incorrectly when changing from the positive to the negative. For instance, the following two statements may be true:

*All citizens of this country pay taxes.*
*Aliens are not citizens of this country.*

But:

*All aliens pay no taxes in this country*

may be false. If they reside in this country, they may be liable for tax. We also cannot convert:

*All typewriters are keyboard machines.*

to:

*All keyboard machines are typewriters.*

This seems very obvious, yet such fallacious reasoning is surprisingly common, particularly in argument where it is easy to think that a proposition that makes a true statement on a subject is also true when reversed.

It can, however, be argued that, as

> *All typewriters are keyboard machines.*

then:

> *SOME keyboard machines are typewriters.*

A long line of reasoning can be conducted using the deductive process, as the following example shows. (The premises are assumed to be true.)

> IF *everyone thought logically there would be no chapter on the subject in this book.*
> IF *everyone thought logically there would be no NEED for such a chapter.*
> BUT *there is a chapter.*
> THEREFORE *not all people think logically* (OR *some people are illogical*).
> *People make decisions.*
> IF *some people are illogical some decisions will be illogical.*
> *Illogical decisions may be wrong.*
> THEREFORE *illogical people may make wrong decisions.*
> *Illogical decisions are often intuitive.*
> *Some intuitive decisions may be right.*
> *Some illogical decisions may be right.*

To carry out a long process of thought using this method is laborious but can be productive. However, it can also be a straitjacket which prevents us from applying other kinds of reasoning, such as arguing from experience, having a flash of inspiration, or deliberately stepping aside to look at the problem from a different angle.


## Induction

Inductive thinking is the process by which we reason from experience, arranging and classifying new information according to its relationship with what we already know. Sometimes we put it into a class or generalisation, sometimes look forward from causes to possible effects, and sometimes make comparisons or analogies.

Conclusions reached by the inductive process will have a high degree of probability but will never have the same kind of certainty as the conclusions arrived at by deduction. Inductive reasoning is sometimes called *empirical*, because it is based on observation and experience, not on theory.

## Empirical generalisation

Generalisation means, as the name implies, classifying things according to an accepted collection of data. For instance, the statement *typewriters have QWERTY keyboards* arises from knowledge that there is a standard keyboard layout on all typewriters (that we know of) which has, as the top bank of letters on the left-hand side, the letters *Q W E R T* and *Y*.

Such a statement can be made with considerable confidence. It cannot be proved to be totally true unless every typewriter in the world has been checked and found to conform, in which case the statement would be based on analytic not inductive reasoning.

To apply this to your own work you need to ask questions such as the following:

> *Is this a reasonable inference judged against existing knowledge?*
> *Has the investigation covered a sufficiently wide area?*
> *Is this particular circumstance/object typical of the general class?*

If these questions cannot be answered in the affirmative, then it is easy to fall into a very common error of reasoning. It is rash to generalise from isolated or special occurrences and equally fallacious argument can arise from ignorance or prejudice. Statements such as:

> *All people from the country of . . . are thieves.*

is clearly more likely (we hope!) to be untrue rather than true.

Facts must never be twisted to fit in with a theory and you must be able to produce evidence to support your argument.

### Cause and effect

Often when we know that events generally follow a certain path we wish to know why, or we wish to assess what may be a future effect of present action, to make forecasts.

Although effect always follows cause and cause always precedes effect, a connection between a particular cause and a particular effect cannot be assumed because of the existence of a time sequence. Superstitious people may do this.

> *He walked under a ladder this morning.*
> *He has been sacked.*

does not mean that he has been sacked *because* of the ladder. We have to find out what other causes might have existed to result in that effect. It is well to remember, also, that the effect may be due to combination of causes.

The cause must not be confused with the occasion. The cause of the destruction of much of Beirut in 1982 was not the Israeli invasion of

Lebanon. That was the occasion. The cause was the much deeper Jew/ Arab hostility over the Palestine issue.

We must also not conclude that there is necessarily a relationship between several possible causes, or effects. The causes of riots in English cities in 1981 may have been the connection between unemployment, bad housing, racial disadvantage, prejudice, growth of politically extreme groups and poor education, but it is very difficult to prove the connection let alone give approximate weight to the different possible causes.

When causal connections are established attempts may need to be made to predict what the effect may be. These forecasts must not be mere generalisations from the particular. They must be based on general observations: for instance, the sales figures for a product over a time sequence, international economic and political information, market research, production capacity, etc. A prediction about sales for the coming year must make a connection between all these variables and produce a forecast which fits all the known data.

*Analogy*

Analogies and comparison can be very useful in making arguments or explanations more intelligible. But what happens when we go further and base our reasoning on, and draw conclusions from, the resemblances which the analogy suggests? It may be a very unsafe process. Analogies can never be used to establish a logical conclusion. Even if we can show twenty similarities between a typewriter and a computer, they obviously have many more dissimilarities than they have things in common.

False analogy is at the root of much specious reasoning. It should only be used to illustrate points made or, perhaps, to indicate possible conclusions.

**Lateral thinking**

This phrase was coined by Edward de Bono to describe thinking processes which require approaches different from those of analytical logic. It includes what Aristotle invented to cover up  the astonishing fact that there were certain phenomena for which he found himself unable to account – CHANCE!

Deductive reasoning can be confining. Some problems simply cannot be solved by its application. Sometimes this is because of a failure to 'see the wood for the trees'. Sometimes one starts trying to solve a problem by making a choice between probable solutions. It is possible to waste much time pursuing what seems the most probable solution to a dead end, rather than realising early on that it would be wise to go back and make a different choice. Sometimes there may be no one right answer, merely a combination of solutions to help reduce the size of the problem.

Aristotle's 'chance' is an intuitive and unconscious thought process –

the imaginative leap which has accompanied so many great scientific discoveries.

Lateral thinking can also follow a series of progressive steps rather like the process of analytical logic, but the steps will merely follow in a time sequence, not as a deductive series. They might include improvisation, experiment, new suggestions.

Lateral thinking can be used very effectively in group problem-solving sessions. It is very notable in 'brainstorming' meetings (where it is often called 'creative thinking'). In these meetings the group has a leader who is responsible for starting the group, recording ideas and switching them to a different track if they get stuck, but there is no formality in the proceedings – quite the contrary. The object is to produce, in ten to fifteen minutes, a large number of ideas, however fantastic, which can be analysed later. It is essential that *no* idea is dismissed as foolish, impractical, already being done, etc., for any one suggestion could generate others that might be useful.

This technique can be used in carrying out value analysis, planning sales and promotion campaigns and devising better procedures and methods of working. There are firms which specialise in thinking up brand names for new products. Recently one of these, faced with a request to name a new car, invited members of the public in from the street, paid them a fee and gave them wine and food, and, at the end of a two-hour session, using brainstorming techniques, had the new name – 'Acclaim'.

## 11.3 DEVELOPING REASONING

Any of the techniques mentioned in section 11.2 can be applied at a simple level by any reasonably intelligent person. Your approach to problems and to their communication will often have been determined by your previous education and training. To develop your reasoning skills it is necessary first to discover how you tackle problems. You will probably find that you use all three approaches but favour one more than the others. This indicates a need to concentrate on introducing other methods.

Also helpful is to try to pinpoint fallacies and errors in reasoning, whether made by you or by others, and determine not to repeat them.

---

### FOCUS

#### SOME FAMOUS FALLACIES

Appeals to pity, force or ignorance:

*The accused has been found guilty of murder but I want the jury to remember that he comes from a broken home.*

---

**Focus** *cont.*

*I want you to work overtime. There are millions of unemployed who would welcome the chance.*

False cause:

*Another bad summer. The Americans and Russians have sent up more satellites.*

Appeals to authority:

*It is a criminal offence in this country. So it must be morally wrong.*

*Our leader said it, so it must be right.*

Ambiguity:

*Left is the opposite of right, so right-wing dictators are preferable to communism.*

Begging the question:

*Have you stopped beating your wife? Answer 'yes' or 'no'.*

---

## 11.4 CONSIDERING THE RECIPIENT

When the thinking process is concluded you should then consider how best to frame your communication. This involves choosing the method of communicating, for example letter or telephone, chart or interview, but, more importantly, it necessitates thinking about the recipient – the person or persons who are going to hear, read or see your message.

Every person and every group possesses individuality, with different background knowledge, attitudes and command of language. Thus you need to adjust your communication to the recipient(s) and that means considering how best to frame communication so that it will achieve the result you want.

## 11.5 PLANNING

Thinking about problems and how we want to communicate often leads us to picking up a pen and jotting down some notes. With letters and other written communication it is common for people to write the document out in full and then edit it and rewrite it. Do you do that? It is a time-consuming process.

The technique we suggest here can avoid the double writing of any document and it can also be used for oral communication. It takes a little time to get used to and at first you may have to exercise some willpower to lose old habits. If you persist, however, you will in the long term save time and money, and communicate more effectively as well.

You will have separated the two main elements of communication: the planning, and the presentation and use of language. The planning of what to say or write being completed, you will be able to give full attention to how you should communicate it. Thus your choice of presentation and use of precise and suitable language will be better.

## Content

You now need to decide on the content. Write it down in the form of short notes, starting each note on a separate line. (For advice on writing notes see Chapter 3.2 and for the planning of long documents see Chapter 2.)

You should already have done the thinking about why you want to communicate, to whom and what is the end-purpose of the communication.

## Format and logical order

Choose a suitable format for your communication. If the format is a simple one, you can now, without rewriting the notes, number them in the order in which you wish to use them (see Chapter 11.6, example 1).

With practice you will be able to write a letter, for instance, from these notes in its final form (or dictate it). Telephone calls can be made direct from original notes. (You will find planning calls helps you to make sure that you do not forget anything and it will keep the cost of the call down.)

If a more complex format is used, it may be necessary to rewrite the notes under chosen headings and with numbers, but if some space is left between the notes and a reasonable left-hand margin, this rewriting would probably only be necessary if the notes were to be used for a talk, interview or similar occasion.

The choice of format is important in written communication. There is a relationship between what the communication looks like on the page and the effect it will have on the person who reads it. A good format and display helps the message, can reinforce it, make it easier to understand and creates a good impression. This is particularly true with advertisements (see Chapter 4), where choice of layout, typeface, etc., is very important, but an effective format also improves other documents.

The following format suggestions apply to most documents. Details of specific systems are found in the relevant chapters of this book.

### Main headings

A definitive subject heading (or main title) is necessary for many documents, desirable for most.

*Intermediate headings*

The now common habit of identifying specific areas by chapter/section headings has made the identification of elements in communications much easier.

*Numbering*

Even within a short document it is very sensible to add a number or letter before any intermediate heading and to number similarly items in a list. Examples of two common systems of numbering were given in Chapter 2.14.

## 11.6 SAMPLE PLANS

Some examples of plans follow. Others are given in Appendix 1, as notes for answers to some of the assignments. (The plans would in practice be written as shorter notes, with words more abbreviated than they can be here for general reading.)

### EXAMPLE 1  PLAN FOR A LETTER

The following shows a plan for a letter. Numbers and letters have been added to indicate the order in which the items are to be included. This would be the second stage in planning.

|  |  |
|---|---|
| *1a* | *Thanks for letter 6.12* |
| *HEADING* | *Subject – order 645321* |
| *2a* | *Cannot supply 6 Model XY4S at moment* |
| *4* | *Discount 5% for cash in 21 days* |
| *3a* | *40 Model XY5P available* |
| *3b* | *Delivery 4 weeks from confirmation of order* |
| *2b* | *XY4S available delivery 1st week Feb* |
| *1b* | *Apologies for delay in answering letter* |
| *1c* | *Reasons – postal strike – received 2.1* |
| *1d* | *Also – own holiday until 2.1* |
| *5b* | *Holding XY5P for 7 days* |
| *6* | *Hope satisfactory and will receive order* |
| *5a* | *Please confirm asap* |

REMEMBER that there is more than one way of putting the items together (for instance, item 5b could go after 3a). Choose an order which will be logical and clear to the reader.

EXAMPLE 2    PARTIAL PLAN FOR A REPORT ON AN INVESTIGATION INTO
A POSSIBLE NEW BRANCH OFFICE IN WESTOWN

1    *Report requested by Board – Minute 10, 11.8.19--*
2    *info collected from:*
     *(a) visit Westown 6-10.8.19--*
     *(b) Chamber of Commerce*
     *(d) Employment offices*
     *(f) Kelly's and other trade directories*
     *(c) Local authority*
     *(e) Estate agents*
3    *General suitability of Westown*
     *Growing town*
     *Market locally*
     *Easy access whole region*
4    *Office facilities*
     *Rent – few suitable premises. Rents very high. 3 possibles –
     especially one in High Street over shop (details to go in
     an appendix)*
     *Buy – on outskirts only. Mainly residential which would have
     to be adapted. 2 possibles (Appendix 2)*
5    *Availability of staff*
     .
     .
     .

And so on . . .

EXAMPLE 3    OUTLINE PLAN FOR TELEPHONE CALL RE COMPLAINT ON
NON-DELIVERY OF GOODS

1    *Collect copies of:*
     *Customer's letter*
     *Order*
     *Invoice*
     *Delivery note*
2    *Note customer's name and telephone number (extension and
     name of contact in company if relevant).*
3    *List:*
     *(a) Date of complaint*
     *(b) Details of goods*
     *(c) Precise complaint*
     *(d) Delivery note details*

*(e) Apology and assurance of swift and satisfactory action (if
complaint justified)*
*(f) Proposed action*

EXAMPLE 4    PLAN FOR A SPEECH TO BE GIVEN AT A RETIREMENT PRE-
SENTATION

1    REGRET BERT OLDAGE LEAVING
*Been here 15 years*
*Popular and cheerful*
*Hard worker*
2    EXCEPT WHEN:
*fell asleep at desk – morning after first grandchild born*
3    BERT PLANS TO REDECORATE HOUSE
*Will do well if as efficient at papering walls as with his office
paperwork*
4    HOPE HE AND MRS O HAVE MANY HAPPY YEARS
5    STAFF CONTRIBUTED TO TANGIBLE REMINDER
*Discreet enquiries made!*
*Portable TV – Bert can watch football while Mrs O sees Coro-
nation Street*
6    ASK THEM TO COME FORWARD
7    PRESENT GIFT AND LEAD APPLAUSE

EXAMPLE  5    PREPARATION  FOR  A  REPRIMAND  INTERVIEW – POOR
ATTENDANCE

1    *Have to hand, if possible:*
*Personnel record*
*Attendance record for last two months*
*Details of any reasons for absence given*
*Report from supervisor on recent work*
*Last appraisal report*
*Copy of company rules on attendance and dismissal pro-
cedure*
2    *Decide approach, e.g.*
*Calm and courteous*
*State reason for interview – quote from attendance record*
*Ask reasons for poor attendance*
*Listen to reasons*
*Probe to establish deeper causes*
*Warn*
*If reasons unsatisfactory, refer to possible dismissal*

*If serious causes, possibly (according to circumstances):*
    *refer to company doctor, or personnel department*
    *withhold decision until further investigation carried out*
    *discuss how matters could be improved, getting employee*
    *to suggest means*

3   *If necessary, list specific questions to be asked, such as:*
    *Why do you have difficulty in arriving on time?*
    *What is wrong with the bus service?*
    *Why can't you catch an earlier bus?*
    *Did you know you have been late X times in the last Y months?*
    *What are you going to do about it?*
    *What do you suppose will happen if you do not improve your timekeeping?*
    *Are there any other problems?*
    *How is/are your wife, parents, children?*

## 11.7 ASSIGNMENTS

1   Which of the following do you consider to be a valid argument? (See Appendix 1 for answers.)

  (a)  *'He's left his wife and moved next door.'*
      *'Well, the Bible says, "Love thy neighbour".'*

  (b)  *Power corrupts. Therefore, absolute power corrupts absolutely.*

  (c)  *No architect is stupid, but there are some stupid people who design houses.*
      *Some house designers are not architects.*

  (d)  *Pierre eats garlic. All Frenchmen eat garlic, so Pierre must be French.*

  (e)  *34 per cent of people in a recent opinion poll favoured capital punishment for murder; 58 per cent favoured corporal punishment in schools. Therefore, the least number in favour of both forms of punishment is 8 per cent.*

2   You read that the ability to communicate successfully is no criterion on greatness. You think, 'Well, that may be so, but we should not know that people were great unless they could communicate successfully.' How would you test the truth of your thinking?

3   What truth is there in the saying that there are 'lies, damned lies and statistics'?

4   Draw up a plan for assignment 1 for Chapter 2 (p. 45). (If you have already completed the assignment, check your plan with your answer and with the suggestions given in Appendix 1.)

5   Plan a speech to be made at a staff association meeting, arguing for complete renovation of the staff recreation room, to be paid for by the firm.

# LANGUAGE

English has many more words than most other languages: for example, the *Concise Cambridge Dictionary* has 300 pages for Italian–English, but 500 for English–Italian.

This wealth of vocabulary is the legacy of its history. The basis of the language is Anglo-Saxon, a relatively obscure Germanic dialect brought to England in the fifth century. The year 1066, the best-known date in English history, brought the Normans, and over the next 200 years Anglo-Saxon (the language of the peasants) absorbed a huge vocabulary of Norman French words and became English. It thus gained a large number of words from the mainstream of Romance languages, from French, Italian, Spanish and other languages descended from Latin.

By medieval times English had become the common tongue of nobleman and peasant alike. But the languages of learning were still largely Greek and Latin. Hence English absorbed large numbers of often technical and scientific words from these languages.

The spread of the British Empire gave English an influx of words from many languages. Some, like *char*, brought back from India by soldiers, remained colloquial, while others, like *bungalow* went directly or indirectly into standard English.

But the greatest modern influence has been American. Especially during the last seventy years there has been a lease-lend of words which, however much we may disapprove of some of its manifestations, has helped to maintain the vigour and versatility of the language. To it we owe hundreds of such useful expressions as *boom, slump, bulldoze, paperback, grapevine, commuter, breakeven*. (We also owe to them the longest word in the English language, *pneumonoultramicroscopicsilicovolcanoconiosis*, a lung disease caused by ultra microscopic particles of sandy volcanic dust.)

English is the most widely used language in the world: 60 per cent of the world's radio programmes and 70 per cent of the letters written every day are in English. It is the international language of air traffic and of the United Nations.

A vigorous language is constantly changing. New words come into use; new meanings evolve (like *escalate*, in the Vietnam war); some words become archaic and disappear, perhaps to reappear. *Obscene*, for example, was dismissed as somewhat archaic by the *Oxford English Dictionary* in 1933 but was restored to general use recently. The structure of language changes, too, and there is no good reason for clinging to rules of grammar which no longer reflect current usage. The function of the structure of language is to support the meaning, not to restrict expression. The English language, like society, manners and fashion, has become more informal since the Second World War, and many words and constructions which would once have been unacceptable in standard English are now established.

For example, *different to*, and *different than*, as well as *different from*, are now acceptable forms, according to that respected authority, the *Oxford English Dictionary*. The distinction between *due to* and *owing to* has disappeared and the rules about *shall* and *will* are fast disappearing. 'Correct English' is, in short, whatever is widely acceptable in current usage. But good English is something else again.

Not only does the English language have a very large vocabulary, so do we. The average vocabulary of a person in Great Britain is a surprising 13,000 words. This figure represents the average person's largest vocabulary, the 'recognition' vocabulary, that body of words which we recognise and understand when we read or hear them. It is a larger vocabulary than our 'recall' vocabulary (on average 8,000 words), the body of words stored in our memory and available for our use. Even this smaller vocabulary is so large that it seems surprising that we should ever have difficulties in expressing ourselves clearly.

But we do. We use the wrong words — those which do not express what we mean, those which are not understood by our recipient, or which antagonise him. Sometimes we merely use so many words that the meaning is lost in them: we can't see the wood for the trees. To be aware of the many ways in which language can be misused is the first step towards using language more effectively.

## 12.1 THE WRONG WORDS

Jargon cannot be better defined than in the words of H. W. Fowler:

> *Jargon is talk that is considered both ugly-sounding and hard to understand; applied especially to the sectional vocabulary of a science, art, class, sect, trade or profession, full of technical terms . . . the use of long words, circumlocution and other clumsiness.*

There are two kinds of language identified here. First, we have the special terminology that develops within any group: social workers, computer staff, shop stewards, and so on. The use of these technical vocabularies can be both irritating and incomprehensible to outsiders, but within the group they act as a kind of spoken shorthand, a concise and precise way of expressing a concept.

Social workers talk of *siblings* rather than brothers and sisters. Computer *hardware* in two syllables contains all the physical equipment associated with computers, while *software* describes the variety of programmes, instructions and procedures which control the functioning of the hardware.

In a world of increasing specialisation and technology, these technical vocabularies are not only defensible, they are necessary. Mathematicians, chemists, lawyers, systems analysts and accountants need the precision and brevity of their own 'languages'.

What is indefensible, however, is to use your special vocabulary on outsiders who are not familiar with your jargon. Not only will you fail to communicate, you will have erected a barrier of frustration, and possibly fear, between yourself and others.

The second variety of jargon, defined by Fowler as *the use of long words, circumlocution and other clumsiness*, is a sure way of losing, or at least mislaying, meaning in a fog of words. There is nothing intrinsically wrong with using long words. *Circumlocution* is certainly one! But it does have the advantage of being more concise than any other expression for *'longwinded and roundabout ways of saying things'*. But too many long words do make it difficult to understand what we are reading or hearing (see the description of the Fog Index on pp. 181-2).

The letter of which the following is an extract won a booby prize of two pounds of tripe from the Plain English Awards Committee:

> *We would advise that our policy does exclude as contingency consequent upon a condition which is receiving or awaiting treatment at the date of issue of the policy.*

The same letter ended ironically:

> *We hope this clarifies the situation.*

Clumsiness is well illustrated in the following extract from a real letter:

> *In response to your card regarding the above order and the non-delivery of one box of 352 Typing Paper, we are writing to inform you that this has currently met an out of stock situation and that delivery cannot be met until the end of February.*

Clichés are those expressions which, when newly coined, had caught the imagination and were adopted and overworked until they became thread-bare, hackneyed and lost all force and vigour. Harold Macmillan's expression, *a wind of change*, which originally referred to a new direction in African politics, but is now applied to any minor event, is an example. Other clichés, often with a less respectable history, may commit the offence of circumlocution too: *at this moment in time* and *in this day and age* for *now* are particularly irritating.

Slang, like cliché, changes with fashion. How many slang words for money can you recall? *Readies, lolly, dough, bread.* Good English is what is appropriate to the circumstances, and slang has its place in familiar chat. It is out of place in most business communication and it is obvious that too informal a choice of language, in, say, a company report would not inspire confidence.

Pompous people seek to add weight (at the expense of losing the point) by using long words, and too many words, for example:

> *Passengers are requested not to communicate with the driver while the vehicle is in motion.*

Pompous writers habitually use such expressions as *in connection with* when *about* might be more appropriate. They *ameliorate, acquaint, terminate* and *assist* when they could *improve, tell, end* and *help!*

The truly great do not need weighty language to add force to what they say. Nelson's famous message at Trafalgar was not:

> *With reference to previous instructions appertaining to naval discipline, it is felt that all personnel in the immediate vicinity of Cape Trafalgar will carry out the navigational and/or combative duties allocated to them, whichever is applicable, to the satisfaction of all concerned.*

He said:

> *England expects that every man will do his duty.*

Churchill used the simplest, most direct, language in a plea for brevity:

> *To do our work we all have to read a mass of papers. Nearly all of them are far too long. This wastes time, while energy has to be spent in looking for essential points.*

A more recent British politician has earned a reputation for misuse of words and delighted audiences with such gems as accusing the opposition of *'going about stirring up apathy'* and by promising *'never to prejudge the past'*.

Negative expressions often give rise to an emotive response from one's listener and need to be used with care:

> *I'm afraid he's not available.*

Is a rejecting statement whose rejection is emphasised by the word 'afraid'. It is better to say *'I'm sorry he's not available'*, which at least implies a polite degree of sympathy.

*But* can be used to arouse an emotive response. *'It's very good but . . .'* is a beginning which may well put the listener on the defensive, and at the least it will initiate a cautious attitude. On the other hand, *but* can arouse hope or optimism, *'It will be difficult but . . . '*. *But* can also be useful to introduce diplomatically your refutation of someone's argument: *'You may well be right but on the other hand . . . '*.

*Disappointment* is a particularly negative word and a sentence beginning *'I'm sorry to disappoint you . . . '* may create more dismay in the listener than he might have felt had the word been omitted.

*Unfortunately* is another depressing expression: *'Unfortunately we were not able to get in touch'* makes a negative statement even more negative.

It is often preferable to avoid negatives altogether. *'We cannot deliver in three weeks'* is flat, rejecting, totally negative and likely to lose you a customer. Put another way, *'Can you give us five weeks for delivery?'*, i.e. as a question, it invites the listener's co-operation.

Ambiguity is a particularly offensive fault in business writing when content is so often factual. *Smith told Jones he had been promoted* is an example of ambiguity caused by careless use of pronouns. (Does *he* refer to Smith or to Jones?) Other kinds of ambiguity may have a second meaning which is contradictory, *Nothing acts faster than . . . .* (a well-known headache pill), or give rise to the sort of double entendre commonly found in comic postcards. Neither of these seriously risks misunderstanding but neither is appropriate in a business context.

## 12.2 EMOTIVE LANGUAGE

It is very difficult to convey information, ideas, and especially opinions, without 'colouring' them with some feeling or emotion. This is often done unconsciously by the communicator. We can scarcely speak or write about any subject without betraying our own opinion or attitudes by our choice of words. It is not wrong to do this, but it may evoke an unfavourable reaction in other people and thus affect their acceptance or rejection of our communication. The following expression exposes the speaker's lack of objectivity:

*I am determined, you are obstinate, he is pig-headed.*

Politicians are natural users of emotive language and it is in their speeches that we so often find fact and reason clouded or lost in the rhetoric. For example, the use of biblical imagery, *the journey through the wilderness, the pilgrimage* to their vision of *the New Jerusalem*, can lend an aura of sanctity, rightness and inevitability to the policies and ideals they describe.

## 12.3 TOO MANY WORDS

Even if we have disciplined ourselves not to use technical words to the uninitiated, have avoided dishonestly using emotive language (rather than reason) to persuade, have used long words with discretion, avoided slang and cliché, there are still many pitfalls in the use of language.

Of these, in business and commerce, one of the worst offences, because it wastes time, is to use more words than are necessary to convey our meaning, as, for example:

*Broadly speaking, this may have the ultimate effect of doubling in numbers the total of orders despatched outwards in a single day.*

This sentence has many superfluous words. '*Broadly speaking*' is surely implied in the rest of the sentence. How else can one double but in numbers? '*Outwards*' is implied in the word '*despatched*'. Tautology is the technical (jargon!) word for expressions like this in which the meaning is repeated, e.g.

*This unique ornamental vase, the only one of its kind.*

A more economical version of the sentence above would read:

*This may have the effect of doubling the number of orders despatched in a single day.*

While the word *single* is implied in the expression *in a day*, it has been retained because it adds *force* to the sentence.

A major cause of 'too many words' or verbosity is the over-use of modifiers, i.e. adjectives and adverbs:

> *The complete implementation of this overall programme will inevitably necessitate extensive demands on the available resources of the appropriate committees and other bodies concerned.*

Not a single noun, *implementation, programme, demands, resources, committees, bodies,* is allowed out unaccompanied, and the verb *necessitate* is chaperoned by its adverb, *inevitably.*

There is no need to point out the difficulty, not to say tedium, inflicted on the readers of such writing. Indeed, the surest way to bore people is to write, or say, too much. Such absurdities as *the true facts* are expressions which immediately create doubts as to the truth of the facts presented.

Another communication which won a 'tripe' award was from a British Rail employee who took 158 words to explain why a particular train had no buffet service. And a third 'tripe' award went to a local government official who devoted 104 words to asking a local resident to trim his hedge.

## 12.4 THE FOG INDEX

The first result of the misuse of language discussed in this chapter was that meaning is obscured. Several methods have been devised to measure the readability of written language; the Fog Index is one such. Readability is affected by:

(a) the average length of the sentences, in words
(b) the percentage of simple words
(c) the percentage of verbs expressing forceful action
(d) the proportion of familiar words
(e) the proportion of abstract words
(f) the proportion of personal references
(g) the proportion of long words.

The Fog Index is based on a count of the number of words of three or more syllables in a hundred-word sample of the passage being checked, as well as of the average sentence length.

To determine the reading difficulty of a passage you will need to:

(a) select samples of 100 words each
(b) calculate the average number of words in the sentences of your sample by counting the number of complete sentences and dividing that into the number of words
(c) count the number of words of three or more syllables, excluding words with a capital letter, compounds such as bookkeeper, and words ending in *-es* or *-ed*

(d) add the average number of words per sentence and the number of words of three syllables or more and multiply by 0.4.

This gives the Fog Index, which is graded as follows:

| Index | Reading level |
|---|---|
| less than 10 | Easy reading |
| 11–12 | the top 20% of 12-year-olds |
| 13 | the top 20% of 16-year-olds |
| 14–16 | first-year university student |
| 17 | university graduate |

This index can usefully be used in checking company communications, for example, to ensure that they will be comprehensible to the work-force.

It is said that a British Leyland memorandum to workers which concerned an ultimatum about productivity had an index of 17: hardly likely, one might think, to be understood or to achieve the co-operation sought. Indeed, it is claimed that the only management-to-worker memorandum which fell below an index of 13 was one wishing all employees a Happy New Year! British Leyland has in the past notoriously suffered from poor industrial relations. Could ineffective communication have been one of the causes?

Some recent American research found that:

only  4 per cent of readers will understand a sentence of 27 words
but  75 per cent of readers will understand a sentence of 17 words
and  95 per cent of readers will understand a sentence of  8 words.

## 12.5 THE RIGHT WORDS

We have already defined the use of good English in business as the use of language appropriate to the circumstances. That is the target, so how is it to be achieved?

First, the reader should be considered. Readability must be balanced so that the reader can easily understand what is said without any feeling of being talked down to. Our relationship with the reader will be another influence. To a stranger there must always be more formality than to a colleague or friend. To someone much higher or lower in the hierarchy than ourselves there is more formality than with our equals.

Use simple words whenever appropriate. Generally prefer to *begin* something not *commence*; don't *transmit* (except in the technical sense) but *send*; agree to *use* not to *utilise*.

Look for shorter expressions. Don't write a letter *with regard to, with reference to, in connection with,* or *in respect of,* but *about* your subject.

Prune modifiers, i.e. adjectives and adverbs, from your writing. Don't let it become inflated by unnecessary words.

Use active verbs, not passive ones, for example:

> not *A meeting will be held by the Board next week.*
> but *The Board will meet next week.*

Generally use personal pronouns rather than the impersonal form, for example:

> not *The task would be capable of determination when the appropriate tools be made available to those concerned.*
> but *Give us the tools and we will finish the job.*

Try to be positive, not negative, for example:

> *The project failed.* not *The project was not successful.*
> *The company has abandoned the plan.* not *The company will not now proceed with the plan.*

Finally, be flexible and keep an open mind. 'Rules' about language are meant to be guidelines, not straitjackets. The long word may express our meaning more precisely than a short one. Modifiers are invaluable in expressing shades of meaning, for example: *I was concerned, I was very concerned, I was most concerned.* The passive impersonal form can be useful: *It has been decided that* may be less damaging to a relationship than *I have decided.* But it is often the coward's way of avoiding responsibility, of passing the buck.

Our choice of words should be governed by considering not *'What do I want to say?'* but *'What result do I want to get?'*

## 12.6 STYLE AND TONE

Style is a combination of choice of words, symptom and structure of language and there are so many possible variations that we each develop a method of writing which can be as distinctive as our fingerprints.

Eric Partridge in *Usage or Abusage* says that 'Style is not something that one assumes on special occasions (like dress clothes) but that which one *is* when one writes; so far from being compelled to seek it, one cannot avoid it.'

Obviously we can, and do, adapt our style to the circumstances, the subject and the reader. But something of ourselves will show through. Our style will communicate to the reader something about ourselves as persons. 'Reading between the lines' is inevitable. A pompous person is likely to reflect pomposity, a good-humoured one affability, and a meticulous, precise person will dot his *i*s and cross his *t*s in even his least formal note. The following examples convey very different personalities:

> *Have you got any jobs vacant at your place?*
> *I would respectfully submit myself for the appointment of clerical assistant advertised in the 'News'.*
> *I was interested to read your advertisement in the 'News' for a clerical assistant.*
> *I am in receipt of details about a vacancy for a clerical assistant in your company.*

Tone is defined in the *Oxford English Dictionary* as 'a particular quality, pitch, modulation or inflexion of the voice expressing . . . affirmation, interrogation, hesitation, decision and some feeling and emotion'. Usually it will in effect underline or emphasise the meaning of the words being used. In written language the tone conveys the feelings of the communication.

The tone of a communication will reflect what is being said, but it can also add a great deal of meaning. A reprimand might be cool, cold, angry, heated, impersonal or detached in tone. A congratulation is likely to be warm and enthusiastic but could be cool and formal. In much business writing a factual, neutral tone is appropriate, but remember that sincerity is an essential of tone however formal the context.

## 12.7 SENTENCE STRUCTURE

In Elizabethan England sentences were about 45 words long. In Victorian England they were about 30 words. Modern sentences average 20 words or less. Short sentences seem more alert and vital than long ones, but if all our sentences were short or simple we would bore our readers by the repetitiveness.

We have four types of sentence structure at our disposal.

(a) *Simple*: one subject, one predicate (see Appendix 3)

> *Eight bandits robbed a train yesterday.*

(b) *Compound:* two simple sentences joined by a conjunction (see Appendix 3)

> *Eight bandits robbed a train yesterday and stole £8,000.*

(c) *Complex*: one main clause plus subordinate modifying clauses (see Appendix 3)

> *Eight bandits who robbed a train yesterday were still being sought by police last night.*

(d) *Compound–complex*: all statements have one or more modifying statements

> *Eight bandits with coshes who tried to rob a train yesterday were foiled by a ganger who threw stones at them and forced them to drop £8,000.*

Varying our sentence structure makes what we say sound more interesting and alive. It also adds a desirable touch of elegance to our writing.

But however long or short a sentence it must contain only one idea, one main thought. A sentence such as the following, though it is grammatically constructed, is so cluttered with detail that the main purpose is almost lost:

> *Saying that, while he accepted medical evidence that asbestosis was associated with the cause of death of a Washington chemical worker, John Henry Thompson, aged 40, of 51 Pattenson Town, the Coroner, Mr J. Williams, indicated at the inquest at Chester-le-Street last night that the final decision whether the disease caused or contributed to death would rest with the Pneumoconiosis Medical Panel.*

A useful rule of thumb for sentence length is to try speaking your sentence aloud. If you can't manage it comfortably with one breath, then it needs rewriting.

## 12.8 PARAGRAPH STRUCTURE

As with sentences, so with paragraphs; the most important quality is unity. A paragraph should have only one theme. This subject can be stated or implied in an opening sentence and then expanded, qualified or illustrated in succeeding ones. Sometimes the so-called *topic* sentence comes at the end of a paragraph, to sum up what has gone before. Too many ideas thrown together in a paragraph confuse. We need to remember that sentence and paragraph structure contribute equally with the choice of words to the clarity of what we write.

---

**FOCUS**

Use: simple words wherever possible
short sentences wherever appropriate
short paragraphs almost always

## 12.9 REFERENCE BOOKS

*Knowledge is of two kinds. We know a subject ourselves or we know where we can find information upon it.*

(Dr Samuel Johnson)

A dictionary is essential. The more up to date it is, the better — one with a supplement containing new words and expressions is ideal.

*Roget's Thesaurus* contains synonyms and is invaluable in helping you to find just the right word to express your idea.

When you wish to check a point of grammar, punctuation and usage, perhaps the most popular choice would be *Usage or Abusage* by Eric Partridge.

The *Complete Plain Words* of Sir Ernest Gowers is recommended reading (rather than reference) for anyone who wishes to improve his command of the English language.

Finally, no list would be complete without a mention of the definitive work, H. W. Fowler's *Modern English Usage* (revised by Sir Ernest Gowers).

---

### FOCUS

**THE ABC OF LANGUAGE**

*Accuracy*  choose the word which exactly conveys your meaning (use *Roget's Thesaurus* if necessary)

*Brevity*  avoid boring your reader and wasting his time — communication is costly!

*Courtesy*  requires additional (to the message) words to avoid brusqueness and convey consideration to the reader

But don't sacrifice courtesy to brevity. George Bernard Shaw was a master of brevity, and also, when he chose, of devastating rudeness. He once received an invitation which read, '*The Countess of . . . will be at home* on . . . ', to which he simply replied, '*So will George Bernard Shaw*'!

---

## 12.10 ASSIGNMENTS

1  Read the following passage and work out its Fog Index. Then rewrite it in much simpler language and calculate the Fog Index of what you have written.

Language is the primary instrument of communication and the extent to which this volume is concerned with language is with that of our native tongue. The observation has been presented in previous sections that the ineffectual utilisation of English can be a hindrance or even a prevention of the process of communication but that the observation of the regulations regarding the usage of English will be of assistance in the conveyance of information. There will be sectional interests who may present the argument that the rigidity of the regulations of language are a deterrent to improved communication.

2   What do you understand by the term 'readability'? How would you assess the readability of a lengthy printed document intended for unskilled workers? [ICSA]

3   What is the importance of concise writing in business communications? [ICSA]

4   Define precisely the meaning of the word 'cliché' and give five example of clichés with which you are familiar. [IAA]

5   Redundancies often creep into written communication. What types of redundancies are the most common in this connection? [IAA]

6   The following notice on a staff notice-board caused great offence. Why?

Rewrite it and compare your version with that given in Appendix 1.

Employees are herewith instructed that any requests pertaining to vacation dates must be submitted to the divisional Personnel Manager, copies to the employee's immediate superior and to the Managing Director. No employee will be given permission to take holidays at any time not already scheduled on the holiday rota unless a month's notice is given and the immediate superior allows it. This ruling is effective immediately and applies to all holidays from Monday of next week. Any employee with holidays booked for the coming month must renegotiate them.

# NON-VERBAL
# COMMUNICATION

All verbal communication is affected by the non-verbal communication that accompanies it. On the telephone the tone of voice conveys nuances of meaning. Face to face, expression, gestures and posture also play an important part. We use demonstrations and models to supplement words, visual aids to clarify lectures, and maps, diagrams, charts and graphs (see Chapter 14) enhance both spoken and written communication.

Often more is conveyed by non-verbal than by verbal communication, yet on the whole it is an aspect of communication that is little considered.

## 13.1 THE NATURE OF NON-VERBAL COMMUNICATION

The major elements of non-verbal communication, excluding models, drawings, etc., can be divided into body language (kinesics), vocal tone, space (proxemics), the senses and time.

**Body language** (see Figure 13.1)
It is obvious that facial expressions and use of gesture contribute much to communication. As important, though perhaps less easy to interpret, is posture. The way we stand, or sit, the position of the head, and hands, can speak volumes. For example, a dejected person tends to slump, shoulders bowed and head held low, while arms crossed and held tightly in front of one's chest indicates a defensive mood. What is interesting is that much of this body language is involuntary or unconscious. When we frown, look puzzled, twist a pen nervously in our fingers, sprawl in a chair, run upstairs, we can convey all sorts of obvious and subtle messages about our emotions, understanding, attitudes and health. Some people are more skilled at hiding these involuntary signs than are others, but we all need to make the effort to do so at times, principally to avoid giving an unfavourable picture of ourselves to others and to avoid letting them feel that we are reacting unfavourably to them.

Fig 13.1  *body language*

## Vocal tone

One of the major differences between the spoken and written word is the addition of vocal tone, stress and emphasis. We can 'say' with a word and a look what it might take a sentence or more to write. For instance, an explosively interrogative *'What?'* accompanied by a look of intense disbelief might need to be written as:

> *'What are you saying? Can you really mean that? I have the utmost difficulty in believing you – in fact I don't believe you!'*

Moreover, we can completely change the meaning of words by the way in which we say them (see also Chapter 7.14), not only by using the pauses and inflections which in writing are replaced by punctuation, but also by our intonation, which can change a reprimand into a joke, or an inoffensive phrase into a deadly insult.

## Space

Each person has an individual spatial relationship with others. The closer the relationship with another person, the less necessity there is to 'keep them at a distance' (see Figure 13.2). There seem to be differences between

Fig 13.2 *personal space*

nations about how they regard personal space. For instance, people from some warm climates tend to move nearer to slight acquaintances to whom they are talking, to show friendship, while other nations (cooler and more reserved) will wish to retain the space as a defensive barrier until friendship is firmly established.

Space is also used to create other impressions, such as status. The larger the office, the bigger the desk or the company car, then the more important the position of the executive is seen to be.

### The senses

Sight, hearing, touch and, to a lesser extent, smell and taste, each plays a part in non-verbal communication:

(a) Sight not only enables us to receive non-verbal communication from other people but also allows us to observe and react to their appearance and clothes, the objects with which they surround themselves and their habits and idiosyncracies, for instance whether their desks are tidy or jumbled.

(b) Sounds other than words reach our ears. A sigh, a laugh, the constant clicking in and out of the top of a ball-point pen, a timid knock on the door – all give us indications about people which add to the communication process.

(c) Touch can produce almost diametrically opposed reactions. On the one hand, it can engender feelings of friendship and warmth; on the other, it may be taken as an infringement of personal space and, for women, as sexual harassment.

(d) Smell can have an effect somewhat other than just the 'b.o.' of the soap advertisement. For instance, perfumes and aftershave present an image of people to our nostrils, sometimes the image of their own choice, sometimes that of the friend or relative who remembered them on their birthdays!

(e) Taste will affect communication through our judgement of people by the food they eat. Tripe and onions, for instance, does not appeal to everyone, and has become associated, unfairly, with the manual workers of the North of England. Similarly anyone who likes tomato ketchup (even former British Prime Minister Sir Harold Wilson) rather than more delicate sauces will be considered by some to be 'lacking in taste', and, for the purist, to drink red wine with fish is a cardinal sin!

## Time

Taking time to talk to or listen to people can given them a sense of well-being, of being valued, of confidence. It also usually leads to better communication.

The timing of communication is also important. However well phrased the message, be it written or spoken, if it is given too early it will be forgotten or appear meaningless. On the other hand, official release of information by management is often too late – the rumours have already spread. Sometimes employees have learnt from the press, radio or television of proposed mergers, closures or changes before being informed by their management, with consequent harmful effects in industrial relations.

Time-wasting can also occur, of course. Communication can be over-long, repetitious or combined with so much social chat that immediate impact is lost.

## 13.2 BEHAVIOUR PATTERNS

Communication between any two individuals will vary in its nature and purpose at different times. It will also vary with non-verbal influences, for instance emotional changes in one of the individuals. Thus each conversation is a unique occasion.

Changes are even more apparent if one considers conversations about the same piece of information between one person and a series of others.

There will be a different tone to the conversations, perhaps even ranging from the friendly to the hostile, from interested to indifferent. Many of these changes will show in non-verbal communication.

Within groups, such behavioural changes may show themselves in a shift of leadership, in the emergence of a 'knowall', in the splitting of the group into sub-groups. In meetings the discussion can be analysed to show five distinct changing and re-forming groups or subjects for discussion:

ME      each person reacting individually
YOU     how each regards the other
US      the meeting working together as one group
THEM    those outside the meeting
IT      the object of discussion

## 13.3 THE EFFECT ON SPOKEN COMMUNICATION

It is clear that what we say is extensively affected by the way in which it is said, by body language, by mood and environment. Non-verbal communication can lead us to make judgements, to erect or destroy barriers. We can use it to create impressions of ourselves, or to change the impressions held by others.

It can supplement or even replace words; modify, change or reverse their meaning; clarify or confuse. Without doubt it is a crucial element in all face-to-face communication.

---

### FOCUS

ELEMENTS IN NON-VERBAL COMMUNICATION
   Body language
   Vocal tone
   Space
   The senses
   Time
BEHAVIOUR PATTERNS
   The individual
   The group
THE EFFECT ON SPOKEN COMMUNICATION
   Judgement
   Barriers
   Supplement to words
   Alterations in meaning

## 13.4 **ASSIGNMENTS**

1  What do you understand by the term 'non-verbal' communication? Indicate, with examples, how oral communication can be modified through non-verbal communication. (See the notes for an answer in Appendix 1.)

2  To what extent and in what ways can non-verbal communication affect human relations within working groups?

3  Manager *A* writes memos or telephones to his subordinates. Manager *B* hold meetings and informal conversations. What temperaments and personalities are their staff likely to attribute to them? Is either approach likely to be successful? (See also Chapter 17.5.)

4  What can our non-verbal communication betray about us in meetings, interviews and telephone conversations?

# CHARTS AND GRAPHS

One simple diagram can convey more information, more quickly and easily, than can hundreds of words. Not only is the visual medium compact, it also has impact, simplicity and variety.

It is said that we remember much more of what we see (see Figure 14.1) than we remember of what we hear or read. That is one reason why we find visual aids an effective support to a lecture, and why charts and graphs are a welcome supplement to the balance-sheets in a company report. Pictures are not only more memorable than a page of print, they are interesting, a way of holding the reader's attention.

Even complicated data, if represented in a diagram, will be easier to understand and more quickly assimilated. An especial advantage of the visual medium is the variety available. While this chapter limits itself to the types of charts and diagrams used in business, there are very many of these.

When we choose to use one of these pictorial methods, we have to consider both our reader and our purpose. If we were describing the output of the company's products in the annual report for employees, we might use pictograms which are interesting, attractive to the eye and which simplify information. But the same information would be better conveyed by line graphs or bar charts if we were producing a detailed analysis for a board meeting. Moreover, our choice between line graph and bar chart would be decided by our purpose and where we wish to place our emphasis. The up-and-down movement of a line graph will emphasise fluctuations and trends, while the solid columns of a block chart will tend to emphasise quantities or amounts.

Despite their advantages, there are some difficulties in the use of charts and diagrams. The first problem is that of perception: we cannot always be sure what will be seen. This is very simply illustrated by Figure 14.2, where the lines $AB$ and $BX$ appear longer than $BC$ and $AC$. Your ruler will show you that this is not so.

**Fig 14.1** *what do we remember?*

Seeing and hearing 50%

Seeing
30%

Reading 10%                    Hearing 20%

It was Disraeli who said that 'There are lies, damn lies and statistics', and a statistician will agree that the same set of figures can be used to 'prove' very different things. Similarly, statistical charts can be drawn in ways that distort the content and may deceive the reader. This kind of misrepresentation is illustrated by Figure 14.3, where the same set of figures is charted to give very different impressions.

Dictionary definitions of the words 'chart', 'graph' and 'diagram' show that the words can be synonymous. For business purposes, we wish to portray numbers and processes in visual form. Thus we may use the words as follows:

(a) *Chart* – the representation of numeric, statistical information.
(b) *Diagram* – non-quantitative illustration such as a flow chart.
(c) *Graph* – applied to the line graph only.

Fig 14.2 *problems of perception*

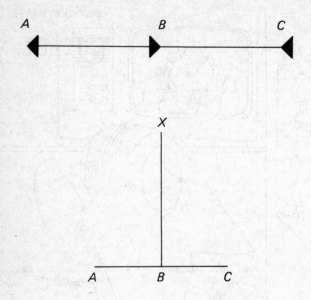

Line graphs can also be used to portray non-quantitative concepts (see Figure 14.4). This merely serves to demonstrate the flexibility of charts and diagrams.

At the end of this chapter you should be able to:

(a) recognise, describe and name different types of chart and diagram
(b) interpret the information they contain
(c) choose the most effective one by which to represent a given set of information for a particular purpose.

You will not produce effective graphic designs merely by making the choice of chart or diagram most suitable for your purpose. You will also need to plan your layout and use of space carefully, just as in other forms of communication. The best way to improve your own technique is to examine critically the charts and diagrams you see in newspapers, books and on television. Look at the diagram shown in Figure 14.31 (p. 223). It has an excellent content, clear, simple and logical, but the display is appalling, muddled and complicated.

## Fig 14.3 *representation and misrepresentation*

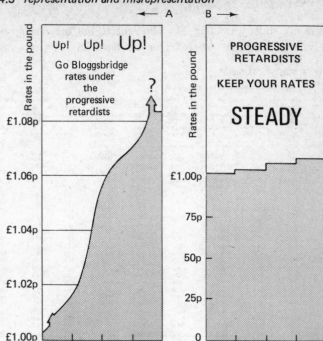

## Fig 14.4 *the Cold War (a non-quantitative line graph)*

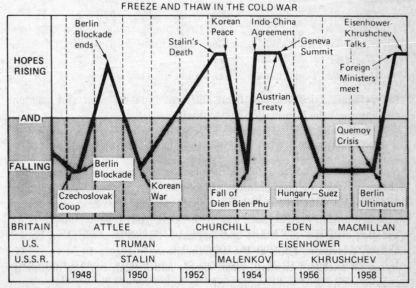

## 14.1 TABLES

Tables are not visually exciting, like some charts, but they are a valuable way of presenting often complex numeric facts in an *orderly* fashion.

**Fig 14.5**  *a statistical table*

Index of average earnings of all employees (new series)

Great Britain. Seasonally adjusted   Classified according to Standard Industrial Classification 1968      January 1976 = 100

| | Whole economy | | Index of Production industries | | Manufacturing industries | | Percentage change over previous 12 months | | |
|---|---|---|---|---|---|---|---|---|---|
| | Actual | Seasonally adjusted | Actual | Seasonally adjusted | Actual | Seasonally adjusted | Whole economy | Index of Production industries | Manufacturing |
| 1977 | 115.6 | 115.6 | 117.2 | 117.2 | 117.1 | 117.1 | 9.0 | 10.3 | 10.2 |
| 1978 | 130.6 | 130.6 | 134.3 | 134.3 | 134.0 | 134.0 | 13.0 | 14.6 | 14.4 |
| 1979 | 150.9 | 150.9 | 154.9 | 154.9 | 154.9 | 154.9 | 15.5 | 15.4 | 15.6 |
| 1980 | 182.1 | 182.1 | 183.9 | 184.0 | 182.5 | 182.5 | 20.7 | 18.7 | 17.8 |
| 1977 October | 117.9 | 118.4 | 119.9 | 120.3 | 119.6 | 120.4 | 8.6 | 9.6 | 9.5 |
| November | 120.1 | 120.0 | 123.4 | 122.8 | 123.8 | 123.1 | 8.6 | 10.8 | 11.2 |
| December | 121.7 | 121.3 | 123.9 | 123.6 | 124.3 | 123.8 | 9.3 | 10.8 | 11.2 |
| 1978 January | 121.5 | 122.3 | 124.2 | 124.9 | 125.1 | 125.3 | 9.6 | 10.8 | 11.3 |
| February | 122.7 | 123.8 | 125.8 | 126.7 | 126.2 | 126.8 | 10.5 | 11.7 | 12.0 |
| March | 125.0 | 125.1 | 128.1 | 127.7 | 128.2 | 127.9 | 10.4 | 11.1 | 11.9 |
| April | 127.2 | 127.4 | 131.7 | 131.5 | 132.2 | 131.8 | 12.4 | 14.9 | 15.5 |
| May | 129.4 | 128.6 | 134.2 | 132.6 | 133.6 | 131.7 | 12.6 | 14.91 | 14.3 |
| June | 133.1 | 132.1 | 136.1 | 135.0 | 135.1 | 134.1 | 15.4 | 16.7 | 16.3 |
| July | 133.6 | 132.0 | 136.6 | 135.4 | 135.9 | 135.1 | 14.2 | 16.2 | 15.9 |
| August | 131.7 | 132.3 | 134.4 | 136.4 | 133.5 | 135.8 | 13.9 | 16.0 | 15.5 |
| September | 134.2 | 134.5 | 137.1 | 138.6 | 135.9 | 137.8 | 15.0 | 16.4 | 15.8 |
| October | 135.2 | 135.7 | 139.7 | 140.2 | 139.1 | 140.0 | 14.7 | 16.5 | 16.3 |
| November | 136.1 | 136.0 | 141.1 | 140.3 | 140.6 | 139.8 | 13.3 | 14.3 | 13.5 |
| December | 138.0 | 137.5 | 142.8 | 142.4 | 142.8 | 142.1 | 13.4 | 15.2 | 14.8 |
| 1979 January | 135.7 | 136.7 | 139.8 | 140.6 | 140.3 | 140.6 | 11.7 | 12.6 | 12.2 |
| February | 141.1 | 142.5 | 143.7 | 144.7 | 144.6 | 145.4 | 15.0 | 14.3 | 14.6 |
| March | 143.7 | 143.8 | 149.9 | 149.5 | 150.2 | 149.9 | 14.9 | 17.1 | 17.2 |
| April | 144.3 | 144.6 | 149.5 | 149.2 | 149.7 | 149.1 | 13.5 | 13.5 | 13.2 |
| May | 146.9 | 146.0 | 153.0 | 151.1 | 154.3 | 152.1 | 13.5 | 14.0 | 15.5 |
| June | 150.9 | 149.8 | 157.9 | 156.6 | 158.6 | 157.4 | 13.4 | 16.0 | 17.4 |
| July | 155.6 | 153.8 | 158.2 | 156.8 | 158.2 | 157.2 | 16.5 | 15.8 | 16.4 |
| August[1] | 153.3 | 154.1 | 153.5 | 155.9 | 151.5 | 154.2 | 16.5 | 14.3 | 13.5 |
| September[1] | 153.6 | 153.9 | 153.7 | 155.4 | 151.9 | 154.1 | 14.4 | 12.2 | 11.8 |
| October | 158.1 | 158.7 | 162.6 | 163.2 | 161.8 | 162.9 | 16.9 | 16.4 | 16.4 |
| November | 162.1 | 162.1 | 167.2 | 166.3 | 167.1 | 166.2 | 19.2 | 18.5 | 18.9 |
| December[1] | 165.1 | 164.5 | 170.2 | 169.8 | 170.3 | 169.5 | 19.7 | 19.2 | 19.3 |
| 1980 January[1] | 163.0 | 164.2 | 167.2 | 168.2 | 166.8 | 167.1 | 20.2 | 19.6 | 18.9 |
| February[1] | 167.3 | 169.0 | 170.0 | 171.2 | 168.8 | 169.7 | 18.6 | 18.3 | 16.7 |
| March[1] | 172.8 | 172.9 | 177.2 | 176.8 | 174.4 | 174.1 | 20.3 | 18.2 | 16.1 |
| April | 175.0 | 175.3 | 178.4 | 178.0 | 176.9 | 176.2 | 21.3 | 19.3 | 18.2 |
| May | 178.1 | 177.0 | 181.6 | 179.4 | 181.4 | 178.8 | 21.3 | 18.7 | 17.6 |
| June | 183.7 | 182.3 | 187.0 | 185.5 | 186.7 | 185.3 | 21.7 | 18.4 | 17.7 |
| July | 185.1 | 182.8 | 189.6 | 188.0 | 188.2 | 187.0 | 18.9 | 19.9 | 18.9 |
| August | 186.5 | 187.6 | 188.6 | 189.6 | 185.3 | 188.7 | 21.7 | 21.6 | 22.4 |
| September | 193.6 | 194.1 | 189.1 | 191.2 | 186.9 | 189.6 | 26.1 | 23.0 | 23.1 |
| October | 189.9 | 190.6 | 190.0 | 190.7 | 187.8 | 189.1 | 20.1 | 16.8 | 16.1 |
| November | 192.6 | 192.6 | 194.0 | 193.1 | 192.5 | 191.5 | 18.9 | 16.1 | 15.2 |
| December | 197.3 | 196.5 | 196.5 | 196.1 | 194.0 | 193.1 | 19.5 | 15.5 | 13.9 |
| 1981 January | 193.3 | 194.8 | 195.6 | 196.8 | 193.5 | 193.9 | 18.6 | 17.0 | 16.0 |
| February | 194.8 | 196.8 | 198.4 | 199.9 | 196.1 | 197.2 | 16.5 | 16.7 | 16.2 |
| March[2] | 197.7 | 197.8 | 202.3 | 201.8 | 198.7 | 198.4 | 14.4 | 14.2 | 14.0 |

1. The figures reflect abnormally low earnings owing to the effects of national disputes.
2. Provisional.

Before you can construct a chart to illustrate, for example, the results of a questionnaire, or a series of production-figure reports, you will need to sort the information into a table. Tables need:

(a) a title which clearly indicates the contents
(b) brief but explanatory headings to the columns and rows
(c) units of measurement (e.g. millions, dollars) clearly shown
(d) if appropriate, the source of the data (often given as a note)
(e) any explanatory comments presented as notes
(f) preferably a vertical arrangement of figures rather than a horizontal one (we are more used to seeing figures in columns not rows)
(g) sets of data which are to be compared placed close together.

The complex table shown in Figure 14.5 demonstrates these guidelines.

## 14.2 LINE GRAPHS

The advantages of line graphs compared with tables are clearly shown by Figure 14.6. The graph retains the detailed information of a table but at the same time trends are obvious and comparisons are simple to make.

In line graphs, the vertical scale should usually start at zero to avoid creating false impressions, and if time is an element, it is always shown on the horizontal axis (see Figure 14.6).

Fig 14.6   *a complex line graph*

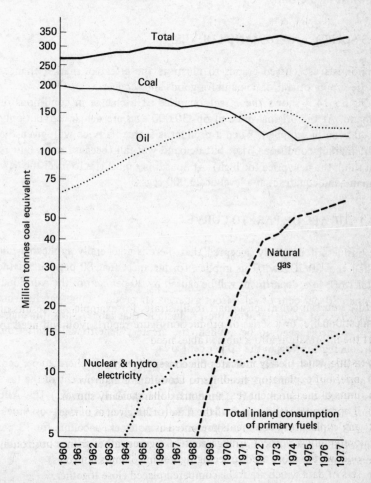

There are many variations to a line graph. A simple line graph would show only one set of information, i.e. one line. The complex line graph shows several sets.

Figure 14.7 is a complex line graph on which the vertical scale is an index scale. (Did you notice that the table in Figure 14.5 used an index, not actual wages?). This graph emphasises the rate of change of data rather than changes in actual amounts. The index scale shows percentage changes which have taken place since the base figure, for 1973, was calculated. The use of a zero line and a negative scale would allow decreases as well as increases to be shown.

*Straight-line graphs* are used when there is a direct variation between two sets of data. Thus hourly paid work involves a direct variation between pay and hours, and if pay is 90 pence per hour, we can draw the graph shown as Figure 14.8.

## 14.3 SUPPLY AND DEMAND CURVES

Economists use curved graphs to illustrate the effect of market changes on the supply of and/or demand for goods and services.

Figure 14.9 shows the effect on price of a change in conditions of demand. At the original price of 6p, 30,000 eggs are demanded, but only 20,000 can be supplied. When a product is scarce its price will, given the right market conditions, rise, but demand will fall (because some buyers will think the new price too high). At 8p, supply must rise to meet the new demand and equates it at a level of 25,000 eggs.

## 14.4 THE ABC OR PARETO CURVE

In business it is widely accepted that there is a generally applicable rule called the '80/20 law'. This implies, for instance, that 80 per cent of the total work in a department will be caused by 20 per cent of the workload, or that 80 per cent of sales from a particular product range results from the success of 20 per cent of the products in that range. Thus if management controls need to be applied, the greatest benefit will result from introducing controls in the 20 per cent area.

In Figure 14.10 this 'law' is applied to stock control, where 20 per cent of high-cost, fast-moving stock items account for 80 per cent of the total cost of all the stock held. (Note that the curve is convex.) The ABC grouping can be clearly seen. Class A is the 20 per cent of high-cost stock. Class B, the medium-cost, medium-movement stock, accounts for 13 per cent of all stock costs. Finally, Class C, slow-moving and low-cost, is only 7 per cent.

**Fig 14.7** *a complex line graph with index scale*

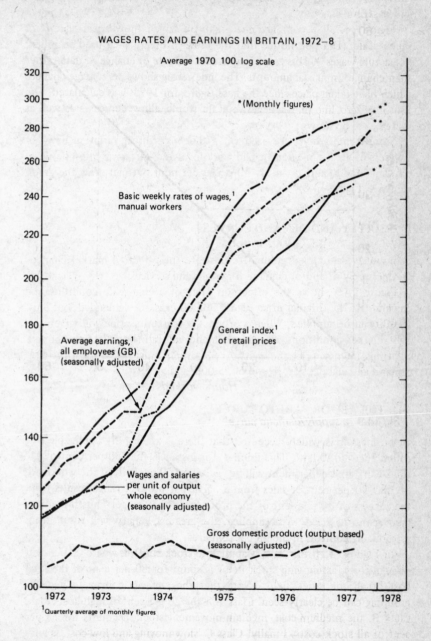

WAGES RATES AND EARNINGS IN BRITAIN, 1972–8

Average 1970 100. log scale

*(Monthly figures)

Basic weekly rates of wages,[1]
manual workers

General index[1]
of retail prices

Average earnings,[1]
all employees (GB)
(seasonally adjusted)

Wages and salaries
per unit of output
whole economy
(seasonally adjusted)

Gross domestic product (output based)
(seasonally adjusted)

[1] Quarterly average of monthly figures

Fig 14.8 *a straight-line graph*

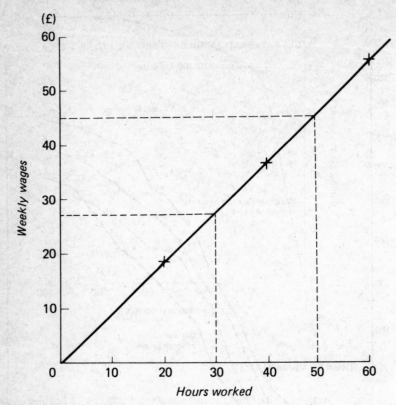

Fig 14.9 *a supply/demand curve*

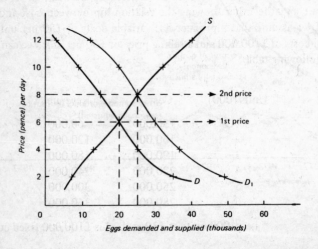

Fig 14.10  *ABC/Pareto curve*

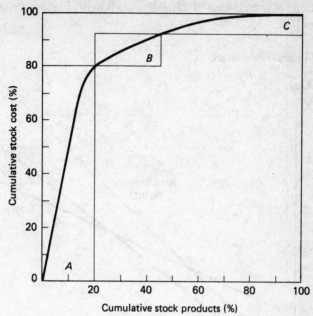

## 14.5 BREAKEVEN CHARTS

A simple breakeven chart like the one shown in Figure 14.11 enables us to show the profit or loss for a given output, and thus is a useful planning tool. It has two lines, one showing the relationship between the revenue and output and the other showing the relationship between cost and output.

If we assume that a product has variable costs of £30 per unit, overall fixed costs of £100,000 and a selling price of £60 per unit, we can produce the following table:

| Units (000) | Costs (£) | Revenue (£) |
|:---:|:---:|:---:|
| 1 | 130,000* | 60,000 |
| 2 | 160,000 | 120,000 |
| 3 | 190,000 | 180,000 |
| 4 | 220,000 | 240,000 |
| 5 | 250,000 | 300,000 |
| 6 | 280,000 | 360,000 |

\* i.e. 1,000 units at £30 each plus £100,000 fixed costs.

This table enables us to construct the breakeven chart, Figure 14.11, which shows that an output of 350,000 units is needed before we begin to make a profit.

Fig 14.11  *breakeven chart*

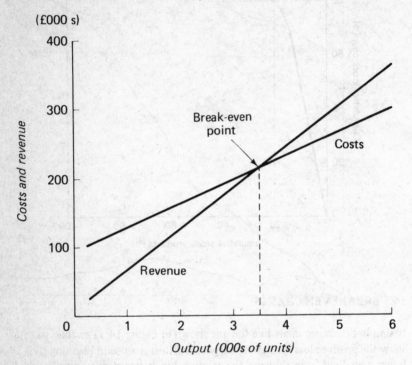

## 14.6 Z CHARTS

Z charts are easily recognised because the three graphs of which they are made up do, indeed, form a 'Z' shape (as shown in Figure 14.12). On this diagram we can show:

(a) the original data, here the current monthly sales figures for company A
(b) the cumulative figures for the period covered
(c) the moving annual total which indicates the trend.

The moving annual total for December in the period covered by Figure 14.12 is the total sales for December plus the sales during the previous eleven months. Similarly, the total for November is calculated by adding November's sales to those of the previous eleven months.

Fig 14.12   *a Z chart*

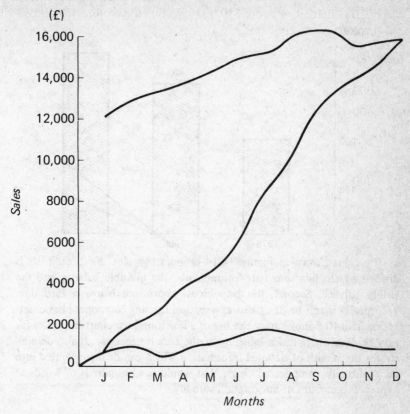

## 14.7 BAR OR BLOCK CHARTS

Bar or block charts are very popular because they have considerable visual impact, especially if colours or shading are used, and this makes them particularly useful for visual aids and the mass media. They can be produced in various formats and thus be adapted to illustrate a wide range of information.

(Strictly speaking, a 'bar' chart uses a single ruled line rather than the 'blocks' shown, for example, in Figure 14.13, but 'block' charts are commonly known as bar charts, the term used in this chapter.)

Figure 14.13 is a simple vertical bar chart, where the height of each bar shows the gross profit for the year, and comparisons are easy, and the trend, though short-term, is clear.

Fig 14.13 *a simple vertical bar chart*

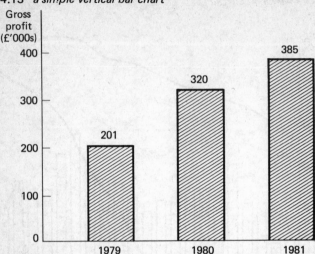

The chart shown in Figure 14.14 is more complex. First, each bar is divided by shading into two 'components, the invisible balance and the visible balance. Second, the bars 'float' above and below a zero line. Technically it can be described as a vertical floating component bar chart.

Figure 14.15 shows how the use of a horizontal bar chart can make for easy reading where much labelling of the bars is necessary. It also demonstrates the wealth of detailed information which can be incorporated into an admittedly complicated chart. You would need hundreds of words to express this amount of information verbally.

## 14.8 GANTT CHARTS

A Gantt chart is really a progress chart. Usually it consists of two horizontal bars for each period of time. One bar indicates the planned, anticipated or target performance, the other the actual figures. Figure 14.16 shows the actual sales of a commodity set against planned sales over a period of six weeks.

## 14.9 **HISTOGRAMS**

A histogram is yet another type of bar chart. It shows the *frequency* of occurrence of the subject being studied, within defined limits. In the following table we are studying the mileage recorded by the 100 salesmen of a company during one week. The class limit or interval is 20 miles. The frequency of occurrence is the numbers of salesmen within each class interval.

Fig 14.14 *a floating bar chart*

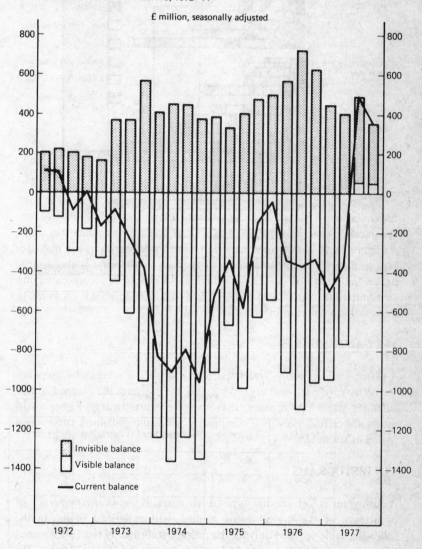

U.K. BALANCE OF PAYMENTS, 1972–77

£ million, seasonally adjusted

Invisible balance
Visible balance
—— Current balance

Fig 14.15 *a horizontal bar chart*

EXPENDITURE PATTERNS: BY TYPE OF HOUSEHOLD

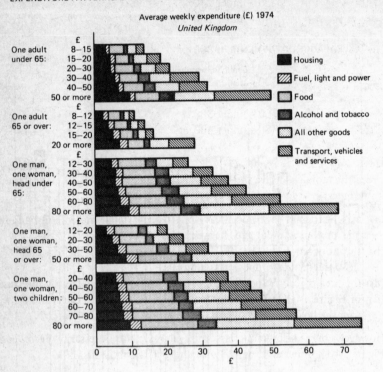

Average weekly expenditure (£) 1974
*United Kingdom*

Fig 14.16 *Gantt chart*

*Production record*

| | Monday | Tuesday | Wednesday | Thursday | Friday |
|---|---|---|---|---|---|
| *Planned production* | | | | | |
| *Actual production* | | | | | |

| Miles | Salesman |
|---|---|
| 200 – under 220 | 4 |
| 220 – under 240 | 6 |
| 240 – under 260 | 10 |
| 260 – under 280 | 14 |
| 280 – under 300 | 18 |
| 300 – under 320 | 15 |
| 320 – under 340 | 12 |
| 340 – under 360 | 9 |
| 360 – under 380 | 7 |
| 380 – under 400 | 5 |

From the table we derive the histogram shown in Figure 14.17. You should note that:

(a) in a histogram (but not always in a bar chart) all the columns adjoin one another without gaps between

(b) the horizontal axis has the usual continuous scale which includes all the units of the grouped class intervals

(c) the area of each block is proportionate to the frequency of the class

(d) in Figure 14.17 the class intervals are even (20 miles each) and there-fore the height of each block is proportional to the frequency.

However, in a histogram class intervals are not necessarily even, and Figure 14.18 shows an example with uneven class intervals.

**Fig 14.17** *a histogram with equal frequency distribution*

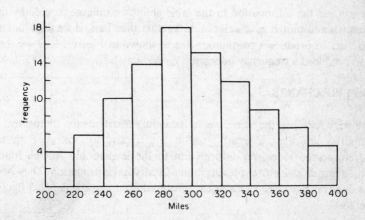

Fig 14.18 *a histogram with unequal frequency distribution*

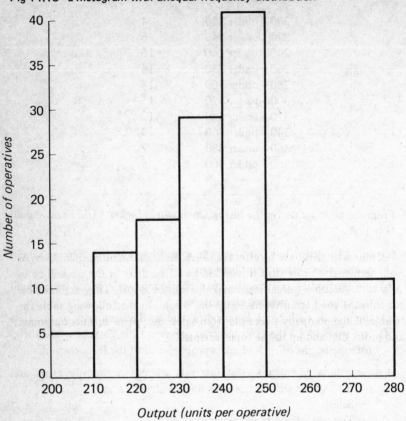

## 14.10 FREQUENCY POLYGONS

We can use the information in the table about the mileage covered by the salesmen and plot it as a series of dots rather than bars. If we then join up the dots to produce a continuous line as shown in Figure 14.19 we shall have produced a frequency polygon.

## 14.11 PIE CHARTS

The pie chart has the same two outstanding merits as the pictogram: it simplifies information greatly, and it is attractive to look at. Both are therefore used to convey information to the layman and will be found in newspaper and poster presentation of statistical information. They have the disadvantage of generalising the information so that the detailed figures are 'lost'.

**Fig 14.19** *a frequency polygon*

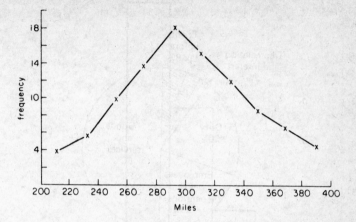

A pie chart will only be effective when there are no more than seven or eight segments – more than this and some of the slices of the pie will be so slim as to become insignificant and the impact is lost. They are valuable for showing the parts that make up the whole. In the following table the 'whole' is the company's receipts from sales, the 'parts' are the outgoings and profit that add up to the total receipts:

|  | £m. |
|---|---|
| Sales | 760 |
| The cost of goods and services | 370 |
| Duty | 149 |
| Employees' pay and pension contributions | 149 |
| Depreciation and interest | 30 |
| Profit before tax | 62 |

We can turn this table into the pie chart of Figure 14.20. First, we have to remember that a circle has 360° and that those 360° represent the total sales of £738m. We can then calculate that the slice of the pie that represents the cost of goods and services is approximately:

$$\frac{370}{738} \times 360 = 180°$$

Similar calculations will give us the slices of the pie which are to represent the other outgoings, and we can use shading to give the diagram, or part of it, more impact.

Fig 14.20  *a pie chart*

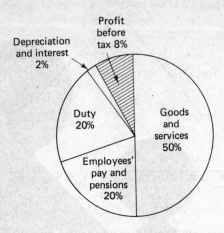

## 14.12 PICTOGRAMS

Pictograms are diagrams which use pictures to represent figures and thus are easily understood irrespective of language or numeracy problems. They are attractive and interesting to look at. Although, like pie charts, they cannot give very detailed information, they can show trends (as in Figure 14.21), comparisons and totals.

The comparative pictogram of Figure 14.22 uses a less satisfactory technique because it is not easy to make quantitative comparisons from the relative sizes of the figures.

Fig 14.21  *a pictogram*

INCREASE IN AIR PASSENGERS

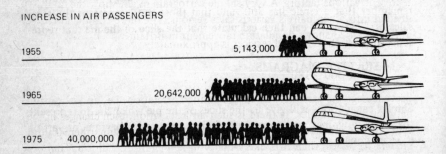

| | |
|---|---|
| 1955 | 5,143,000 |
| 1965 | 20,642,000 |
| 1975 | 40,000,000 |

Fig 14.22 *a comparative pictogram*

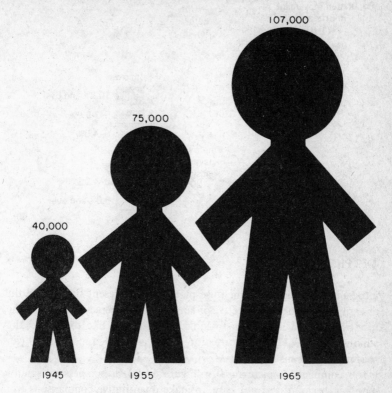

TOTAL MALE STAFF EMPLOYED BY ELECTRONICS CO.

107,000

75,000

40,000

1945          1955                    1965

## 14.13 CARTOGRAMS

These are maps on which we superimpose symbols, shading, figures, etc. to represent various factors. A very simple cartogram might show the country divided into a company's various sales regions. The more complicated one in Figure 14.23 shows population movement in Britain.

## 14.14 SCATTER DIAGRAMS

Scatter diagrams are one way of indicating correlation, i.e. an association between two variables. If there is such an association, then changes in the value of one are associated with changes in the value of the other. If your income increases, then it is likely that your expenditure will too. That is a

**Fig 14.23** *a cartogram*

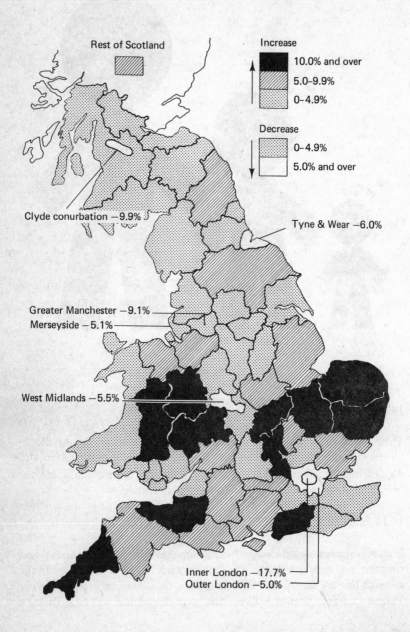

Population movement
in Britain,
1971–81

Rest of Scotland

Increase

10.0% and over

5.0–9.9%

0–4.9%

Decrease

0–4.9%

5.0% and over

Clyde conurbation −9.9%

Tyne & Wear −6.0%

Greater Manchester −9.1%
Merseyside −5.1%

West Midlands −5.5%

Inner London −17.7%
Outer London −5.0%

simple everyday correlation. If a company spends more on advertising, its sales may increase (but not necessarily, since other factors, like competition, are involved).

A scatter diagram (or scatter graph) simply provides a means of deciding whether or not there is association between variables. Figure 14.24 shows

Fig 14.24 *a scatter diagram*

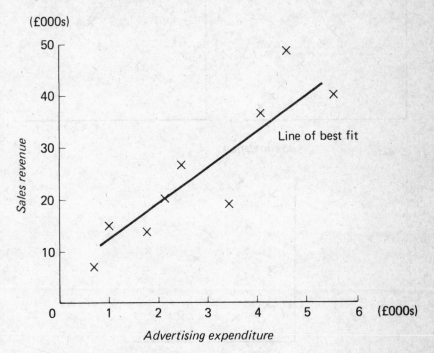

a scatter diagram with the scale for one variable, advertising expenditure, on the horizontal axis, and the other scale, for sales revenue, on the vertical axis. Each pair of figures is then plotted as a single point on the graph. Having plotted our points, we must look to see if there is any pattern among the points.

In Figure 14.24 there is such a pattern, and we have drawn a 'line of best fit' which has the same number of points on each side. Our line indicates a *positive* correlation, i.e. as advertising expenditure is increased, so sales revenue tends to rise. The graph does not 'prove' a causal relationship but indicates that there may be association between the variables. In other words, the scatter diagram gives an indication which may be the first piece of evidence in an investigation.

Other types of correlation are shown in Figure 14.25.

## Fig 14.25 *types of correlation*

*perfect negative correlation*

*perfect positive correlation*

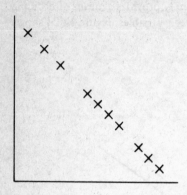

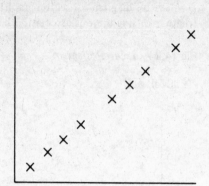

*no correlation*

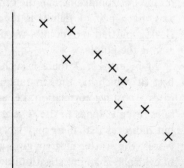

*positive correlation*

*negative correlation*

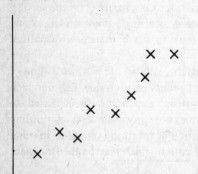

## 14.15 ACTIVITY CHARTS AND FLOW CHARTS

Activity charts are a diagrammatic representation of the flow of work through the various operations of a system, and flow charts provide the best example of this type of chart.

Flow charts give a graphic picture of the logical steps and the sequence involved in a procedure. They help the systems analyst (see Figure 14.26) and the computer programmer (see Figure 14.27) to break down a problem

Fig 14.26   *paperwork flow chart*

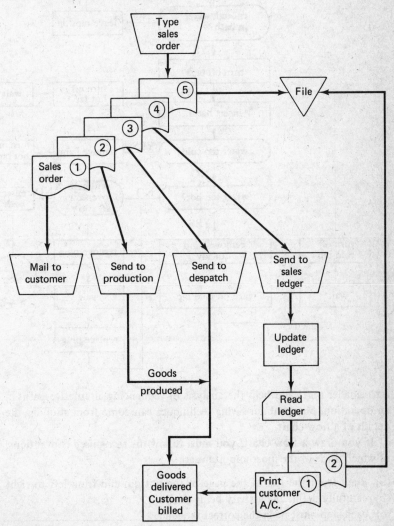

Fig 14.27  *a flow chart*

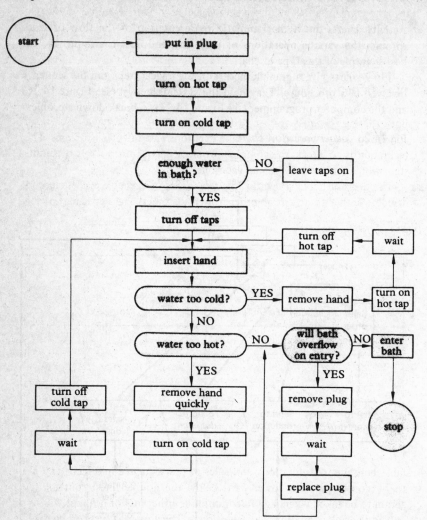

into smaller parts and help the analysis of sequencing alternative paths in an operation. Many labour-saving techniques can come from studying the details of a flow chart.

If you draw a flow chart, you must follow the recognised conventions, of which some of the most important are:

(a)  draw from the top of the page to the bottom and from left to right
(b)  carefully define the activity being shown
(c)  each step must be in the correct sequence

(d) the single start and end points must be clearly shown
(e) the conventional symbols should be used, for example arrows to indicate the direction of flow
(f) decision points must be clearly distinguished from actions by the shape of the box.

## 14.16 DECISION TABLES AND ALGORITHMS

Both these techniques are used to help people find the way easily through complex rules of procedure, to take decisions and to solve problems. The technique is to break the complex problem down into a series of simple steps which require only yes/no decisions.

The decision table shown in Figure 14.28 would enable a sales clerk to decide whether to accept an order from a customer. The upper part of the

Fig 14.28 *decision table*

| ORDER PROCESSING<br>1. Acceptance procedure | RULES/ACTIONS | | | |
|---|---|---|---|---|
| Is the order within the credit limit? | Yes | No | | |
| Is the payment record good? | | Yes | No | |
| Are quantities above minimum order level? | | | Yes | No |
| Approve order | X | X | X | X |
| Reject order | | | | X |

table contains the questions and rules in the sequence in which they are to be considered. The lower part, below the double lines, contains the action to be taken when a given condition is either met or not met.

The sales clerk first answers question 1. The answer is 'yes', so he reads down the column to the X and sees that he can approve the order. Had the answer to question 1 been 'no', he would next check question 2. If the answer is 'yes', he again reads down the column to the X and finds that he can approve the order. If the answer to question 2 were 'no', he would move on to question 3 and again read down the column to the appropriate X and the decision. In this particular table he would only reject an order if the answer to all three questions had been 'no'.

The algorithm shown in Figure 14.29 takes the reader through a series of simple yes/no responses to the answers to the complex question, 'What

Fig 14.29  *an algorithm*

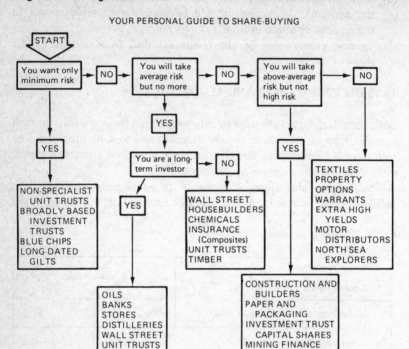

YOUR PERSONAL GUIDE TO SHARE-BUYING

shares should I buy?' Such diagrams can also be used for complex procedures like finding the fault in a TV set.

## 14.17 ORGANISATION CHARTS

These are the family trees of the organisation and are used to show:

(a) levels of authority and responsibility from the top to the bottom of the organisation
(b) divisional, departmental interrelationships in the organisation
(c) the lines of formal communication channels
(d) the relative status and prestige of employees.

Figure 14.30 shows an example. What it does not show is the informal organisation that may have developed. Some individuals will have come to command status, even authority, through the force of their personality, and this will not be shown on the chart. For mainly psychological reasons, and to improve human relations, organisation charts are often shown in a circular or horizontal form.

**Fig 14.30** *organisation chart*

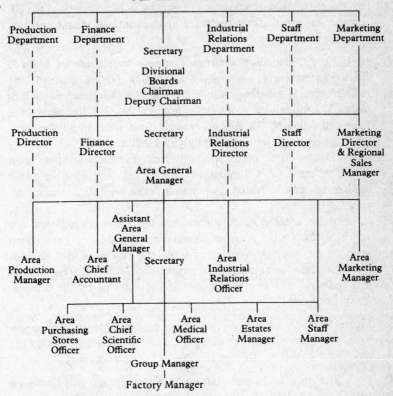

PLASTIC NOVELTIES BOARD

Chairman
Deputy Chairman
Full- and Part-time Members

| Production Department | Finance Department | | Industrial Relations Department | Staff Department | Marketing Department |

Secretary

Divisional
Boards
Chairman
Deputy Chairman

| Production Director | Finance Director | Secretary | Industrial Relations Director | Staff Director | Marketing Director & Regional Sales Manager |

Area General Manager

Assistant
Area
General
Manager

| Area Production Manager | Area Chief Accountant | Secretary | Area Industrial Relations Officer | | Area Marketing Manager |

| Area Purchasing Stores Officer | Area Chief Scientific Officer | Area Medical Officer | Area Estates Manager | Area Staff Manager |

Group Manager

Factory Manager

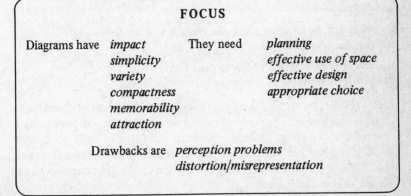

## FOCUS

Diagrams have  *impact*    They need  *planning*
*simplicity*      *effective use of space*
*variety*      *effective design*
*compactness*    *appropriate choice*
*memorability*
*attraction*

Drawbacks are  *perception problems*
*distortion/misrepresentation*

## 14.18 ASSIGNMENTS

1  Describe a suitable type of chart or diagram to show each of the following and append an illustrative sketch of any one of them:
   (a) progress of work being made in completing a plan
   (b) the circulation of a national newspaper in each county of the UK
   (c) the division of total cost of a product into its main categories.

   [IAA]

2  In 1970, 1,090 million passenger journeys were made on Bloobell Railways, yielding £137.6 million in receipts. Of the journeys, 351 million were at full fares, 426 million at reduced fares and an estimated 313 million by season-ticket holders. By 1973, journeys at full fares had fallen by 78 million, reduced fares went up by 9 million, while season-ticket journeys went up by 4 million.

   During the same period, receipts from full fares went up from £59.7 million to £74.0 million, reduced fares went up from £46.1 million to £54.1 million and season-ticket receipts increased by £5.9 million.

   Draw up a table which summarises the above information and which brings out the principal changes between the two years. Comment on any ways in which you think the data given in your table are inadequate for purposes of interpretation of the progress of Bloobell Railways and any subsequent decision-making by the management. [RSA DPA]

3  Figure 14.31 shows a flow chart whose content is logical and appropriate but whose layout is disorderly and does not conform to the required conventions. Redraw it, using an improved layout.

4  Look at Figure 14.32 and choose the three symbols you find most apt. (You will find the ones which performed best in tests listed in Appendix 1.)

5  What are the advantage and disadvantages of the following?
   (a) bar charts
   (b) tabular presentation
   (c) flow charting
   (d) Gantt charts

**Fig 14.31** *a flow chart*

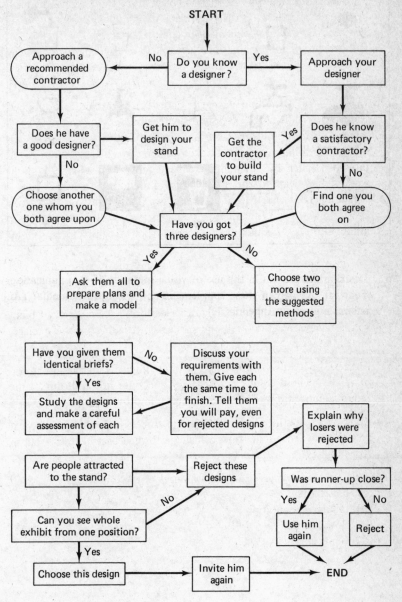

HOW TO OBTAIN A WELL-DESIGNED EXHIBITION STAND

Fig 14.32 *public information symbols*

6   Describe the growth in the use of visual methods of communication. To what extent can these supplement or replace other media? (An answer is given in Appendix 1.)

# ANALYSIS AND INTERPRETATION

The natural extension to the process of talking and writing, listening and reading, is the ability to understand, analyse and interpret communication. This skill is constantly needed in all aspects of work and it is therefore tested in most examinations, not only those specifically concerned with communication skills.

This chapter is thus concerned with two aspects: the practical application of analytical and interpretative skills, and the approach required in examinations.

## 15.1 APPLICATIONS AT WORK

In our normal working lives we are asked to look at, understand and use a very wide range of information and data. Much of it is familiar and presents little difficulty, but the following examples will show some of the problems that can occur:

1. *You have been asked to prepare proposals for the reorganisation of the layout of a factory floor, or a large office, or a shop. As you are not familiar with the laws and regulations governing the environment, and health and safety at work, you have to read the appropriate sections of the various statutes.*

PROBLEMS

(a) Legal language is notoriously complex and difficult to understand.
(b) From among the lengthy and numerous statutes you have to establish which particular portions are applicable to your problem.
(c) You must then be able to show exactly how each regulation would affect your proposals for the new layout. For instance, where there is a general formula for determining the number of people who can legally work in a room 10 metres square, there will also be require-

ments about size of gangways, and so on. There may, however, be a 'grey' area when it comes to deciding to what extent the working area of the room is in law considered to be diminished by the amount of equipment contained in the room.

(d) Having completed your analysis, you will then have to present your conclusions to management in a succinct and clear manner, 'translating' the complicated wording of the original where necessary.

> 2. *Your firm has decided to make much more financial information available to its employees. As one of the employee representatives you have been given the end-of-year financial information and have been asked to explain it to your colleagues at a forthcoming meeting.*

PROBLEMS

(a) You may have limited or no accountancy knowledge. Even if you have it, your colleagues will not necessarily be as well informed. So you will have to seek methods of presenting the complex information simply, and this means having a very clear understanding of it yourself, if necessary researching the subject.

(b) Many people find figures easier to understand than words, but the converse is also very true. You may be figure-blind, so how can you possibly comprehend a balance-sheet?

> 3. *You have been asked to analyse the last five years' sales to determine any market changes reflected in them. The information is only available to you in the form of computer printouts giving daily sales by regions, itemised by product (a range of small hardware items).*

PROBLEMS

This example combines many of the problems in the two earlier examples: complexity, amount of material, figures as well as words.

## 15.2 EFFECTIVE APPROACHES

Each individual must determine the particular approach that must be adopted for any one problem. There are, however, certain general principles that can help.

(a) Make a practice of carrying out consistent background study relevant to all aspects of your job; for example, reading textbooks, financial papers or specialist journals, attending courses or conferences, listening to radio or watching television programmes that may give you a wider background.

(b) Think carefully about the information you are trying to obtain so that you will be able to determine quickly which portions of any document will be relevant to your purpose. (See also the techniques on reading suggested in Chapter 9.)

(c) Expand your knowledge of language by using a dictionary when you come across unfamiliar words and by reading more widely.

(d) To overcome 'figure blindness' treat the numbers as words and try to see the pattern that is emerging rather than working out precise figures. For instance, in the following passage there are many figures.

*The pattern of machine-tool production is highly cyclical; deliveries last year were valued at £190 million, including numerically controlled tools worth £19 million. Exports of complete machines had a value of £97 million, 11 per cent up on the previous year. Of the orders on hand at the end of last year (£96 million), 56 per cent were for export; Australia (£9 million), the Federal Republic of Germany (£8 million). France (£7 million) and Italy (£6 million) were the main overseas markets last year.*

*Seven of the industry's 200 or so companies provide over half of total deliveries, though because of the high degree of specialisation small firms provide the remainder.*

Suppose you were asked to estimate the average exports of an average small machine-tool firm. The crucial parts of the passage are the second and last sentences, and the analysis and interpretation process would be the following.

(i) Total exports were £97 million.

(ii) Seven of the 200 companies provide a little over half of total deliveries

(iii) Thus 193 (200 − 7) small companies provide just under half of the £97 million. (A complicated calculation now looms in front of our eyes. Let's simplify it — you were only asked for an *estimate*.)

(iv) 193 is nearly 200: £97 million is nearly £100 million. Half of £100 million is £50 million.

(v) So the estimated average exports of an average small firm would be:

$$\frac{£50 \text{ million}}{200} = \frac{£5 \text{ million}}{20} = £\tfrac{1}{4} \text{ million}$$

(e) The analysis of charts and graphs is made easier if you apply the suggestions made earlier and also familiarise yourself with the various types of charts and graphs (see Chapter 14). By understanding how to compile and present data you will more easily be able to comprehend and interpret them.

---

**FOCUS**

Expand your knowledge
Determine what you need to know
Increase your vocabulary
Treat numbers as words
Become familiar with charts and graphs

---

## 15.3 EXAMINATION QUESTIONS

This and following sections are primarily concerned with the answering of comprehension questions in communication examinations. The advice given and techniques discussed are, however, applicable to most other examination questions which demand the ability to interpret and comment on data.

## 15.4 THE NATURE OF COMPREHENSION QUESTIONS

It is very difficult to reproduce in an examination paper the practical working applications discussed earlier. The assessment of different aspects of your ability to understand, interpret and use information has to be made on the basis of specific written answers. Thus comprehension questions are often academic in nature, requiring: definitions of words and phrases, to assess understanding; replacement of vocabulary by synonyms, to illustrate language capability; comment on argument, to show analytical ability; compression of parts of the passage, to show ability for concise expression; and so on.

A methodical approach and an ability to recognise the implications of each question are needed and the following suggestions may prove helpful.

## 15.5 METHOD

(a) Read the passage through at least twice, or until you have really understood it.
(b) Read the questions very carefully.

(c) Re-read the passage, searching for answers to the questions. It may be helpful to mark the appropriate points of the passage by putting the question numbers in the margin.

(d) Write your answers.

(e) Check your work for omissions, unnecessary information and accuracy.

## 15.6 GENERAL ADVICE

(a) Number your answers accurately.

(b) Avoid presenting your answers out of sequence if possible.

(c) Set your answers out clearly. Look at the worked answer to assignment 1 of this chapter to see how this may best be done.

(d) Write in complete sentences except, for example, in vocabulary questions or when you are asked to give a list.

(e) Use your own words, not those of the passage, whenever possible.

(f) Recognise the limits of each question. Resist the temptation to write at length. Some students use the 'shotgun' technique of including everything that may conceivably be relevant in the hope of somehow hitting the target. Such a technique will lose marks. Your answers must be as brief and to the point as possible.

(g) Confine yourself to the information given in the passage unless you are asked a general-knowledge type of question.

(h) Your answers should rarely overlap. If you find yourself giving the same information in answer to more than one question, the chances are that at least one of your answers is wrong.

## 15.7 TYPES OF QUESTION

If you can recognise the different types of question you may be asked, it will be easier to produce an answer which is to the point and which conforms to the limits of the question. The main types of question are listed below.

### Vocabulary

Typical questions may be phrased as shown in the following examples:

> *Explain the meaning of the following words as they are used in the passage* . . .
> *Explain, in context, the meaning of* . . .
> *Give an alternative word or phrase for* . . .

(a) Your answer must be set out to include the original word used and your own alternative, for example:

| ORIGINAL WORD | YOUR ALTERNATIVE |
|---|---|
| *connotations* | *implications* |

(b) Your answer must use the same part of speech, or its equivalent, as the original. Test this by checking that your answer can replace the original word in the passage. For example, either (but not both) of these answers would be appropriate:

> *hurriedly – with haste* (or) *quickly*

(c) Give one answer only. If you give more than one, the examiner will mark the first and ignore others. Do not give an answer like these examples:

> *lure – attraction, enticement*
> *lure – attraction or enticement*

It is permissible, if there is no one synonym available, to give two words linked by the conjunction *and*, provided that your answer obeys rule (b) above, for example:

> *anarchic flux – chaotic movement and change*

### Re-expression

The questions are similar to vocabulary questions but you are required to give the meaning of a phrase or sentence from the passage rather than the meaning of one word only. Such questions may be expressed as follows:

> *What does the author mean by . . . ?*
> *What do you understand by the following expression . . . ?*
> *Rewrite in your own words the following sentence . . . ?*

(a) Figures of speech should be changed into literal expressions, for example:

> *blue skies – free from problems*

(b) Your answer may be written either as a phrase which could replace the original one in the passage, or as a complete sentence.

### Interpretation

Such questions usually take the form of direct questions referring the student to the passage, for example:

> *Why does the author contend that . . . ?*
> *What reasons does the author give for . . . ?*
> *What conclusions does the author draw . . . ?*
> *Explain . . .*

The answers to these types of questions may be found in one sentence, or even a single phrase, in the passage. However, check carefully through the whole passage to ensure that you do not omit any relevant information.

## Summary

The questions are usually easily recognisable, for example:

> *Suggest two abstract nouns to describe . . .*
> *Describe in two or three sentences . . .*
> *Describe in about forty of your own words . . .*
> *Summarise in your own words . . .*

Do not waste any words in your answer. Your ability to express yourself concisely is being tested. Give your summary a heading if possible.

## Reasoning

These questions are among the most difficult to answer. They may take many forms, for example:

> *Do you agree with the author when he states . . . ?*
> *What are your views on . . . ?*

The marks will be awarded to students who demonstrate a logical approach even though the conclusions reached may vary. The reasoning in your answer should be supported by evidence and example wherever appropriate.

## General knowledge

Although comprehension exercises primarily test a student's understanding of a passage, some examinations include general-knowledge questions. Two such questions might be:

> *Name one or two Middle East nations.*
> *What do you understand by solvency?*

Students who are well read and keep themselves informed on current events by regular reading of newspapers will not usually find difficulty with these questions. Do not waste too much time on trying to work out or guess the answer.

---

### FOCUS

Recognise the implications and limits of each question
Present answers clearly, correctly and concisely
Questions are of the following types:

> **Focus** *cont.*
>
> | *Vocabulary* | *Re-expression* |
> | *Interpretation* | *Summary* |
> | *Reason* | *General knowledge* |
>
> Be orderly  – number answers carefully
> – set them out attractively

## 15.8 ASSIGNMENTS

1   The following extract is taken (with modifications) from *Video and Audio-Visual Review*, vol. 1 no. 10:

> For an industry whose prime concern is communication, the audio-visual aids business is remarkably ineffective at conveying its own image. Too many times we have attended demonstrations of new video recorders, tape systems, cine projectors, etc., where *paradoxically* anything but the equipment itself has been used to convey the sales message. One importer recently went so far as to use 16 mm cine film to portray its company identity, which would have been encouraging had the company not been launching a colour video tape machine.
>
> Not that we are ourselves beyond criticism. The *logical media* for *Video and Audio-Visual Review* might arguably be video tapes, video disc, film-strip or *microfiche*. However even in these days of rising publication costs, cold print remains substantially cheaper than any plastic-based magnetic format.

(a)  Would it make any difference to the sense, and why, if the first sentence had spoken of 'primary concern' instead of 'prime concern'?

(b)  In your own words, say what you understand by the following words or phrases in the extract: *paradoxically*; the *logical media; microfiche*.

(c)  If someone suggested that the extract was taken from an editorial, explain briefly what he meant and say whether you agree, and why.

(d)  In a word or two, give an example from the extract of a '*plastic-based magnetic format*'.

(e)  If a typewriter manufacturer sent out a beautifully designed sales letter written by a leading artist in superb italic script, what connection would this have with the ideas in the first paragraph of the extract?

In a few lines say how far you regard such ideas as valid or invalid.

[LCC PSC]

[See Appendix 1 for an answer.]

2   Read the following (amended) extract from *New Scientist* and then
    answer the questions below it.

### HOW DO GOVERNMENTS SUPPORT MICROELECTRONICS?

The President of France presented an *erudite* technical paper about
the development and use of microelectronics during a nationwide
campaign in France involving the *mass media* and special conferences
to examine the social impact of new technology. It coincided with a
major computer and electronics exhibition in Paris, which the
President and senior cabinet members attended.

In British terms, this is the equivalent to the Prime Minister giving a
paper to the British Computer Society and taking a personal initiative
in encouraging TV and Fleet Street to make a *concerted* attempt at
explaining the nature and effect of computers, microelectronics and
telecommunications.

These efforts by the French people to *augment* their information
industries stem from a desire to safeguard their national independence.
The particular event which is always *invoked* to explain this attitude
was the refusal of the United States in 1963 to allow France to import
a large computer in case it was used to develop nuclear weapon capability. Ever since, the French have believed it essential to have their
own *indigenous* capacity to build large computers.

The capability was one of the selling points stressed by the French
in their successful *overtures* to the USSR over the computer system
for the news agency TASS. 'No problems over a possible American
*embargo* because we make the components as well', was the line the
French put forward.

On the international level, France realised some time ago that a
flourishing computer and telecommunications industry would be a
passport to foreign currency through export earnings. On the home
front, information activities are politically much more sensitive than
in the UK. At one end of the scale there are constant outcries against
government control of the media. There have been many fears, too,
about the effects of information banks and computing facilities on the
balance of power within French society. If the *administration,* or
large industrial concerns, acquire vast data storage and are the only
ones able to afford the powerful computers to process the data,
what will happen to the balance of power between the citizen and
these bodies?

There is also much more concern over privacy and data protection
in France than in the UK. Another major political *issue* is the impact
of computers on employment, leisure patterns and life-styles in
general. All these topics have been grist to the French politician's

mill and food for the French press, which rivals some parts of the British and American press for inward-looking chauvinism. In other words, the political profile of data processing, telecommunications and other information sector activities in France is extremely high and explains why this sector receives so much government attention.

(a) The original article ran as follows' . . . 'for the newspaper TASS'. This is an error since TASS is a news agency, and the mistake has been corrected in the extract. However, if the mistake had to be retyped exactly as it stood, there would be various methods of indicating to the reader of the text that there was an uncorrected error. Name and describe TWO possible methods that might be used.

(b) TEN words or phrases in the extract have been shown in *italics*. Choose any *five* of them and explain briefly (in one or more words) their meaning as used in the passage. Particular importance is attached to your ability to answer precisely, aptly and clearly.

| | |
|---|---|
| erudite | indigenous |
| mass media | overtures |
| concerted | embargo |
| augment | administration |
| invoked | issue |

(c) Assume that you are the assistant to the sales manager of a computer firm which is hoping to export to France. He is shortly visiting France for preliminary discussions. However, he has not been there before and admits that he knows little about the attitudes of the French.

Having read the extract you decide he might be interested to see a photocopy of it. Draft a covering memo in which you explain to him what you have done and why you think it may be helpful, drawing attention to the main points.

(d) In a few lines say to what extent you consider the French approach to microelectronics is or is not commendable when compared with the British approach. There is no 'right answer', but your intelligent analysis of text is looked for.

(e) What is your opinion of the style of language used in the sentence beginning 'All these topics . . . ' (last paragraph), given the context?
[LCC PSC]

3  Inflation Accounting is becoming more widespread. Show your ability to understand the subject by answering the questions printed below:

Accounts generally record actual historical market transactions rather than estimated current values. They do not try to reflect the 'true worth' of a company. Although accounts have traditionally been prepared on a historical cost basis there is now an increasing desire to allow for the falling value of money over time. A generally conservative approach is a feature of accounting treatment, although companies are increasingly inclined to become more realistic.

(a) Why are the market transactions called 'historical'?
(b) In what way do conventional accounts not reflect 'true worth'?
(c) Why should there be any need to allow for the falling value of money?
(d) What is the implication of the word 'realistic'? [LCC PSD]

4 Study the following table and then answer the questions below it:

PUBLIC EXPENDITURE

£ million

|  | This year | Proposed cuts |
|---|---|---|
| Defence | 3;818 | 110 |
| Overseas services | 741 | 12 |
| Agriculture, fisheries and forestry | 853 | 152 |
| Trade, industry and employment | 1,421 | 3 |
| Nationalised industries | 2,394 | 100 |
| Roads and transport | 1,781 | 91 |
| Housing | 3,583 | 115 |
| Other environmental services | 1,558 | 85 |
| Law, order and protective services | 1,156 | 27 |
| Education and libraries, science and arts | 4,753 | 86 |
| Health and personal social services | 4,093 | 75 |
| Other public services | 507 | 17 |
| Social security | 7,625 | – |
| Common services | 1,582 | 28 |
|  | 35,865 | 901 |

(a) What approximate percentage of the total public expenditure is accounted for by *social security*?
(b) By what percentage approximately is it proposed to cut expenditure on *education and libraries, science and arts*?
(c) Which one of the areas of public expenditure listed above has suffered the greatest proportional cut?
(d) Use the information in the table to draw a suitable statistical diagram to be published in a newspaper under the heading 'Public expenditure – the proposed cuts'. Before drawing the diagram, simplify the information by reclassifying the areas of expenditure given in the table under no more than six appropriate headings. (See also Chapter 14.)

5 Using Figure 15.1, answer the following questions:

(a) What factors could help to account for the pattern of consumers' expenditure on alcoholic drink, as shown in the diagram?

(b) What advantages do seasonally adjusted figures of expenditure have over non-adjusted figures? [UNIVERSITY OF LONDON 'A' LEVEL ECONOMICS]

Fig 15.1  *consumers' expenditure on alcoholic drink*

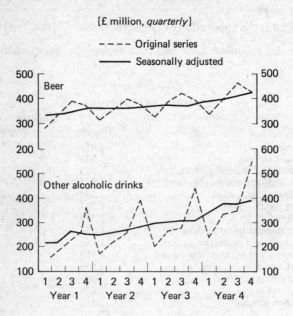

[£ million, *quarterly*]

– – – – Original series
——— Seasonally adjusted

# EXTERNAL AND INTERNAL COMMUNICATION

## 16.1 EXTERNAL COMMUNICATION

Since the Second World War business has had to live in an increasingly difficult and hostile climate. Through increasingly tight government control it has lost much of its autonomy.

A series of technological accidents (air disasters, thalidomide, Three Mile Island, asbestosis — the list could be extended almost indefinitely) and the less dramatic spread of pollution have caused tremendous public concern and led to a corresponding increase in legislation and control of commerce and industry's activities and products.

Currently the world recession, growing unemployment and the realisation that the new technologies will seriously limit future employment prospects have also contributed to the suspicion and distrust with which industry, reasonably or not, is surrounded.

### Public image and reputation

Industry needs to influence the climate in which it has to function. It has to demonstrate how it serves the public in providing it with employment and goods. It not only has to project an image which fulfils those essential functions but must also be aware of its responsibilities towards individuals as well as society in general.

There are several facets to this image. One is product quality; and our concept of quality is changing. Once it was sufficient for cars to be good-looking, comfortable, have high performance and be value for money. Now there is great emphasis on the safety of the design too. That demand for safety indicates another aspect of image, the producer's concern for the consumer.

Other positive facets of image are strength of management, financial strength, a contribution to the economy, export performance and the provision of local employment.

## The outside world

The outside world towards which the company image is to be projected has so far been referred to as the public. In fact, of course, it is a whole variety of publics, each with its own concerns.

(a) The most influential is government at its many levels, local, national, even supra-national, like the EEC.

At national level government policy and legislation control every aspect of business activity: wages, prices, dividends, product content and quality, safety, environmental protection, taxation. Government also controls large sectors of commerce and industry through ownership, by nationalisation, or less directly through holding companies like the British National Oil Corporation. Such government control exists in every country to a greater or lesser degree.

Government policies on, for example, trade, foreign affairs, finance, location of industry, etc. are also a powerful influence.

Companies need to improve both the amount and effectiveness of their communication with government and politicians: first, to keep in touch so that they can anticipate and adapt to changes of policy; and second, to keep government informed. Government should be aware of the needs of industry or its policies may have unforeseen and unsought effects. Speedy information and advice can avoid difficulties.

(b) The financial public includes not only individual shareholders whose capital finances industry but also other interests such as pension-fund administrators, unit trusts, banks and stockbrokers. The information they look for includes earnings records, estimates of future earnings, the company's competitive position, the competence of management, the growth potential of markets.

(c) Educators and students are another special section of the public. They have been largely ignored by business in the past, and this may be one reason why the most able students (in Britain at least) have preferred academic or civil service careers to industrial ones. Teachers generally have a lack of business or industrial experience; they go through the educational system from school to college/university and then back to teach in schools or colleges. Not surprisingly, it is difficult for them to give young people realistic attitudes and expectations about work in industry.

(d) The environmental and consumer protection groups which developed during the 1960s were the spearhead of popular concern which has already led to much new legislation (for example, the Trade Descriptions Act 1972). The consumer groups are so well established in many countries that they have expanded their field of interest from the comparative testing of products to cover commercial, welfare and health services, taxation, citizen's rights and more, and have had a tremendous influence on advertising practices, for example. Such groups are represented by publications like *Which?* in Great Britain, *Test Achats?* in Belgium and *Que Choisir?* in France. Their activities have been copied in newspapers, radio and television by many popular series which champion the individual against the 'anonymous' organisation.

Public concern with environmental problems has emerged as a grass-roots movement, local and voluntary, but also in the form of national organisations funded at least partly by government grants. Much of the concern has been with matters which affect industry directly: pollution, the hazards of new technology, the location of factories, the use of energy and its sources.

Industry is regarded with distrust by both consumer and environmental organisations. To overcome these barriers industry needs to show its willingness to meet and talk, to put its case, and to be more willing to spend money on co-operation rather than wasting it on defending law suits.

(e) Other 'special' groups within the public are women's organisations (and the UK Equal Pay Act 1970 and Sex Discrimination Act 1975 bear witness to their influence), and at a local level residents' associations seek to exert an influence on local firms.

(f) Finally, there is the great mass of the general public which provides the market for products and services and the employees for the labour force.

## 16.2 CONTACT WITH THE PUBLIC

### The mass media
Without doubt the mass media are the most effective channel through which industry can improve its image, make its case and influence special publics like government and finance.

The information needs of the media are many and varied. Even newspapers are not homogeneous. They may be national or local, daily or weekly, popular, serious or specialist, and each type will have its different interests and priorities.

The press has little regular need for information, except perhaps at local level, since what is 'news' is necessarily the irregular and unusual event. Television news looks for the dramatic event also, but many features programmes will spend time and money on producing in-depth studies of industries or firms.

A common-enough occurrence, a factory strike, will demonstrate the different needs of the media. Television news will seek a few key facts and frequently will wish to dramatise the conflict, to make more entertaining viewing. This may be done by using a managerial statement and matching it with a contradictory view provided by a worker or union representative. The local newspaper is also interested in personalities but will want more names and details of the people involved. It will also want to assess the impact on the local community.

The industrial or financial editor of a national newspaper will likewise be interested in the social and economic implications, but he will be looking far wider and will be more interested in the problems than the personalities.

Timing is important, too. Television news and the national press have urgent deadlines to meet, but the reporter from the local press is not under the same constraints.

Commerce and industry have to be able to respond to these occasional demands, but they also need a more regular and continuous relationship with the media. However, this cannot be based merely on a regular flood of press releases, because too much information is as unhelpful as too little. Editors who are swamped by more information than they have time to handle will soon learn to ignore the regular press releases of that particular firm.

What is needed is an understanding of the needs of the media, a recognition of what their various interests are and a willingness to be co-operative.

Press releases need careful timing to give a good impression to the media (for their composition see Chapter 4). Too often they are produced as news items when they are days too late — stories have been leaked and published already.

If the subject of the press release is of sufficient interest, it will result in further enquiries from the press. To avoid misunderstandings and mis-reporting it is essential that press enquiries in person or on the telephone should be answered only by someone authorised and competent to do so.

When reporters and photographers arrive to cover an event at the factory they should be given every assistance. Someone should be detailed to escort and inform them and some basic written information may be presented as a press kit in a folder. For example, the kit prepared for the visit by a Minister of Transport to a local bus company contained the following information sheets:

> *The Minister's programme*
> *A bus ride for the Minister*
> *Minister sees the company's computer terminal in action*
> *Computerised schedule planning*
> *Grants save many rural bus services*
> *Modernised single-deck buses (with photograph)*

Photographers will be helped by having someone appointed to escort them, to help in the setting up of groups or scenes for the photographs and to give them particular details, such as names for the captions of the pictures.

Another method of briefing reporters is the *embargo* press release. This contains information released to the press on the understanding that it will not be published before the date specified. Such a release has two objects. First, it enables editors to plan ahead, thus ensuring that they have space to publish the information on the most appropriate date. Second, it can brief reporters covering the event so that they know what further information to seek.

Relations with the press are usually handled in a large firm by the public relations or publicity department. Smaller firms are likely to find it more economical to become the clients of a firm of public relations specialists. Even large organisations, such as county councils, often use such consultancy services.

One such agency, for example, is Universal News Services, which especially serves business and trade associations. It disseminates information from its subscribers over a teleprinter network to the national and provincial newspapers, to radio and television stations and to the London bureaux of international news agencies. Additionally it provides a mailing service for the world's trade and technical journals, has a special 'Enternews' unit handling arts, entertainment and leisure industries, and offers a shorthand reporting service to cover, for example, company meetings.

## Other contact

### Company annual reports

These are an effective method of communicating with those who, like shareholders and financial editors, have a particular interest in the organisation. There is a welcome trend towards more attractive designs using graphics and photographs to make company reports more readable. At least one British weekly newspaper gives a small prize monthly for the best company report. Such reports will be sent as a matter of routine to the media and their publication will coincide with advertisements in the financial pages which announce the company results.

### Company newspapers

They have a somewhat wider influence than the employees at whom they are primarily aimed. Many companies send them regularly to local paper editors so that they can pick up any stories they feel will interest their readers. They are also seen by employees' families.

### Direct advertising

This is obviously a key element in the image-building process and often represents a very large investment indeed of company resources. (Almost a third of the price of a packet of soap powder is spent on advertising.)

### Indirect advertising

Job advertisements which contain the company name, logo or symbol help to keep the company in the public eye. Such advertisements can help in image-building, especially if they are prestigious display advertisements containing carefully detailed job descriptions for jobs carrying high salaries.

### A company's letters (see also Chapter 1.1)

Letters to customers, clients, suppliers and others can help the company image. An organisation which takes care to answer complaints with courtesy and perhaps a little generosity can gain itself much goodwill. So can courteous replies to the many requests for information which come from so many sources, like students and researchers, though these can be very time-consuming and expensive.

### Trade exhibitions and conferences

A specialised form of communication, they are mainly aimed at customers, but are also useful as a means of keeping in contact with one's competitors.

### Sponsorship

On a national level this is widespread, and many major sporting events, racing, cricket, golf, etc., rely heavily on such assistance.

### Local activities

There are many local functions through which a company can enhance its reputation. Open days enable employees' families and prospective employees to learn about the firm, its products, policies and premises.

Participation in community affairs can take many forms: company teams can compete in local leagues and competitions; companies can sponsor local events and organisations by advertising in fête programmes, by active participation, by the donation of prizes and the like; they can offer prizes to local students, or occasional gifts to local institutions – educational, old people's homes, and the like.

---

## FOCUS

Business in a HOSTILE climate
The importance of IMAGE-BUILDING and REPUTATION

**Focus** *cont.*

The outside world
  governmental, financial, educational, environmental and the general public

Channels of communication:
  the mass media, direct and indirect advertising, press releases, letters, company reports, open days, local participation, sponsorship, trade exhibitions and conferences

## 16.3 INTERNAL COMMUNICATION

The complexity of internal communication systems and information flow coincides with the growth of administrative and clerical functions and the size of organisations.

In a small organisation with perhaps only six or seven staff, all in one room, communication is simple and straightforward with people talking face to face to one another. There is no need to send innumerable memos or use the telephone. However, there will still be a need for some internal written communication.

### General written communication

Information which will be used more than once must be kept in written form, such as reports, financial information, order and purchase records, stock control forms. Legal obligations will require other internal records to be kept, such as individual staff pay and pension details or accident reports. For control purposes, costings and forecasts may also be required.

As soon as the organisation expands, so does the communication system. More written communication is needed, with information being transferred from one document to another according to the needs of different departments. These will not all require the complete information, for instance a sales ledger clerk might no longer have to retrieve information for preparing customers' accounts direct from the invoices, but will take it from the already prepared ledger postings and customer account cards.

Similarly, separate sections will need to use other combinations of information, for example, Sales Department, Despatch or Production, while the financial section will want the overall picture.

Even the same information will need to be communicated in different ways to different groups. For instance, the wages department will need weekly and/or monthly details for individuals in order to make up the payroll, while management may wish to have annually the totals of wages and salaries paid. The information may have to be presented in a different form either because it will be used differently or because it must be intelligible to the reader (for instance, the Managing Director will understand the annual balance-sheet, but in companies where financial information is communicated to employees, a simplified format might be needed).

Management reports for decision-making may have to be prepared anew for each major decision, including all the information needed for that particular decision but omitting all unnecessary detail. Management also requires records of how decisions are arrived at, exactly what the decision was and the action agreed on: in other words, minutes of their meetings. These are often also required by law.

### Notice boards

Some communication with employees will be carried out by using notice boards. All sorts of internal memos, general notices, safety posters, internal job vacancies can be posted. To encourage staff to read notices, the boards should be strategically placed where staff can see them easily (in a recreation area, for instance, or near the main exits). Notices should be well displayed and the board regularly cleared of out-of-date information so that new items show clearly. The board might be divided into sections for different types of information or there might be a 'Today' or 'Urgent' section.

There is a tendency for people to read a notice and then ask 'Why are they doing this?', or 'What does it mean?' This happens because the giving of information is only one part of the communication process. Staff should be given the chance to ask their questions of an appropriate person, preferably the writer of the notice. Notices must also be very carefully phrased to avoid as much misunderstanding as possible.

### House magazines and newsheets

A better way of giving detailed information to staff may be by way of the company magazine or newsletter. This can be a simple A4 duplicated sheet or, in very large organisations, a glossy magazine or full-size newspaper. It can contain general news items as well, so telling people in one part of the organisation about their colleagues in another.

### Handbooks and manuals

These are considered in detail in Chapter 5. They include general handbooks for staff, particularly new staff, special booklets with instructions on how to use a particular piece of equipment (for instance, a dictating-machine), manuals detailing work procedures to be followed, and instruction manuals used in training.

### Inter-branch communication

Written communication between branches of an organisation can be sent using the public postal system: telexes, facsimile transmission, etc., and private mailbags can be used so that internal correspondence does not need to be individually enveloped and stamped or franked.

## Distribution of written communication

Many large companies employ internal messengers to collect and distribute internal (and external) mail. Automatic conveyors also exist — variations on the conveyor-belt principle — and pneumatic tubes, such a feature of Victorian shops, are still sometimes used.

## Telephones

An internal telephone system will most commonly be linked into the external system (possibly with a dictating system included), but the big organisations may have separate internal systems within, for example, a factory employing thousands. Private lines can be used, through the public system, for communication between branches of the same organisation.

Confraphone allows managers to hold internal company meetings by telephone over long distances (using the private line or the public system). If there is a group at either end of the line, it will have a loudspeaker attachment for the telephone to allow everyone to both hear and talk easily.

## Meetings

Many meetings are simply conversations between two individuals, very informally, or are interviews. However, the bigger the organisation, the more the communication system calls for formalised meetings. Chapter 7 looked at meetings procedure and practice in detail, while Chapter 6 was concerned with all the written communication connected with meetings. 'Meetings breed meetings, breed meetings' is a criticism constantly levelled. Meetings are necessary and often very useful but can be expensive and time-wasting if not conducted efficiently.

## Other systems

Inter-communication systems (walkie-talkies, telephones in the car) also exist. Public-address systems can be used for making announcements, calling a member of staff to the telephone and even for playing music. Bleep systems and coloured light signals can also be used to page staff.

## Computer communication

Data can now easily be transmitted from a visual display unit to another hundreds of miles away, using the public telephone system (or, in very sophisticated organisations, a satellite dish aerial). Private viewdata systems can be similarly used and have the facility for communications to individuals being included as and when desired.

## Safeguards

(a) All communication, in however sophisticated a form, is between individuals, and human relationships must be maintained. The pieces of paper or the machines do not communicate, people do.

(b) The increase in complexity has added greatly to the amount of communication. Hundreds of needless papers float around organisations. Duplication abounds. (One university sought to reduce the amount of paper being used. The senior administrator sent a memo to each member of the academic staff requesting their co-operation. Unfortunately, he forgot to tell other managers that he had communicated with all staff. Consequently, each lecturer received five memos on the same subject from different levels in the organisation). The larger the organisation, the greater the need for control to be exercised over the flow of information. Simplification of procedures can help.

(c) There are times when it is both quicker and easier to pick up the telephone than it is to go and talk to someone at the far end of the building. However, over-use of the telephone adds to the remoteness and distancing of one person from another which is one of the drawbacks in widespread organisations. It certainly could often be replaced by direct contact between people who are geographically close.

(d) Control must be maintained over the number, purpose, length, organisation, recording and results of meetings.

(e) Handbooks and manuals should contain only necessary information, be kept as simple and short as possible and be updated regularly.

(f) Costs of communication between branches through private lines, telexes, computer links must be monitored and kept as low as possible.

(g) Confidentiality and security must be maintained, both with papers or with computer information being transmitted via a public system.

---

### FOCUS

THE MAIN INTERNAL COMMUNICATION SYSTEMS

*written* — memos, reports, forms, noticeboards, house magazines, manuals

*telecommunications* — internal telephones, dictating systems, private lines, confraphone, telexes, computers, viewdata

*meetings* — informal conversation, interviews, formal meetings

## 16.4 **ASSIGNMENTS**

1   What major developments have occurred in the mass media in the last thirty years? What implications do these developments have for the professional administrator? [ICSA]

2   The board of directors of a large company have asked you for advice on how their company can establish better relationships with the local and national press. What steps would you advise them to take, and what would your recommendations be designed to achieve [ICSA]

3   What are the most important differences between the different forms of the mass media which exist in your locality? How do these differences affect their coverage of and approach to the affairs of business and government organisations?

   What are the most important implications of your analysis to the professional administrator who is concerned about the quantity and quality of media coverage of his/her organisation? [ICSA]

4   Find out what internal records are legally required in your company?

5   To what extent do you consider that paperwork will be replaced in offices by data communication via computer within the next twenty years? (See also Chapter 18.) What effect may this have on internal communication?

# CHAPTER 17

# MANAGEMENT COMMUNICATION

By its very name *participative management* implies that all parties in an organisation should take an active role in the business to maximise its success. This is a contemporary style of management which seeks to increase employees' involvement in management decision-taking, while not necessarily removing in any way management's right to make the final decisions. It can be implemented through worker directors, union consultation, non-union staff consultative groups, a better informed workforce (through written information and regular briefings) or informal encouragement of employees to present ideas, suggestions and constructive criticisms to their immediate line managers.

None of these is possible unless there is effective vertical and horizontal communication and feedback.

## 17.1 THE NEED TO IMPROVE

In very many organisations this necessary effective communication does not exist or is sketchily implemented.

Poor communication is one of the main reasons why many workers feel indifferent or even hostile to their employers. It is also a reason why workers resist change – if they do not understand why changes are being made, it is natural for them to believe that the moves could be against their interest. Hence the improvement of communication can have a direct bearing on profitability.

Then we need to overcome the problems caused by the growing size of organisations and the impersonality which can develop in them. This both results in developing remoteness and also in the breakdown of communication structures which are often closely linked to the organisation structure. As the latter grows in complexity, so the lines of communication become stretched, tangled and (sometimes) broken.

Restructuring of the organisation consequent upon growth, merger, or even retrenchment to combat recession, is seldom accompanied by the necessary replanning of the communication structures.

Of comparable importance is the trend towards industrial democracy, which means giving workers a say in the formation of industrial policy and practice. The growing demand by workers in the Western world for participation in management has several causes: political, educational and technological. Since the Second World War there has been in the West a drift towards socialism, towards greater egalitarianism which makes workers feel entitled to have some say in company policies which can affect them greatly.

Also the work-force is much better educated than previously, and thus is much more competent to participate in management decision-making.

This better-educated work-force often has to do work which, because of automation and other developments, tends to be repetitive and boring. The need for work satisfaction finds expression in a desire to participate in decision-making and policy-formation.

Among EEC countries this trend is so well established that a recent EEC document was able to comment that *employee participation is a political, legal or social reality throughout the Community*', ('Employee participation and company structure', *Bulletin of the European Communities*, supplement 8, 1975.) In Sweden the co-determination law gives workers the right to negotiate on all matters affecting them and also access to books, accounts and other documents which relate to their employer's business. In West Germany firms over a certain size have, by law, a supervisory board which consists of ten shareholder representatives, nine union representatives and one staff representative. This board has the power to appoint the board of directors and to approve company accounts and investment plans.

In many other countries, even if there is as yet no participative legislation, there is none the less a large body of law which demands a tremendous amount of management communication, including the regulation of company and directors' meetings; contract law, which gives employees the right to specified information; financial regulations, on pension schemes for instance; strict rulings on the observation of safe working practices and health standards (the British Health and Safety at Work Act 1974, for example, requires firms over a certain size to set up safety committees) and laws governing the protection of employment which will require, or at the very least recommend, the communication procedures to be followed before workers can be dismissed.

Thus managements need to improve communication.

## Structures
The organisation of the structures of communication must be reviewed and strengthened to ensure that the greater flow of communication will reach those for whom it is intended.

The revised structures must allow for greater flexibility and informality to suit the more egalitarian climate, while retaining clear lines of communication and indicating *clearly* who is responsible for what areas of communication.

Job specifications need to be revised to show individual managers' duties, responsibilities and authority for communication.

## Analysis of communication needs

There must be *more* communication, on some matters, to *more* people. If this additional communication is not to be the pumping out of a mass of information with no opportunity for feedback, additional to the often too great a hailstorm of paperwork already deluging staff, then an analysis must be undertaken of communication needs.

Such an analysis should take into account the nature of the communication it is desired to give, the reasons for communicating it, the needs of the recipients and the medium (media) to be adopted. It must also consider of what importance a particular communication is and how it will fare among all the others. Finally, the method of obtaining feedback must be organised.

Employees need several levels of communication. At the primary level they need communication:

(a) of immediate concern to enable them to perform their work — job training, changes in working procedure
(b) information about related departments and work
(c) background information about the working environment — safety regulations, unions, canteen
(d) personal data — rates of pay, pensions, holidays, other benefits.

(The communication will naturally vary according to the level of the job — a process worker will not *need* financial information, an accountant will not *need* to know how to make floggle toggles.)

Additionally, many employees have an interest in and curiosity about many other facets of their organisation. Some Japanese companies, indeed, insist that all managers should have production work experience, and in many management training programmes the world over trainees spend time in a range of departments. Job rotation, enlargement and enrichment also incorporate this concept.

These may be considered secondary needs, but there can be no denying that the well-informed employee can make a more positive contribution than one who is ignorant. The whole focus of participative management thinking is on improving the knowledge of employees so that they will perform both more efficiently and with greater job satisfaction.

There are many classic examples of employees whose knowledge is limited and whose communication even with peripheral departments is so poor as to have caused serious difficulties.

A state-owned company organised training for its supervisors. At first, supervisors from comparable transport departments in the region were brought together. Certain common problems emerged. One of these was a complaint that the maintenance sections were completely unappreciative of the transport problems, were inefficient and unco-operative. A subsequent course brought together the service supervisors, whose major grumble was – you guessed! – that the transport supervisors were completely unappreciative of the service problems, were inefficient and unco-operative.

Both groups admitted that they never went to talk over problems with their opposite numbers, merely sent notes or at best picked up the telephone.

The company was concerned at the feedback received from these courses. An experimental meeting of combined transport and service supervisors was held to discuss the situation. Both groups toured each other's premises, detailed their own problems and began to understand the interrelationship of their work and to appreciate one another as human beings. Finally, the company set up regular information-giving and problem-solving meetings of line management, from all departments, with great success.

More communication requires careful thought and organisation of communication channels and more time to be spent on communication.

### Controlling the information flow

To ensure that the additional communication proposed does not overload the system, checks and controls must be applied and questions asked of both existing and new communication, such as the following:

> *Is it needed?*
> *Who needs it?*
> *In what form and detail?*
> *What methods are available to us?*

A variety of methods will be available: newsletters, employee reports, manager training (in communication techniques), briefing sessions, induction programmes, joint consultation committees, suggestions, and so on.

### The main areas of communication

*What* we are to communicate falls conveniently into three categories: instructions, information and consultation.

#### Instructions

Commands and directives must pass swiftly along the lines of communication, most usually phrased as 'requests', but nevertheless instructions that employees are expected to comply with, since they are designed to improve performance. There should, however, be opportunities for consultation before policy directives are taken and for explanation, feedback and review afterwards.

## Information

Matters on which workers should have information are mainly company performance and management strategy. Company performance includes company profits and their relationship proportionally to wages and investment, and the company's future prospects. On management strategy employees should, for example, be informed of any organisational and management changes which are likely to affect them. Again, prior consultation and suitable explanation and provision for feedback must exist.

## Consultation

Topics for consultation will relate to those matters which affect workers immediately and directly, though they should also be consulted at times on wider policy issues. The extent of the topic area will depend on the nature and organisation of the consultative process. (See also Chapter 17.2.)

Inevitably there are problems in improving communication. First, it takes time. Companies which have implemented successful employee consultative schemes say that little perceptible improvement occurs during the first two years following the establishment of the programme, and even then participation is slow. Americans complain that it takes a very long time to get a decision from Japanese management, whereas an American manager can take decisions very quickly. On the other hand, in Japan so many people have been involved in the decision-making that their co-operation and hence implementation is assured. The American manager's quick decision frequently meets opposition from other managers and from employees and its implementation can be delayed.

It has also been said that giving workers full information (for example, on the state of the company's order book) gives them power which may undermine management's position in collective bargaining. This argument is refuted by the findings of a Confederation of British Industries (CBI) study in 1976 which found that well-informed workers and unions were more realistic in wage negotiations.

Other critics imply that there would be possible leaking of confidential information which could endanger the competitive position of the company.

Perhaps simply getting the information across is the most real problem. Complex financial information needs translating and the use of pictorial methods if it is to be meaningful to the shop-floor worker. Very often the first barrier is getting people to read the company newspaper and report, to look at notice boards, to contribute suggestions.

The CBI study showed that it is worth making the effort. It found a strong relationship between workers being well informed and having a high level of job satisfaction — with all that that implies for morale, absenteeism, and so on.

---

### FOCUS

Improved communication is needed because

    employees must be motivated
    large organisations are remote
    workers wish to participate in arriving at decisions
    laws require it

Improvement requires
    good organisation
    increased communication on relevant matters
    control of information flow

Employees need
    instructions
    information
    consultation

---

## 17.2 STRUCTURE AND LINES OF COMMUNICATION

There is an undeniable link between the organisational structure of any concern, large or small, and the communication structure. By and large, vertical communication follows the line of command, whether downward or upward, but even the organisation chart will often not show horizontal organisation clearly. The communication structure, however, will be much more complex.

### The communication structure

Figure 17.1 shows a part of a line and staff organisation. Figure 17.2 shows the communication structure needed for the Training Department, which is in a staff position, to communicate with just one of the other areas, Production. As you can see, the pattern is very different from the organisation chart and is far more complicated. Yet this is only the tip of the iceberg, one very small portion of the complete communication picture.

On an even smaller scale, the structure of communication within a

**Fig 17.1** *section of a line and staff organisation chart*

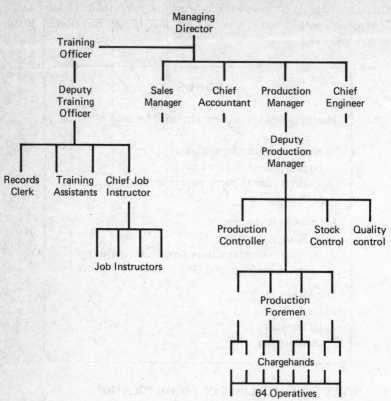

working group may be quite complex and at variance with the structures in other groups in the same organisation. For example, a group with a very strong leader will probably have a structure where there is relatively little communication between the members of the group but each will have a direct line of communication to the leader.

Communication will be swift but morale in the group will be low as they will not be working as a team.

Conversely, the group with no discernible leader, working by consensus, will have a close communication structure, with everyone being informed and consulted. This reduces the speed of communication and can also limit efficiency, but morale will be high.

**Lines of communication**

The structure shown in Figure 17.2 also illustrates the length of lines of communication if they follow the organisational structure. For instance, an agreed change in the training of operatives, if the line structure is

255

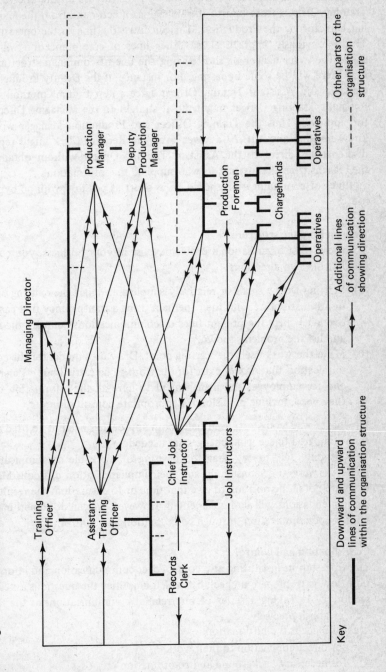

Fig 17.2 *lines of communication*

Key

━━━ Downward and upward lines of communication within the organisation structure

→ Additional lines of communication showing direction

- - - Other parts of the organisation structure

followed, would have to go from the Job Instructors up the line to the Training Officer, from him to the Managing Director and from the Managing Director via the Production Manager down the line to the operatives. This is obviously impractical, so other lines of communication will be used. The main danger of shortcutting the line of command structure is that there will be some bypassing. For instance, if the Deputy Production Manager and Assistant Training Officer agree a new training method, the Assistant Training Officer might put it straight to the Managing Director for approval. Thus the Training Officer and Production Manager would know nothing about it. At a lower level, the Records Clerk might report discrepancies direct to the Assistant Training Officer without obtaining the reasons from the Instructors who supplied the information.

Lines of communication should be as short as possible, with no bypass routes.

## Reorganising the structure

To assess what organisational problems exist in your business, you could attack from two directions.

(a) Starting with a small or relatively simple area, chart the existing organisation structure, and then (perhaps using a transparency that can be overlaid) chart the present lines of communication. Compare the two and list the problems shown.

(b) Make the work itself the starting-point. Draw up a model for the communication that *should* exist for the work to be carried out efficiently and for employees and management to have all the information that they need. Include provision for appropriate consultation.

Whichever way you start, eventually both approaches need to be tried and then compared to see what changes are needed.

It is only fair to say that the devising of workable communication models is very time-consuming and their implementation difficult. Many of us are not in the position to give that time or to ensure that the resulting recommendations will be implemented. However, we can do something to improve communication, through co-ordination and control.

## Co-ordination and control

The first step in instituting any control over communication and information flow is to prepare a check-list which amplifies the questions asked in section 17.1. Taking a series of interrelated communications as the first step, establish precisely:

(a) Who needs the information:

for direct application to their work

for necessary background and co-ordination purposes.

(b) Whether the people identified in (i) receive the information.
(c) Whether it is presented to them in the best medium (spoken, written, etc.) and in the most suitable way (format, language, tone, etc.).
(d) If suitable opportunity is available for prior consultation, discussion afterwards and assessing feedback.
(e) Whether the information is also being sent to people who neither have a need nor an interest (remove them from the circulation list).

This will enable you to establish what the lines of communication should be, assess consultation and feedback requirements and decide on the manner of communicating: formal or informal, choice of medium. Co-ordination with other sections involved will then be necessary so that any system or revision introduced will fit in with their requirements. They may well, also, be able to help solve some of your problems and the resultant system should meet with general acceptance.

The system must then be controlled through a series of checks. First of all, managers and supervisors must include the overseeing of communication within their duties and must be quick to spot deviations from the agreed structure, identify the reasons and either make any necessary adjustments or lead staff into following the existing procedures.

### Practical control techniques

With written communications, controls can be applied to forms and to letters and memoranda.

### Form control

Forms should be regularly reviewed to find out if they are still necessary, if they are being completed correctly (and, if not, why not), and whether the information required needs amending.

### Correspondence

It is a salutary exercise to take, for a period of six weeks or so, an extra copy of every letter, telex or memorandum sent out of one office.

At the end of that time, the thickness of the pile may given an early indication that all is not well. Reading a sample of the correspondence may show up major faults such as undue length, illogical procedure, failure to answer queries clearly, and poor grammar, punctuation and tone.

So a correspondence audit is the next step. To each letter should be attached a slip showing the main areas in which faults occur, for example:

> *poor appreciation of company policy*
> *lack of company/product knowledge*
> *incorrect information*
> *poor ordering of content*

*queries unanswered*
*inaccuracies*
*excessive length*
*poor format*
*errors in use of language*
*unsuitable tone*

A tick could then be placed against any fault which the particular document shows. A combined picture can then be built up, which will show faults common to the whole group and identify problems with individuals.

Such an exercise can only be really useful if the results can be communicated to staff, suitable changes implemented and training given. To do this means involving the staff and gaining their co-operation at the beginning, even before the collecting together of the correspondence begins.

They must be told why the exercise is being undertaken and what it is hoped to achieve, for instance the reduction both of the excessive time they have to spend on drafting communications and of the cost savings if fewer letters and shorter telexes can be sent. They must also be convinced that no one is 'gunning' for them and that help will be available if they are asked to make changes.

It is often useful to enlist the services of your organisation and methods specialist, if there is one, or to call in an outside consultant. Either of these will be in a better position to present unbiased criticism and can also advise on the basis of knowledge of similar problems. The audit should be followed by further checks at six-monthly intervals.

### Standardisation

A standard pattern (house style) for written communication can be useful, coupled with a short handbook of helpful tips on writing documents and dictation practice.

Some documents which are often repeated can be turned into standard forms or letters, or a series of standard paragraphs can be composed. This removes the problem of several different people adopting varying styles in similar documents and also problems of relevant content being sometimes omitted. (See also Chapter 1.1.)

Standard documents and paragraphs should be originated by a member of staff who can combine the requisite level of knowledge with good communication skills. There must also be a regular review procedure.

### Charting

Responsibility charts can be drawn up to show clearly who is responsible for the different phases of a communication, for example who institutes the communication, drafts or dictates it, edits, types, checks, duplicates and mails it.

## Oral communication

Control of telephone use may be needed. The size of the telephone bill will indicate if the problem is serious. It is possible to find out, either through detailed telephone accounts or through machinery attached to the telephone exchange, both the duration and frequency of calls.

This can lead to an examination of why so many calls are being made, whether their duration could be reduced through proper planning (see Chapter 11.6, example 3) or whether some action must be taken to reduce the number of private calls.

Effective planning of interviews and meetings is also a necessary control, reducing the time spent on communicating but increasing efficiency. (See Chapters 7 and 8.)

## Consultative machinery

The process of consulting staff, whether about a correspondence audit, or on other matters, should be achieved by a mixture of formal and informal methods. (The consultative procedures involving unions are not considered here for reason of their specificity to the UK.)

The simplest form of consultation is the informal talk between a manager and an individual member of staff, where the manager is seeking information and views before taking a decision, perhaps on a suggestion made by the employee, perhaps on a change which the manager is considering. This informal consultation can be extended to include all or some of the group, on an *ad hoc* basis.

Similar informal consultation takes place between departments and between groups of managers. However, there is often a much more formal consultative machinery, mentioned in section 17.1. Organisations will have joint consultative committees or works councils whose major purpose is to provide for the participative element. Generally such bodies are composed of elected representatives of all employees (including management), together with appointed senior managers, with the Managing Director frequently in the chair. Topics for discussion will include:

(a) the pattern of work, working hours, shifts, breaks
(b) matters of discipline and behaviour, rules
(c) amenities – the canteen, recreational facilities, welfare funds and their administration
(d) ways of improving productivity, including the administration of suggestion schemes
(e) training and further education

(f)  safety and employee health
(g)  grievances
(h)  absenteeism
(i)  redundancy.

Members will be informed by management of progress and of plans and of changes consequent on external influences (like new laws) and will have the opportunity to comment on proposals. They will also be able to put forward their own recommendations and offer advice. They will have no executive function, however, nor will their wishes bind management, though management may ignore such advice at its peril.

---

### FOCUS

The communication structure is:
 more complex than the organisation structure determined by management and leadership patterns

Lines of communication can be:
 too long
 bypassed

Co-ordination and control must:
 start with analysis
 have good management and supervision
 use suitable control techniques.

Consultation may:
 range from the everyday, informal, to formal consultative groups
 include freedom to comment on management policy
 allow recommendations on topics of immediate relevance

---

## 17.3 THE PLACE OF INFORMAL COMMUNICATION

Consultation is only one of the areas where informal communication is used, albeit within the accepted structure. We have seen, however, that the organisational structure is cumbersome, making for long lines of communication wherein messages, especially oral ones, simply get lost or where, to speed the process, people are bypassed.

Simpler and shorter lines of communication encourage an informal approach and more personal contact. You can go next door and have a brief talk with Joe about an immediate problem — and solve it in five minutes. You can call Bill in to your office for an informal meeting, ostensibly to ask if he's recovered from his bad cold perhaps, but also to pave the way for telling him that his work has been below standard for quite some time and get him to make a fresh start. You can spread good news quickly: *'Harry, let everyone know that we're finishing at 3 p.m. on Friday before the factory closes down for the holiday!'* That news will be widely released quickly and accurately.

Such informality is quick, it is accurate and it makes for good relationships with employees. If properly used, informality can improve overall communication, overcoming management's occasional failure to communicate properly in the first place, and allowing employees to talk about their feelings and reactions — to 'let off steam' — without fear of repercussions.

On the other hand, informal communication often takes place when the correct lines of communication have not been used and it is then that the facility of the *grapevine* for spreading information alarmingly fast, but distorting it and introducing rumour, adverse comment and even untruth in the process, is demonstrated, as the following case illustrates.

(*Note*: the word *'grapevine'* is often wrongly used to describe all informal communication. Its use should be limited to the sense in which it is used here.)

An organisation was considering introducing flexible working hours for office staff. Management had agreed the method to be adopted and had also agreed that the only satisfactory method of recording staff time worked would be to install time clocks.

Confidential discussions had taken place with all the unions concerned and agreement had been reached on the method and the date of starting. A date was also set for informing middle and line management and the staff of the new scheme.

The time clocks were purchased and, a week before the date on which the staff were to be informed, installation commenced in the General Office. Staff quickly recognised what the machines were for. Their union representative was on holiday so could not give them information and the manager knew nothing.

When he sought information from the workmen installing the equipment he was told, 'It's for the new working hours. You'll hear all about it in due course.'

A member of staff overhead this and repeated it to a colleague adding, 'I bet they're going to make us work longer.'

Two hours later, the general office staff held an unofficial union meeting to discuss the management proposal to lengthen their working week by one hour and fine them if they were more than five minutes late or left early!

A deputation was sent to the Managing Director to inform him that all staff were refusing to go back to work until the time clocks were taken down.

Such a situation is manifestly the result of management incompetence and a creaking formal information structure.

People always put the worst possible interpretation on the information they receive, the rumours which are passed, through the grapevine. The result of ignorance of what is happening and the cynicism engendered by the grapevine lead to lowered morale; this can affect staff turnover and production. It is not possible to prevent the operation of the grapevine, but the harmful effects of rumour can be avoided if management keep staff informed.

(a)  Tell people what is going on, before the grapevine starts.
(b)  Talk to people – in groups, not individually, so that they all get the same message.
(c)  Use the proper channels, i.e. the chain of command, not the union representatives.
(d)  Hold briefing groups regularly –
     encourage questions
     give information in writing
     consult the workers – this will improve co-operation.

---

## FOCUS

Informal communication is fast, personal and improves human relationships
The grapevine (rumour) points to management deficiencies:
    it is very quick, usually distorted, sometimes untrue, suspicious and often dangerous
    management cannot prevent it but can minimise its harm by positive communication

---

## 17.4 THE CHOICE OF MEDIA

No communication will be effective unless it is presented through the best medium or combination of media.

### The choice available

The primary choice will be between oral or written or non-verbal presentation, but within these broad categories further decisions must be made, as the possibilities given below suggest.

### Oral communication

This may be face to face, or by means of the telephone. Between individuals it can be used for discussing problems, interviewing, training, or providing information.

Groups will meet together for any of the reasons discussed in Chapters 7.1 and 11.2 (p. 167), and for lectures and conferences. The purpose of any meeting should determine the way in which the oral medium is used in that case.

All face-to-face communication will be modified by non-verbal communication and may also be supplemented by visual aids — plans, models, charts, graphs.

Telephone communication, however, relies solely on the combination of the words spoken, the tone of voice and delivery. It can only be supplemented by visual information if it is connected into a computer VDU system or allied with facsimile transmission (FAX). (See also Chapter 18.)

### Written communication

The major types of written communication can be classified as: internal/external correspondence; forms and questionnaires; reports; general information in notices, leaflets, booklets and manuals; instructional material; publicity material; itineraries, programmes and agendas; regulations and constitutions.

It is often combined with visual material and linked with oral presentation.

### Non-verbal communication

Non-verbal communication also has a specific role in the visual presentation of material (see Chapter 14).

### Approach and tone

The choice is very extensive and must be made with care and forethought for the resulting communication to be most effective. Within the chosen medium, also, there is a further possible division — of approach and tone. Is the approach to be formal or informal? Should the tone be authoritative, genial, sympathetic, harsh, light-hearted, non-committal or persuasive?

### Time, place and amount

Finally, three other matters affect the choice of medium. The timing of the communication may well mean that it has to be oral — there being delay if a letter, for instance, were to be sent. Also, the time at which one communicates must be suitable — people doing urgent work should not be interrupted for non-urgent messages, nor can a busy manager be expected to listen on the telephone to personal problems when he is in the middle of an important conference. Too early a communication will be forgotten; too late and it sometimes becomes an expensive error.

The place in which the communication is being made will affect the method used. Sign language or showing someone what to do might be necessary in a very noisy workshop. A personal or confidential message should not be announced in front of a large group of staff. The examples are easy to find.

The amount to be communicated at any one time must be determined by how much the recipient will be able to assimilate, the time needed to plan the communication and the correct medium to match the volume of information to be conveyed.

## 17.5 THE EFFECT OF COMMUNICATION ON HUMAN INTERACTION

Or perhaps it should be the other way around − the way in which communication is affected by human relationships, for it is these relationships which so often determine the success or otherwise of communication.

Communication is like a two-way street with cars coming and going in both directions. Information is the one-way street. Both can lead to a dead end, because essentially the process of sending or receiving messages is more truly that of people relating to one another. Without this process, no organisation could exist. It could not tell its workers what it wants done, how, when, why or by whom. It could not motivate or lead.

### Structural barriers

Throughout the whole field of communication, the dead ends, the barriers, lie waiting to stop the messages. Within the structure of the organisation itself many of these man-made barriers can be identified. Lack of unity of command, too great a span of control and unclear levels of authority, linked with inadequately expressed or inconsistent corporate objectives and policy, result in poor management and leadership, in lines of communication that are too long or unclear, in bypass routes and in too great a reliance on the 'grapevine'.

Sometimes the top executive is either unwilling to communicate or does not appreciate the need. Such an attitude will be echoed by other managers. There may also be problems of geographical distance or organisational complexity.

Doubt may exist about who has the functional responsibility for communication, and thus it may either be duplicated or not be done at all. There may be conflict between the staff role of communication specialists and the line role of the managers. The former tend to be concerned with 'persuasion' directed to matters of morale, hygiene and human relationships, while the line manager is interested in productive effort and problem-solving. Communication is concerned with both, but persuasive communication tends to be used when mistrust and resistance already exist and so it can be counter-productive, be seen as propaganda, as an effort to persuade employees to accept what they do not want.

Communication is best when it arises as a natural response to effective work and problem-solving, as a result of trust, job satisfaction, recognition and good morale.

To improve organisation communication, the structure may need to be clarified and simplified. Management will have to be persuaded that purposeful communication, openness, clarification of responsibilities and careful selection and training of people is essential.

Managers must be chosen whose characters and personalities, intelligence and knowledge, sympathetic approach and consistent and fair treatment will allow them to build the trust essential if communications are to be accepted.

### Lack of trust

The barriers that can be seen when that trust is not in evidence include selective listening, preconceptions, closed minds, devious responses, distortion of feedback, camouflaging of response, the building of facades, the development of strategies to manipulate others, and engaging in extra communication.

### Other barriers

Fear also breeds from mistrust. It may be fear of losing status, of showing gaps in knowledge, of being criticised or reprimanded, of being misrepresented, or even of reprisals.

Selective listening, preconceptions and prejudices can result in the communication being interpreted incorrectly and in limited recall.

A further barrier is that of intelligibility. This in particular results from a communication either being of such substance or couched in such language that the recipient either cannot understand or is not sufficiently interested to try. So we get the notice on the board that no one bothers to read, the training lecture that no one remembers; the joint consultative committee meeting where ten minutes are spent in discussing company plans for computerisation of stock control and fifty on the quality of the canteen tea, and the contract with the complex legal terminology that is unread because it is incomprehensible.

### A positive approach

Many of these difficulties can be overcome, as earlier chapters in this book have suggested. Successful communication can be achieved when there is:

(a) a sincere wish to communicate
(b) a properly organised management structure
(c) clear lines of communication and well-defined responsibility
(d) an understanding of the what, how, where, when and why of communication
(e) a willingness to explain, consult and consider individual feelings and reactions
(f) high communication skills.

Communication cannot necessarily change attitudes, perceptions, value systems, behaviour or motivation. People hear what they want to hear, forget what they wish to forget. It is only through the development of conditions of mutual respect and trust that relevant and effective communication can emerge.

---

### FOCUS

Communication and human relationships are indivisible
Organisational, managerial and individual barriers constantly limit effective communication
Good communication results from the positive development of trust, mutual respect and openness

---

## 17.6 ASSIGNMENTS

1   Explain the importance of good communication for the maintenance of sound relations between management and employees. Comment on the relative values of informal and formal methods of communication. (See Appendix 1.)

2   The management of a national company communicates various types of information to its employees. Discuss the merits of the different methods likely to be used.

3   'The best system of communication is that achieved with the least paperwork.' Say how far you agree with this statement and explain the advantages of (i) oral and (ii) written communication in business. [ICSA]

4   What is meant by the distinction between *formal* and *informal* systems of communication within organisations? What are the most important implications of this distinction for the administrator? [ICSA]

5   What are the main barriers to effective communication that occur in
    large business and government organisations? How can they be over-
    come?

6   A company manufacturing a consumer product with highly technical
    equipment decided that their existing premises were too old and
    cramped to cope with further expansion and that they should move to
    a new £4 million, 16-acre site, 2½ miles away. The following facts may
    be relevant:

    (a) the company employed nearly 2,000 employees on production
        and distribution
    (b) enormous stocks were held — worth about £5 million
    (c) they had 30 per cent of the existing market for similar products
    (d) the company had a high proportion of long-service employees
        whose expertise they valued
    (e) the company's products went to some 4,500 dealers
    (f) choice of site was made in the summer of 1970
    (g) rumours of the move were already current at this time
    (h) the move was proposed for June 1972 (usually a slack period)
    (i) production was to be gradually transferred over a four to eight
        week period
    (j) to avoid distribution problems it was decided to transfer the bulk
        of stock in advance with immediate stocks being transferred over
        a long weekend
    (k) there would be no redundancies
    (l) industrial relations had been good over the past few years with
        some very satisfactory negotiations over both payment systems
        and working arrangements

    Consider the following:

     (i) What information should have been given and to whom?
    (ii) What opportunities for discussion should there have been?
    (iii) Timing. What should the time-table of communication have been?
    (iv) What media of communication should have been used at various
         stages?
     (v) What are the main problems that could have arisen from com-
         munication failures and what might the consequences have been?

# CHAPTER 18

# INFORMATION TECHNOLOGY – THE FUTURE

Offices in many countries are now buzzing with noisy machinery. There are telephones and telexes, reprographic machines, electric typewriters and many kinds of computers. Electronic typewriters, micro-computers, word processors and viewdata systems have already made their impact in large organisations and are spreading fast to smaller concerns.

## 18.1 THE TECHNOLOGICAL DEVELOPMENTS ALREADY IN USE

### Electronic typewriters and word processors
The electronic typewriter is the halfway house between the electric typewriter and the word processor. Different models have different capabilities but all tend to offer an easy switch between typeface sizes, a self-correcting facility and a limited memory.

Word processing is, however, the use of true computing for the preparation and editing of text. The word-processing choices may be broadly categorised as follows.

(a) *A word-processing package for use on a micro-computer.* Such packages are already sophisticated but tend to be somewhat limited compared with the *dedicated* word processor.

(b) *The dedicated word processor.* This is a computer which is designed solely for word processing. It has complex software which allows for inputting text and numbers, displaying them, altering typeface, margins, etc., and editing on a full A4-shaped screen before printing. Often additional software packages are available for form design, report writing or graphics presentation, for example.

(c) *Linked systems.* The concept of electronic mail is now a practicality. Both word processors and computers can be linked between offices, branches and countries by telephone, now increasingly using high-capacity fibre-optic cables, or satellite (and the latter is likely to

Fig 18.1 *the impact of information technology*

develop most speedily within the next twenty years). *Intelligent* teleprinters have also been developed. The word *'intelligent'* is used in the computer industry to indicate that the computer has been given a built-in ability to analyse data and make decisions, within given limits.)

So it is already not necessary to print out a letter and post it. Instead it can be sent electronically from one terminal to the other.

## Micro-computers

Very sophisticated micro-computers can now be bought for a few hundred pounds. For a few thousand an office could have a linked system.

Documents of all kinds can be stored in large data bases, recalled at speed, updated or erased. So the job of the filing clerk is being replaced by that of the computer operator.

## Working from home

As the use of linked systems of computers and word processors grows, so it becomes possible for some workers to avoid the journey to work and back every day, working instead on computer terminals in their own homes. To a limited extent this already happens. Some computer programmers, particularly women with small children, work at home, as also can research workers who are using computer links to obtain and select information.

### Newsprint transmission
Computer technology already allows newspapers to be transmitted electronically from, say, England to West Germany and printed there so that copies of foreign newspapers can be available in other countries on the day of publication. This is valuable for businessmen who wish to see, for instance, the *Financial Times*, and for the tourist trade.

### Facsimile transmission (FAX)
It has long been possible to send 'wire pictures', but these tended to be of poor quality and transmission was relatively slow. Now the picture can be transmitted in a different way, as a series of digital pulses, just like computer information. Transmission is fast and of excellent quality; and technological innovations are improving it all the time.

Long-distance conferences can be held, using closed-circuit television, computer transmission of data and facsimile transmission of complex plans and diagrams, thus reducing the need for executives to travel long distances, at great expense, for meetings.

### Viewdata (teletex) systems
Three main systems are now in use.

(a) *The information systems available on special television sets* (such as the BBC 'Ceefax' and ITV 'Oracle' systems). These present constantly updated information on a wide variety of topics but are mainly aimed at home viewers and are of limited capacity compared with Prestel.

(b) *National systems.* The national systems are led by the British-developed 'Prestel'. This links the television via the telephone with computer-stored information, but it is also an interactive system. For instance, it is possible to book an air flight or order goods from stores or make donations to charities. Businesses find the system very useful for its financial information, and travel agencies also use it.

(c) *Private systems.* Some companies have developed their own viewdata systems which can also be linked to 'Prestel'. In addition to other facilities, private systems allow messages to be transmitted to individuals.

### Other information systems
The contents of libraries are now recorded on computers. Sometimes it is only the index, but sometimes the text is also electronically stored. Until

recently, access to the computerised information was restricted, but now some public libraries, for instance, offer access to legal information, while anyone with a computer terminal and a telephone can, for a fee, be linked to the British Library data.

## Other developments

The application of computers to industry at large has already changed and is changing the role of the office in business. For instance, sales and purchases, payroll and stock control are early candidates for computerisation. In consequence new procedures and documentation are generated, computer operators replace clerks engaged in writing and accounting machine operators must learn new skills.

Other technological innovations are helping in the change. For instance, the replacement of ordinary telephone cables by fibre-optic lines has already begun to expand considerably the capacity of land lines, while the development of commercial satellite use, with small dish aerials for transmission and reception, makes world-wide data transmission even easier. Even the silicon chip looks as if it will be replaced by a new and better material, aluminium gallium oxide.

By the time you read this book there will be other major developments affecting the way we communicate — so fast is the speed of progress.

## 18.2 DEVELOPMENTS FORESEEABLE THIS CENTURY

It is possible to look forward over the next twenty years and predict what might happen, based on the changes that have already taken place and on the developments already at research or prototype stage. However, the real rate of change will be restricted and uneven in its effect. The restrictions will be those of cost, availability of trained personnel, a constant and reliable electricity supply and the development of telephone-line and satellite capability.

As different countries have different needs, growth in their use of sophisticated electronic tools will also be limited by other priorities. However, the pattern of communication in the next twenty years contains the possibility of considerable extension of linked computer and word-processing systems with world-wide transmission of documents and newspapers. These latter may come into our homes on the viewdata systems, perhaps eventually replacing the newspaper. The former may lead to more home-working, thus changing the pattern of our working lives and emptying the office blocks in our towns and cities.

It is already possible to put a book on a small and cheap micro-chip. If we become accustomed to reading from a screen, we may begin to assemble our own micro-chip libraries of business and technical information, as well as leisure-time reading.

Systems of direct speech input into computers and word processors are likely to be commercially practicable by the next decade – thus eliminating the need for typing – and also the simultaneous translation of text into other languages is being developed. There are sure to be many other as yet unforeseen innovations with the introduction of what are called the 'fifth-generation' computers, and keen competition is likely to bring much of the technology within the reach of even small firms.

## 18.3 THE EFFECT ON THE PROCESS OF COMMUNICATION

The precursor to this modern communication revolution was the introduction of the printing press 500 years ago. That made it possible for information to be made easily and fairly cheaply available to everyone. Now the television has come together with the computer to affect not only our leisure time but also our working lives.

The effect of the technology on the actual process of communication is difficult to assess but it looks as if there will be.

(a)  An increase in the volume of information communicated.
(b)  A reduction in personal contact, either face to face or over the telephone.

**The increase in information flow**
Many people will say that this increase will be beneficial: people will know more about what is happening.

Experience tells us, however, that this is not necessarily the case. There are certain categories of information that people need in the course of their work. If they are presented with too much information they will either spend too long in reading it, and thus fail to complete their work, or they will ignore it, or read it only superficially, which is worse.

A further potential difficulty is that some people experience problems when they have to look at a VDU for long periods of time. Initial studies have indicated that eye trouble, headaches and even epileptic fits can be caused. People also find difficulties in editing material on a screen. Indeed, one leading word-processor manufacturer recommends printing out a draft copy and editing from that.

One wonders whether there were similar reactions to the printed word. Certainly many people forecast that eyesight would suffer as a result of watching television, but there seems little evidence that this has happened. Perhaps many of the symptoms complained of result from psychological reactions to the new and different rather than from real physical problems inherent in the new technology.

There are many tangible benefits to be derived from this new availability of information. Managements, in particular, no longer have to work on outdated facts, so their forecasting is made easier. They also can have more pertinent detail.

Communications are speedier and, even the printed ones, can be visually more easy to read and absorb. Because so much more is 'written', new skills in the use of languages are demanded. It will not be enough to be able to talk fluently. People will have to be able to spell, punctuate and use acceptable grammatical structures more competently than at present (and accept that their present level of competence is often lower than they realise). This may well make communication more precise.

### The reduction in personal contact

With added emphasis on the written word, with some people working from home, there is likely to be a reduction in telephone and face-to-face contact. This will suit people who find impersonal contact easier but may well not be attractive to those for whom direct contact with people at work is one of the bonuses of their working lives. This social aspect is discussed later in this chapter.

## 18.4 THE EFFECT OF ADVANCED TECHNOLOGY ON COMMUNICATION

### On the economy and business

Setting aside the problems of computer fraud, the results of a greater volume of communication are likely to be shown in two areas where there is already concern.

### *International markets*

Modern technology already brings fast and reliable information about international events into the money, bullion and commodity markets of the world, affecting rates of exchange and prices swiftly. Soon such news will reach into many more offices via viewdata and computer links. The complexity of international business, of importing and exporting, will be heightened by the need to react swiftly. The premium on very good management information and high management skills will rise.

### *Security*

With computer-linked systems and many people with access to the computers the need for tight security of information is paramount. Otherwise confidential company and personal data can all too easily pass into the wrong hands. Companies such as banks, and even some countries like Sweden, are very aware of the problems and have taken steps to ensure confidentiality, by limiting access and introducing security codes for example. However, this is not true everywhere and it is a danger area.

## On society

People working in offices will experience the social changes of reduced personal contact and changes in working conditions. For some there may be a deskilling of their work; for others retraining to acquire new skills will be necessary.

In general high technology in industry has led to fewer jobs in modernised factories, but there has been a growth, not only in electronics and its peripheral industries, but also in service industries. The effect on offices in the future is likely to be a reduction in the number of jobs but a greater need for staff with high communication skills.

In the already highly developed and industrialised countries the general effect on the population will be to generate considerable social change. Allied to the high levels of unemployment already forecast for other reasons, the effect of high technology is likely to intensity the divisions between the skilled and the unskilled, to require very many people to face periods of unemployment or retraining during their lives. The working week may shorten, and also the working life. There should be a corresponding increased emphasis on the provision of leisure and community facilities so that those not at work can lead rewarding lives.

It is more difficult to foresee the effect of introducing sophisticated communications technology into countries which at the moment have scarcely a national telephone system and in whose offices the electric typewriter and the pocket calculator represent considerable progress. However, much of the new technology, in its simplest forms, is not expensive and may be expected to spread as quickly as telephone links, electricity supplies and the education and training of the population will allow. There should then be an increase in employment opportunities.

One noticeable social change which has already taken place in industrialised society is the widespread availability of news and information through the medium of television particularly. Supplemented by viewdata systems, video cassette, satellite television bringing foreign TV programmes into the home, and home computers, it seems possible that our leisure time will be spent receiving a wide variety of visual information, while at work we shall be using the same satellite and telephone links for computing and for written communication.

Either way, we are likely to have to become used to reading from a screen, instead of from a page, and to typing into a machine rather than writing by hand, or even to dictating material to a computer or word processor instead of to a secretary.

Whatever the methods we shall be using in the future for our communications, we need to remember that the intrinsic message is the communication and that the sophisticated technology is of no use if the basic communication is poor.

---

### FOCUS

THE PAPERLESS OFFICE

   word processors
   micro-computers
   FAX
   viewdata

THE PEOPLELESS OFFICE?

   systems linked via satellites; data bases; terminals in the home;
   direct speech input

---

## 18.5 ASSIGNMENTS

1   Choose *one* major recent innovation (for example, micro-processors, word-processing machines, audiovisual aids, etc.) and analyse how this will affect:

  (i)  communication in business organisations
  (ii)  the role of the professional administrator. [ICSA]

2   Discuss the effects that information technology is likely to have on employment.

3   How is the 'paperless office' likely to affect (a) business practice, (b) working life?

4   How is the new technology being used already in your own office? Describe any other applications that would be beneficial.

5   How is management communication, as discussed in Chapter 17, likely to be changed by technological developments?

# ANSWERS/NOTES FOR
# ANSWERS

## CHAPTER 1

### Assignment 1

See the example below for the complete answer. You will note that:

(a) a heading (the order number) has been added to ensure that the reader knows immediately what the letter is about and can, if necessary, look up the order
(b) the unbusinesslike vague references to a *telephone call of recent date* and to a letter have been given more specific detail
(c) the order chosen is 'good news first, bad news later'
(d) the letter ends by indicating to the reader the next step, i.e. a decision has to be made about whether to order items D996, D935, D995.

Dear Sirs

ORDER NO 665544

We confirm the telephone conversation with Mr Brown of your Purchasing Department on 15 October, 19-- and are pleased to give you the following information on the outstanding items of your order.

1. Items delivered
   The following items have been delivered and Proof of Delivery has been requested from our Despatch Department:

   | Item | Document No. |
   | --- | --- |
   | 992945 | 267339 |
   | D315 | 282390 |

2. Items to be despatched shortly
   Documentation for the following items has been completed and they should be delivered within ten days:
   994130
   A6007 (despatch date 28/29 October)
   49493

3. Overdue order
   The following items are not available at present and we cannot give a delivery date at the moment, as we explained in our letter of 31 September.
   > U1300
   > A6005
   > A6011
   > D330

4. Discontinued range
   We regret that D104 is no longer available – this was also explained in our letter of 30 September.

5. Minimum orders
   Please note that the following items must be ordered in a minimum quantity of 20 each:
   > D996
   > D935
   > D995

If you decide to order in these quantities please let us know. We shall be able to deliver them immediately.

Yours faithfully

## CHAPTER 2

### Assignment 5
*Writing a report*

MEMORANDUM

To:   Mr S Wilson                     Date:    11 December 19--
From: A B Jardine

I attach for your consideration the report which you requested on the redecoration and reorganisation of the Sales Office.

ABJ

-----------------------------------------------------------

THE
REDECORATION AND REORGANISATION
OF THE SALES OFFICE

As you requested I have examined the improvements needed in the Sales Office to accommodate an increased number of staff, and I suggest the alterations and additions detailed below. A plan is attached to the report as a guide to layout (appendix 1), together with a colour scheme (appendix 2), and a detailed estimate of costs (appendix 3).

## 1 NEW OFFICE EQUIPMENT

(a) Desks. The existing desks are in good condition and can be retained. New desks will be needed for the shorthand typist who will join us shortly and for the two new sales representatives. As the desks in present use are of teak, it would maintain uniformity if similar desks were ordered.

(b) Cabinets and cupboards. The office filing cabinets and cupboards are in very poor condition. It would therefore be preferable to order six new cupboards in a bright colour. One of the new circular filing systems would prove indispensible to the secretarial staff and would not take up as much space as the old filing cabinets.

(c) Carpeting. The existing floor covering seems to be quite adequate; this grey corded carpeting is hard-wearing and will fit in with any colour scheme.

(d) Chairs, telephones and typewriters. The appearance of the office would be improved if new chairs were ordered in some bright colour, the same colour perhaps as the filing cabinets. These chairs must be comfortable. The three existing telephones are adequate for the needs of the office, but a new typewriter will have to be ordered before the new shorthand typist begins work.

## 2 OFFICE LAYOUT

I have included a diagram of the proposed layout (appendix 1), which is self-explanatory. I should, however, like to make the following comments on the reasons for my choice of layout:

(a) Windows. I have made every effort to ensure that desks are placed as near to windows as possible so that all employees are aided by a certain amount of daylight. The present lighting is adequate.

(b) Doors. I have placed the desks in such a way that anyone entering the office may immediately see all members of staff at work.

(c) Heating. By next month under-floor electric central heating will have been installed in the entire office block. I have not proposed any air-conditioning system as this would prove very expensive. However, electric fans would be most useful in the summer months.

## 3 REDECORATION

In deciding upon a colour scheme (see appendix 2) I had to consider several factors. Too much bright colour would be overwhelming and so I confined this to chairs and cabinets. Walls should be painted with a vinyl paint so that they can be cleaned easily, and walls and ceilings should be of a colour that is light but easy on the eye.

## 4 ESTIMATE OF COSTS

The total estimated cost of these alterations is £2,750. A detailed breakdown is given in appendix 3.

I hope that the plans for the reorganisation meet with your approval and that this total estimated cost does not appear to be excessive.

A. B. Jardine
11 December 19--

# CHAPTER 3

## Assignment 1
The question specifies a brief explanatory memo. The memo should mention: subject (the effect of increased fuel prices), source of information, content of summary (cars and driving habits).

SUMMARY NOTES
(a) Car buying
new cars — registration down 10 per cent (Econ. Intell. Unit)
effects of credit control
second-hand dealers' returns — considerable sales small cars
returns suspect
(b) Alternative transport
thought cars less used or just to get to local rail — probably negated by fares' rises, particularly London Transport
(c) Company cars
40 per cent company-owned/subsidised
Only 60 per cent to judge changes
(d) Leisure motoring
environmentalists' vain hope less road and parking congestion
people restricting length of journey
visiting local attractions
leisure motoring affected by other than fuel prices

SUMMARY

### Memorandum

| To | Transport Manager | From | M Robinson |
|---|---|---|---|
| Date | 18 June 19-- | Subject | The effect of increased fuel prices |

I recently read an article in the March 19-- edition of New Society and, as it concerns cars and driving habits, I thought you might be interested in the attached summary of its contents.

MR

# THE EFFECT OF INCREASED FUEL PRICES

The article makes the following points:

CAR BUYING
New Cars
Registration has fallen by 10 per cent (Economic Intelligence Unit) but this may have been affected by stricter credit control.
Second-hand Cars
Dealers' returns show considerable activity in sales of smaller-capacity cars but, with some evidence of bulk-buying of large cars, the returns are suspect.

USE OF ALTERNATIVE TRANSPORT
It was thought that cars might not be used, or merely used to drive to local stations. However, this trend is probably negated by rises in other transport fares, particularly the London Underground.

COMPANY CARS
40 per cent of cars are company-owned or subsidised. Thus changing trends will only show in the remaining 60 per cent.

LEISURE MOTORING
Environmentalists hoped vainly for less road and parking congestion. It seems likely either that people are restricting journey length and visiting more local attractions, or that weekend motoring is governed by factors other than higher fuel prices.

[154 words]

## Assignment 2
SUMMARY OF CORRESPONDENCE

Summary of correspondence between J Maggs, 5 Maple Grove, Bingley, Wilts, WB4 6LM, and the Reliable Insurance Company, Broadgate, Bradford, BD1 5CX, about a comprehensive motor insurance policy, between 14 and 28 March 19– –

Mr Maggs queried the quotation of £65, asking for a no-claim bonus and a reduction for his agreement to pay the first £25 of damage.
    The Reliable Insurance Co. agreed to a no-claim bonus allowance of £18.50 on receipt of proof of the bonus from Mr Magg's previous insurers, plus an allowance of £10 for his acceptance of responsibility for the first £25 of any damage.
    Mr Maggs accepted the revised quotation of £36.50 and enclosed proof of his previous no-claim bonus.
    The Reliable Insurance Co. confirmed the revised premium and sent proposal forms for Mr Magg's signature.
    Mr Maggs returned the signed forms, and enclosed his cheque for £36.50. He requested that cover should be arranged as soon as possible.

[123 words]

# CHAPTER 4

## Assignment 6
NOTES FOR ARTICLE

(a) Attention-getting title; indication of authorship; clear paragraphs; section headings would be appropriate.

(b) Content should include:
> need for good human relationships — and their maintenance
> effective oral communication skill
> some of:  organisation structure and function
>> positions of different people
>> relationship with colleagues
>> dealing with callers and customers – reception
>> maintenance of good company image
> conclusion summarising the main points.

(c) Tone and style should be:
> simple and straightforward, with language aimed at new entrant
> appreciative of new entrant's lack of experience
> persuasive, showing the logic of the practices mentioned indicate prospects for progress for new staff.

# CHAPTER 5

## Assignment 5
Conference form should include the following:

(a) HEADING: name of conference
>> name of organisation
>> venue and date

(b) SUBHEADING: enrolment form

(c) phrase stating *'please enrol'*

(d) block asking for names, initials, job titles and organisation of delegates, total conference fees at . . . per person

(e) business address and telephone number

(f) accommodation required: single, double, private bathroom (unless assumed for all delegates), for which nights, prices, total price for all delegates

(g) annual dinner and cost: number and names of those attending and total cost

(h) to whom cheques must be made out and space for total enclosed

(i) if credit cards accepted, which ones and space for insertion of card information

(j) space for date and signature

(k) to whom completed form to be forwarded.

## CHAPTER 6

### Assignment 3
(a) MINUTING A RESOLUTION

> It was therefore resolved by 15 votes in favour, 4 against, with 1 abstention
> THAT the new suggestion scheme should be adopted and implemented from 1 January 19--.

(b) AN AMENDMENT TO THE PREVIOUS MINUTES

> 2. *Minutes of previous meeting*
> The minutes of the meeting held on 1 May 19-- were taken as read and approved, with the following amendment:
> *Minute No. 5.* The balance reported by the Treasurer should read £113.00 not £11.30.
> The minutes were then signed by the Chairman.

(c) RECORDING DISSENT

> The motion was approved by 7 votes in favour, 2 against with 1 abstention. Mrs Crisp asked that her dissent be recorded.

(d) A CHANGE OF CHAIRMAN

Insert the following paragraph into the minutes at the point in the discussion where the change took place:

> At this point Mr X, the Chairman, had to leave the meeting and the Chair was taken by Mr Y, and the Vice-Chairman, for the remainder of the meeting.

## CHAPTER 7

### Assignment 1
OUTLINE ANSWER

*Advantage of committees*
(a) People can become expert in certain fields and can sometimes devote attention to affairs for which they have aptitude.
(b) Greater variety of experience. More useful information can be pooled.
(c) Ideas are brought to light by discussion.
(d) Personnel have the chance to make worthwhile contribution to the organisation.
(e) The feelings and reactions of employees can be made known to management.
(f) Lines of communication are improved.

*Disadvantages of committees*
(a) Delay — postponement of decision-making.
(b) Irrelevant discussion.
(c) Delay — notice of meetings.
(d) Dominant chairman or secretary can have too much power.

(e) Weak chairman cannot control meeting
(f) Lack of proper preparation.
(g) Cost.

Size is an important factor. On the one hand, it should be sufficient to enable all views to be represented but, on the other, it should be kept to a minimum.

The first part of the question is straightforward and should cause little difficulty. The second part, however, requires *an example* of each of the situations outlined. You would lose marks if you did not give *one specific example of each*. Areas from which examples might be chosen are suggested below, but this is not intended as a comprehensive list:

(a)  (i) joint consultation
    (ii) specialist co-ordination
    (iii) problem-solving
(b)  (i) imposition of policy
    (ii) forum for chairman
    (iii) need for speed.

There are, of course, many other areas which could be chosen. It must again be emphasised that the question asks for one example only of *each* of (a) and (b).

# CHAPTER 8

## Assignment 5
NOTES FOR ANSWER

(a) An acceptable format must be used — either fully blocked with open punctuation or semi-blocked.
(b) Own home address; date; their reference; recipient's name and address.
(c) Salutation: Dear Sir/Yours faithfully preferable as formal letter but Dear Mr Johnson/Yours sincerely would be accepted.
(d) Subject heading desirable; enclosure.
(e) Clear and logical structure should not repeat details on the application form, but amplify them or draw attention to them in the light of the details on the advertisement:
    experience/knowledge of personnel functions; office systems and procedures; supervision; meetings; qualifications and experience; particular specialisms or interests; availability for interview
(f) Letter should open with formal statement of application and close courteously. Language and style should be courteous, interestingly phrased; accurate; aim to seek and hold attention without being conceited. Narrow dividing-line between the application that understates the case and the one that overstates it.

# CHAPTER 9

## Assignment 1
A GOOD LISTENER

Willingness, preparation (background knowledge), attentiveness, concentration, an open mind, patience and courtesy, integrity.

# CHAPTER 10

## Assignment 1
THE MISTAKES THE PRESENTER MADE

(a) He prepared far too much visual material for the time available for presentation (twenty transparencies for fifteen minutes!) Possibly some of the transparencies were overloaded with information too. Tables of costings may well be too detailed to be assimilated by the audience in the short space of time available.
(b) He did not familiarise himself with the equipment, or check it, beforehand. Thus his audience was distracted by his efforts to make it work.
(c) To indicate key features of his transparency, he should have used a pencil or pointer to identify them on the transparency as it lay on the projector. Walking over to the screen to use his pointer would have resulted in loss of audience concentration. Turning his back on them it would lead to a loss of contact.

# CHAPTER 11

## Assignment 1
VALID OR INVALID ARGUMENTS

(a) NO
(b) NO
(c) YES
(d) NO
(e) YES. (*Explanation*: to get the *least* number who are in favour of both, we assume no overlap between the 34 per cent and the 58 per cent. Therefore, we add them together (92) and subtract from 100, which equals 8, which is the minimum number who are both.)

# CHAPTER 12

## Assignment 6
A REWRITTEN NOTICE

A new procedure has been agreed for organising the holiday rota. If you wish to take some holiday, please send a memo to the divisional Personnel Officer with copies to your manager and to the Managing Director.

We should like a month's notice of your holiday plans (and these must of course be agreed with your manager to avoid overlap of holidays).

The new procedure should be used from now on. If you already have holidays booked for the next month, please check with your manager that he has a note of them.

Personnel Officer
18 April 19– –

# CHAPTER 13

## Assignment 1
NOTES FOR ANSWER – TWO-PART QUESTION

(a) Required to define 'non-verbal communication' – do so in first paragraph:
EXAMPLE: In this context, non-verbal communication means all methods of communicating in which words are not used, including gestures, posture, facial expressions, movement, demonstration, charts and graphs.
NOTE: 'non-verbal' *must* exclude anything which is 'verbal', i.e. which uses words – therefore excludes both oral and written communication.

(b) Modification to oral communication – 'modify' means alter slightly.
Start with general comment, then try to give an example of each of several different types of non-verbal communication, showing in each case how modification is achieved. Keep examples practical and choose from ones relevant to business.
EXAMPLES

(i) *Diagram showing process flow*
Modification – may alter sense of oral communication through presenting information more accurately and concisely.

(ii) *Sales graph*
Modification – impact; reduction of words needed; permanent record.

(iii) *Facial expression*
Modification – amendment to meaning, for example sarcasm softened by smile.

(iv) *Gesture and demonstration*
Modification – can alter focal point – recipient watches hands first and listens to voice second.

(v) *Body movements*
Modification – indication of attitude or emotion.

NOTE: Answer needs careful format with clear distinction between the different points.

The second part might start like this:

The combining of two media of communication usually entails the modification of one or both. Where the second medium employed is as varied as is non-verbal communication, then its employment with oral communication can cause infinite modification of the latter. For instance, the use of a diagram of the process flow in a production department can make the presentation of information by a speaker at a meeting both more concise and more accurate and, therefore, easier to understand. [And so on . . . ]

## CHAPTER 14

### Assignment 4
PUBLIC INFORMATION SYMBOLS

The symbols which performed best in appropriateness ranking tests were nos 7, 8 and 11.

### Assignment 6
THE GROWTH IN THE USE OF VISUAL AIDS

  (i) Have had posters, graphs, etc., for long time. Now make better use of them; e.g. safety posters, sales graphs.
 (ii) Use for disseminating information to laymen.
(iii) New uses — ergonomics, flow charts, closed-circuit television, video, OHP, computers, VDUs, light pens.

SUPPLEMENT   (a) giving statistics to support a report
             (b) giving a clearer description of a state of affairs or action
             (c) as visual aids to focus attention — include gestures, etc.

REPLACE      (a) Some items are more clearly stated in pictures or diagrams.
Not often total replacement.

## CHAPTER 15

### Assignment 1
MODEL ANSWER

(a) Both 'primary' and 'prime' can mean 'of first importance'. However, 'primary' has the sense of 'first in time' so its use in the first sentence would have changed the meaning.
(b) *paradoxically* — contrary to expectations
    *the logical media* — the most suitable means of communication
       (NOTE 'medi*a*' is plural; therefore 'mean*s*')
    *microfiche* — postcard-sized positive film on which some eighty A4-size documents can be recorded
(c) An editorial is a passage in a journal or newspaper in which the editor expressed his views. Since the first sentence in the second paragraph uses the expression 'we ourselves' and then continues to discuss what might be the logical media for use by the *Review*, it seems very likely that it was taken from an editorial.

(d) Video tape. (NOTE: The question asks for 'a word or two' so such a brief answer is correct. Other choices could have been video disc or film strip — provided it had a sound magnetic stripe — but not microfiche.)

(e) The first paragraph suggests using the equipment itself to convey the sales message. By analogy the typewriter firm should use typewriters in their sales technique; therefore, a typed sales letter would be more appropriate than a handwritten one, however beautiful.

The argument is valid up to a point, but, for instance, a video tape describing how to use a video-recorder would be useless unless the operator had already been given some basic instruction in another medium.

# CHAPTER 17

## Assignment 1
OUTLINE ANSWER — TWO-PART QUESTION

(a) *Importance*

Employees today expect to be consulted.

They must be told what need/want to know but not just information — communication must be two-way.

Attempt to remove barriers or prevent their erection

Create better relationships — leading to better productivity.

Larger concerns — more impersonal — better communication of even more importance.

(b) *Informal vs formal*

   (i) INFORMAL — a desirable style of communication:

           improves personal contact and working relationships often more successful than formality

           speedy and direct

      BUT: 'grapevine', i.e. fragmentary, inaccurate and distorted communication not through correct channels, is unreliable and unstable. Sets up attitudes of irritation, disbelief and cynicism.

  (ii) FORMAL — uses well-defined channels through managment levels desirable for passing of instructions

           recognisable

           prevents bypassing of management

           normally fairly accurate and reliable

           necessary for important communication, for example, when written record needed, decision-taking meetings.

# GLOSSARY OF MEETINGS TERMS

**ad hoc**   Literally 'to this' or 'for this': that is, 'for this purpose', e.g. a committee formed for a special purpose and usually disbanded after that purpose has been achieved.

**addendum**   A resolution which adds words to a motion.

**adjournment**   The act of extending or continuing a meeting for the purpose of dealing with unfinished business, or of deferring the debate on a motion which is before a meeting.

**agenda**   Literally means 'things to be done', but commonly used to describe the agenda paper which lists the items of business to be discussed at a meeting. The agenda lists items in the order in which they are to be taken.

**agenda paper**   This term is also used of papers of supplementary information relating to items on the agenda which are circulated for the information of members of the committee.

**amendment**   A proposal to alter a motion which has been submitted to a meeting, e.g. by adding, inserting or deleting words of the original motion.

**ballot**   A method of voting used when secrecy is required, e.g. by the use of a voting paper.

**bye-laws**   Local laws set up by local authorities or the internal regulations of an organisation.

**casting vote**   A second vote usually allowed to the chairman, except in the case of a company meeting, and used to break a deadlock.

**closure**   A motion submitted with the object of ending the discussion on a matter before the meeting.

**committee**   A person or body of persons to whom general or specific duties and authority have been delegated by a parent body, e.g. authority and duties are delegated by the shareholders of a company to its board of directors.

**co-opted**   Invited to join the discussions of a meeting, part of a meeting, or a series of meetings but not entitled to vote. (Co-optative members have a vote.)

**debate**   Discussion on a motion put before a meeting, prior to putting the matter to a vote.

**ex officio**   Literally 'by the virtue of office or position', as, for example, when a person attends a meeting not in his capacity as a member but because of the position he holds.

**executive committee**  A committee with powers to put decisions into effect.

**form of proxy**  A document by which one person authorises another person to attend a meeting and vote on his behalf.

**formal motion**  A motion intended to alter the procedure of a meeting, e.g. to adjourn the meeting.

**in camera**  Held in private — the public excluded.

**intra vires**  Within the power of the person or body concerned.

**majority**  Unless otherwise indicated, this may be taken to mean a simple majority, as opposed to an overall majority.

**minutes**  A written record of the business transacted at a meeting.

**motion**  A proposal put forward for discussion and decision at a meeting.

**nem. con.** (*nemine contradicente*)  Without dissent, but implying that though no one voted against the motion, there were abstentions.

**nem. dis.** (*nemine dissentiente*)  Without dissent.

**open voting**  Any method of voting 'in public', e.g. a show of hands.

**order of business**  The intended order in which items of business, as set out in the agenda, are to be taken. This order may be altered by resolution of the meeting.

**point of order**  A question regarding procedure or a query relating to the rules (e.g. constitution, standing orders) raised during the course of a meeting and decided on by the chair, e.g., lack of quorum.

**poll**  The taking of a vote; the number of votes recorded.

**previous questions**  A formal (or procedural) motion usually put in the form 'THAT the question be *not* now put.' By this motion the proposer is seeking to postpone voting on the matter concerned.

**procedural motion**  *See* formal motion.

**proxy**  A person authorised to attend a meeting and vote on behalf of someone else *or* the document which authorises him to do so.

**quorum**  The minimum number of people entitled to be present at a meeting which the regulations require to be present in order that the business of the meeting may be transacted validly.

**resolution**  Although the words 'motion' and 'resolution' are often used indiscriminately, a 'motion' is a proposal put to a meeting, whereas a 'resolution' is a proposal which has been accepted by the meeting.

**rider**  An additional clause or sentence added to a resolution, and proposed, seconded and voted upon in the same manner as the motion.

**right of reply**  The right of the mover or proposer of a motion to reply once to discussion of it before the vote. (In effect, it allows the proposer to speak twice to the motion, while other members may only speak once.)

**sine die**  'Without an appointed day': indefinitely. Thus a meeting adjourned *sine die* necessitates fresh notice for the adjourned meeting.

**special business**  All business defined by the rules as other than 'ordinary business'. Meetings convened to consider 'special business' usually require a longer period of notice than 'ordinary meetings'.

**standing committee**  A permanent committee (the opposite of an *ad hoc* committee), such as the housing department of a local authority.

**standing orders**  The name given to rules regulating the conduct and procedures of certain bodies, such as the permanent standing order of local authorities.

**status quo**    The existing state of affairs. The more conservative members will vote to preserve the status quo unless they are persuaded of the necessity for change.

**sub-committee**    A committee appointed by a parent body for a certain specific purpose or to relieve the larger body of some of its routine work. It usually consists of some of the members of the appointing committee, but specialist members are often co-opted.

**ultra vires**    Beyond the legal powers possessed by the organisation. (*See also intra vires.*)

**unanimously**    A motion carried unanimously has been agreed by all present at a meeting.

# GRAMMAR, PUNCTUATION AND SPELLING

This section has been written to help with the mechanics of language: grammar, punctuation and spelling. (There is a glossary of grammatical terms which might be helpful starting on page 296.)

## GRAMMAR

### Sentences
A sentence is the expression of a complete thought. To be grammatical even the shortest sentence must contain a subject and a finite verb. Errors in sentence structure are most often made in the introduction and conclusion of letters. Neither of these expressions is a sentence:

> *In reply to your letter of 8 May.*
> *Looking forward to your early reply.*

The first contains neither subject nor verb.

> CORRECT VERSION
> *In reply to your letter of 8 May I have pleasure in enclosing our quotation.*

The second has what at a casual glance seems to be a verb, *looking*. However, it is a participle, not a finite verb, and there is no subject.

> CORRECT VERSION
> *I look forward to your early reply.*

### Agreement of subject and verb
Not only must a sentence have a subject and a verb, but these must also agree: that is, a singular subject must have a singular verb, and a plural subject a plural verb.

> INCORRECT
> *Details of the new contract is to be found overleaf.*

Here the subject *details* is plural, so that the verb must also be made plural, *are*.

> INCORRECT
> *Each of the typists are to have her own stationery.*

The subject here is *each*, NOT *typists*, and so the verb must be made singular, *is*.

NOTE: *every, either, neither, each* are all singular.

The following is a very common type of error:

*This is one of the papers that is to be enclosed.*

The relative pronoun *that* refers to *papers*. Since *papers* is plural the pronoun and verb must also be plural.

CORRECT
*This is one of the papers that are to be enclosed.*

Collective nouns are usually singular, unless the members of the group are behaving as individuals. However, practices are changing and, provided the number remains constant, either singular or plural is acceptable.

## Agreement of demonstrative adjectives
Demonstrative adjectives must agree with the noun they qualify:

INCORRECT
*He could not agree with these sort of proposals.*
*He could not agree with this sort of proposal.*
CORRECT
*He could not agree with these sorts of proposals.*

## Subject and object
Look at the following sentences:

*You and I will meet our consultant, Mr Brown, next week.*
*Mr Brown will meet you and I next week.*

The first sentence has *you and I* as the subject and is correct, but the second version has *you and I* as the object and is incorrect. The sentence should read:

*Mr Brown will meet you and me next week.*

This error is easily avoided. Think of it this way. You would never say:

*Mr Brown will meet I next week.*

## Gerunds
A gerund has the same form as a present particle but serves as a noun. It frequently gives rise to grammatical errors. Consider this sentence, for example:

*We apologise for him not contacting you earlier.*

This should be:

*We apologise for HIS not contacting you earlier.*

## Matching pronouns
It is necessary to be completely consistent when using pronouns. Look at this sentence:

*One should always read a hire-purchase agreement carefully before he signs it.*

Here the writer has changed horses in mid-stream. He began the sentence using the pronoun *one* and then changed to *he*. The CORRECT version is:

> *One should always read a hire-purchase agreement carefully before one signs it.*

## Relative pronouns

There is some confusion over the use of the relative pronouns *who/whom*, *which* and *that*. The general rule is:

> *who/whom* refers to persons only
> *which* refers to objects and all other creatures
> *that* may refer to persons, objects or other creatures

These pronouns are used to introduce relative clauses — see also p. 298 on commas.

(a) To define a preceding clause (the antecedent):

> *Uneasy lies the head that wears the crown.*
> *This is the play that Oscar Wilde wrote.*
> *This is the boy who told me the news.*

(b) To give further information about an already defined antecedent:

> *The play, which was directed by Peter Hall, is excellent.*

The above examples show that in defining clauses (i) *that* is usually preferable to *which*.

Following a preposition *whom/which* is preferable:

> *He is a man for whom I have the greatest regard.*
> *The box from which she took the chocolate was large.*

## Shall — will

The use of these two words is governed by specific rules.

(a) In a statement expressing simply the future tense:

> *I, we* are followed by *shall*
> *you, he, she, it, they* are followed by *will.*
> *I shall be glad if you will come tomorrow.*

(b) If determination or intention is to be expressed, the rule is reversed:

> *I, we* are followed by *will*
> *you, he, she, it, they* are followed by *shall.*
>
> *I will pass the examination however many times I have to take it.*
> *I will drown and no one shall save me . . .* is definitely suicidal!

## Should – would

Like *shall* and *will*, these two words are not interchangeable. Similar rules apply.

(a) In a statement expressing uncertainty or doubt, or where one action is conditional upon another:

> *I, we* are followed by *should*
> *you, he, she, it, they* are followed by *would*

*I should be grateful if you would visit me.*

Note the difference between this sentence and:

*I shall be grateful if you will visit me.*

The second sentence contains a hint of command, whereas *I should . . . if you would* suggests the asking of a favour.

(b) When the rule is reversed *should* and *would* express regret, a hint that something is unlikely to happen and may also suggest a sense of obligation or duty.

*I would come but I am unable to take the time from work.*
*He should visit his relatives but he does not wish to see them.*

Do not confuse *would* and *could*:

*I should be grateful if you would . . .* means 'if you are willing to'
*I should be grateful if you could . . .* means 'if you are able to'.

## Split infinitive
This is an awkward expression that occurs when an adverb is placed between the word *to* and the other word(s) which together with it form the infinitive:

*We must not fail to carefully consider our future development.*

The better version is:

*We must not fail to consider our future development carefully.*

## Fewer – less
Less is most commonly used but *fewer* can convey a different meaning, for example:

*There are fewer and less-skilled technicians than there were five years ago.*

## Use of prepositions
(a) Avoid the use of compound prepositions when simpler expressions may be used, for example:

*Employers were warned to obey the regulations in respect of [about] safety.*
*Greater efficiency could result from an improvement in regard to [in] industrial relations.*

(b) A preposition at the end of a sentence is often clumsy and should usually be avoided. In the following sentence, however, Sir Winston Churchill showed that unnatural English can result from following this general guide too closely:

*This is a practice up with which I will not put!*

(c) Many words may be followed by more than one preposition. However, certain words are linked with certain prepositions. Some of the most common are:

| | acquiesce in | estranged from |
| | amenable to | exonerate from |
| | coincide with | indicative of |
| | compatible with | initiate in |
| | conducive to | subordinate to |
| | conscious of | negligent of |
| | debar from | relevant to |
| | dependent on | oblivious of |
| | similar to | different from (than/to now acceptable) |

## Forms of reported speech

| | Direct speech | Reported speech |
| --- | --- | --- |
| VERBS | reports | reported |
| | is reporting | was reporting |
| | has reported | had reported |
| | shall (will) report | should (would) report |
| | may | might |
| | can | could |
| | must | had to |
| PRONOUNS | I, you (sing.) | he, she |
| | we, you | they |
| | me, you (sing.) | him, her |
| | mine, yours (sing.) | his, hers |
| | ours, yours | theirs |
| | myself, yourself | himself, herself |
| | ourselves, yourselves | theirselves |
| | this, these | that, those |
| ADVERBIAL | now | then, at that time |
| EXPRESSIONS | today | that day |
| | yesterday | the day before |
| | last week | the week before |
| | tomorrow | the next day |
| | next week | the following week |
| | here | there |

## GLOSSARY OF GRAMMATICAL TERMS

**adjective**  A word that qualifies or describes a noun, e.g. a *competent* chairman.

**adverb**  A word that modifies or describes a verb, adjective or other adverb, expressing a relationship of place, time, circumstance or manner, e.g. *greatly, gently, so, now, where, why.*

**clause**  Part of a sentence which contains its own subject and verb. In the sentence *He went to the bank when he needed to cash a cheque* there are two subjects, *he* and *he*, and two verbs, *went* and *needed. He went to the bank* is a main clause because it can stand alone to form a simple sentence, but *when he needed to cash a cheque* cannot; it is dependent upon the main clause for its own existence and is a subordinate clause.

**collective noun**  A word used in the singular to express many individuals, e.g. *herd, crowd, committee.*

**conjunction**   A word which links or joins other words, or groups of words, together. *And* is the most common one.

**demonstrative adjective**   An adjective which points out or stresses a particular noun, e.g. *that* dog, *those* people.

**finite verb**   What is said of the subject of a sentence, limited by number and person, e.g. he *walks*, I *said*, they *will go*, she *has spoken*, you *were saying*.

**gerund**   A form of verb which serves as a noun, ending in *-ing*, e.g. *hiking* is an energetic pastime, *eating* is a pleasure.

**infinitive**   A form of verb which is not limited by number or person. It is always composed of at least two words, including *to*, e.g. *to walk*, *to discuss*.

**modifier**   An adjective or adverb.

**noun**   A word used as a name of a person, thing or abstract idea, e.g. *table, chairman, Africa, religion, hope*.

**object**   A noun or noun-equivalent governed by an active verb or by a preposition, e.g. I kicked *him*, he saw *the man*, I waited in *the car*.

**parenthesis**   A word or passage of comment inserted in a sentence which is grammatically complete without it, e.g. he said, *and I agreed with him*, that he could never condone such behaviour.

**participle**   A verbal adjective qualifying a noun, e.g. a *talking* doll, the *spoken* word.

**predicate**   The rest of the sentence when the subject has been removed (*see also* **subject**). The predicates of the following sentences are in italics. The majority of the committee *voted in favour of the motion*. The motion *was approved by the rest of the committee*.

**preposition**   A word serving to mark the relationship between the noun or noun-equivalent it governs and another word, e.g. I found him *at* home, wait *in* the hall, the bed that he slept *on*, won *by* waiting, came *through* the door.

**pronoun**   A word used instead of a noun to designate a person or thing already known, e.g. the man saw *it, we* were at home, *who* is there? *I* refuse to read *this*.

**relative pronoun**   A form of pronoun which attaches a subordinate clause to an expressed or implied antecedent, e.g. the man *whom* you saw is my father, the prominent chin *that* characterises the Hapsburgs.

**sentence**   A set of words complete in itself and including, or sometimes implying, a subject and a finite verb, and conveying a statement, question or command, e.g. *I go, Will you go? Go (you)*.

**subject**   The part of a sentence (a word or group of words) which is responsible for the action named in the verb, or the receiver of the action if the verb is passive, e.g. *the majority of the committee* voted in favour, *the motion* was approved by most of the committee (*see also* **predicate**)

**subordinate clause**   *see* **clause**.

## PUNCTUATION

### Full stops

A full stop is used (i) at the end of a sentence, (ii) after abbreviations, for example *B.A., Co., Capt*.

Note that if the first and last letters of an abbreviation are the same as those of the word for which it stands, for example *Mr, Mrs*, the full stop is usually omitted. It is also now usually omitted from the abbreviated names of organisations, for example *BBC, IBM, ICI, Plc.*

## Commas

(a) Commas must be used to separate *commenting* (or non-defining) clauses from the rest of the sentence. For example, in the following sentence the relative clause *comments* on the purpose of the *nut*, which is defined or identified by the word *larger*:

> *the larger nut, which secures the high-tension lead, must now be loosened.*

However in this second example:

> *The nut which secures the high-tension lead must now be loosened.*

the relative clause is a defining one which identifies and completes the subject, *the nut*, and no commas are used.

There is a clear difference in meaning between these two sentences:

> *The two passengers who were seriously hurt were taken to hospital.*
> *The two passengers, who were seriously injured, were taken to hospital.*

(b) A parenthesis must be separated by commas, brackets or dashes from the rest of the sentence, for example:

> *The Chairman, Sir Henry Golding, opened the conference.*
> *No one, I am convinced, could have solved so difficult a problem.*

(c) Finally, commas must be used to separate nouns, adjectives, verbs or adverbs in a list, for example:

> *She bought ham, eggs, cheese and bread.*
> *She typed the letter, read it through, signed it, put it in the envelope and sealed and addressed it.*
> *He summed up the situation concisely, accurately, quickly and without prejudice.*

In addition to these cases where commas are necessary there are many occasions where good style and personal taste call for the use of commas to mark a short pause. Modern practice is to minimise the use of commas where this does not obscure the meaning.

## Apostrophes

(a) Apostrophes are used to indicate omissions and contractions, for example:

> *I wouldn't, I've, o'clock.*

(b) Finally, they are used to indicate possession or ownership (belonging to). With singular nouns the apostrophe comes before the *s*, for example:

> *the girl's handbag*

a handbag belonging to one girl. With plural nouns the apostrophe comes after the *s*, for example:

*the secretaries' typewriters*

typewriters belonging to more than one secretary. Note that such expressions as:

*in a fortnight's time*
*two years' guarantee*

require apostrophes. Words whose plural form does not end in *s* have the apostrophe before the *s*, for example:

*the children's toys*
*men's ties*

Note that when a proper noun ending in *s* takes the possessive case there is no one rule for the position of the apostrophe. Most proper nouns ending in *s* require *'s*, for example:

*Charles — Charles's*

(c) *its and it's. Its* is a possessive adjective:

*Each typewriter has its own cover.*

*It's* with an apostrophe indicates an omission, i.e. *it is*.

## Semi-colons

Although they are not greatly used nowadays, semi-colons can still be useful. They represent a pause midway in length between a comma and a full stop. In the following sentence Winston Churchill found that the two expressions were too closely related to be separated by a full stop. At the same time a comma was hardly sufficiently emphatic a pause.

*Do not let us speak of darker days; let us rather speak of sterner days.*

Note that there are cases where, to avoid ambiguity, a semi-colon must be used to separate items in a list because a comma is also being used in the sentence:

*The clothes in the shop window included two dresses, one with a pleated skirt; two skirts, two blouses and matching accessories.*

## Colons

A colon is used to introduce a list or to amplify a previous statement:

*A good secretary needs many qualities: intelligence, common sense, a neat appearance and patience.*

It is also used before a quotation to give added emphasis:

*What Dr Johnson said is worth remembering: 'Knowledge is of two kinds. We know a subject ourselves, or we know where we can find information upon it.'*

## Exclamation marks

They are rarely used in business communication. They may be occasionally used to express surprise, or for emphasis.

## Question marks

A question mark is used after a direct question:

>*Where have you put the report?*

An indirect question does not have a question mark:

>*He asked where she had put the report.*
>*I wonder where you have put the report.*

## Dashes

Dashes may be used in several ways.

(a) They may indicate an interruption:

>*'And in conclusion I might say —'*
>*'And about time too,' interrupted the heckler.*

(b) They may indicate a break or hesitation in direct speech:

>*'Come,' replied the stranger, 'stopping at Crown — Crown at Muggleton — met a party — flannel jackets — white trousers — anchovy sandwiches — devilled kidneys — splendid fellows — glorious.'*

> Mr Jingle in *Pickwick Papers* by Charles Dickens

(c) They may also be used with a colon to introduce a list. Nowadays, however, the dash is usually omitted.

>*Please supply the following: — two reams of A4 paper, a packet of paper clips and a roll of tape.*

## Inverted commas

These are used in four ways.

(a) They indicate direct speech.

>*The chairman said, 'Our company has made great progress this year.'*

A capital letter is used to open the actual words spoken. A separate paragraph is required for the words of each speaker.

(b) They enclose titles of, for example, books, plays, names of ships, trains, houses, trade names, in typed or handwritten material.

>*'The Observer', 'Cellophane', 'Queen Mary', 'Dunromin'.*

Note the use of inverted commas in the following sentence where the title of a film occurs within direct speech:

>*He said, 'I went to see "Julius Caesar" last night.'*

(c) They also enclose direct quotations.

(d) Finally, they are used to indicate words used sarcastically or slang expressions, for example:

>*so-called 'experts', 'with it'.*

## Capital letters

The following list indicates the main uses of capital letters.

(a) The first letter in a sentence and the start of direct speech:

> *This is my book.*
> *She said, 'This is my book.'*

(b) The pronoun *I* and the interjection *O*.

(c) The forenames and surnames of people:

> *Margery Smith, Peter Jones.*

(d) Nicknames and pet-names of people and animals:

> *Dusty Miller, Spud Murphy, Fido, Rover.*

(e) Registered Kennel and Jockey Club names:

> *Red Rum, Arkle.*

(f) Titles of people and organisations:

> *Her Majesty, The London Chamber of Commerce and Industry*

(g) Abbreviations of (v):

> *HM, LCI.*

(h) Geographical place-names including countries, areas, rivers, mountains, cities and towns:

> *England, United States of America, Paris Basin, Nairobi, River Thames, Mount Everest.*

(i) The names of languages and peoples:

> *Russian, Chinese.*

(j) The names of political and administrative divisions within a country:

> *Berkshire, Gwynedd.*

(k) Words used instead of relatives' names as titles when addressing the persons:

> *Father, Grandmother.*

(l) Deities and pronouns referring to them (also when referring to Jesus Christ):

> *God, Our Father Who art in heaven.*

(m) The days, weeks and months of the year:

> *Monday, February.*

But not the seasons unless they are being referred to as part of a specific title or date:

> *spring, Autumn crocus, Spring 19--.*

(n) Religious and other festivals:

> *Easter, May Day.*

(o) Legal documents:

> *Will, Act of Parliament.*

(p) Bills and Acts of Parliament:

*The Health and Safety at Work Act.*

(q) Trade names (whether or not they are the names of companies):

*Aspro, Papermate.*

(r) Ships and other means of transport:

*Ark Royal, Concorde, Flying Scotsman.*

(s) Stars and planets:

*Mars, Venus.*

(t) The technical or specific use of common names:

*the Monarchy* (referring to a specific monarchy), *the Standing Committee.*

(u) Books, plays and film titles:

*Under the Greenwood Tree, Close Encounters of the Third Kind.*

Note the less important words such as the articles *a* and *the*, pronouns, prepositions and conjunctions such as *of, by* and *for* only have a capital letter if used at the beginning of the title.

## SPELLING

If you find problems with spelling you should keep a dictionary handy and use it whenever you are in doubt. There are many useful spelling books which will help you (see, for example, Patrick Thornhill, *Spelling Made Easy*, Hodder & Stoughton).

The list which follows contains some of the most commonly mis-spelled words. You will certainly need to use them, so learn them.

| A | B | C |
|---|---|---|
| absence | beginning | certain |
| accommodate | believed | choice |
| acquainted | business | colleagues |
| all right | | coming |
| among | | committee |
| appearance | | completely |
| arrangement | | correspondence |

| D | E | F |
|---|---|---|
| decision | especially | faithfully |
| definite | essential | familiar |
| disappointed | excellent | |
| | exercise | |
| | expenses | |
| | extremely | |

| G | H | I |
|---|---|---|
| guard | height | immediately |
| | | independent |
| | | instalment |

**K**
knowledge

**L**
losing
lying

**M**
maintenance
minutes

**N**
necessary
noticeable

**O**
occasionally
occurrence
omitted
opinion

**P**
planning
possess
preceding
privilege
procedure
professional

**Q**
quiet

**R**
really
received
recommend
representative

**S**
scarcely
secretary
separately
similar
sincerely
successfully
surprising

**T**
transferred

**U**
undoubtedly
unnecessary
until
usually

**V**
valuable
view

**W**
Wednesday

# EXAMINATION TECHNIQUES

## TIME

(a) To gain the maximum number of marks possible, you *must* complete the paper; you must answer every question required (or at least attempt them). You can do this by planning your time. Never simply start writing and stop only when you have finished or time runs out. Allow at least five and possibly ten minutes at the beginning for reading your question-sheet and, at the end, for checking what you have written.

(b) Then allocate a suitable period for each question. You can judge how much time to allow by looking at the number of marks allocated to each question. For example, if a question carries a quarter of the marks, you should spend a quarter of the available time devising and writing the answer. Within the time you allow for answering each question, at least a third should be spent on *thinking* and *planning*.

## PLANNING

(a) First of all read the question very carefully to be quite sure you know what the examiner wants. Check how many parts there are to the question. Inspect every word.

(b) Now make a plan. Write out in note form — each new idea on a new line — what points you are going to make. Then put the ideas in order by numbering them, adding bits, deleting anything you reject.

(c) If you are writing in essay form, remember that you will need an introduction and a conclusion. Try to attract the examiner's attention. Remember that he is only human and may have to read scores of essays on the same topic. A 'fresh start' will help both him and you.

(d) Write your answer directly from your notes. Deviating from them wastes time and you may lose the logical flow. Never waste time by writing answers out twice.

(e) Set them out attractively. Use lots of space. Neat underlining with a ruler, capitals for headings, careful numbering, all give a good impression. Remember that first impressions do count.

(f) When your answer is complete, cancel rough notes with a diagonally ruled line. Don't worry about their spoiling the neatness of your script — the examiner won't look at them.

## MISTAKES

(a) Small errors can be corrected by using a typist's liquid eraser or by a neat cancellation with one line through the offending word(s).

(b) If near the end of the examination you realise that you have left out a whole paragraph of an answer (or more than you can insert legibly), then write the paragraph at the end of the script, labelling it carefully, for example 'please insert into Q4 at the point marked with an asterisk'.

## REVISION

Always have a few minutes at the end of the examination to check your work. Have you labelled answers correctly? Check grammar, spelling and punctuation. Check the content. Remember what your own weaknesses are and look especially hard for these.

---

### FOCUS

Read the examination paper carefully
Choose the questions you intend to answer
Choose the order
Allocate time for each question
Plan your answers in rough note form
Write them up neatly and attractively
Cancel rough notes
Check carefully what you have written

---

# INDEX